THE HISTORY OF AN APPALACHIAN FAMILY

by

Nancy Richmond

TABLE OF CONTENTS

Forward

Chapter One: **A Family History**   **1**

Chapter Two: **Family Tree Charts**   **23**

Chapter Three: **Historical Documents**   **73**

Chapter Four: **Photographs**   **121**

FORWARD

From the time I was a little girl growing up in one of West Virginia's aging 'coal camps' I have been fascinated with history. I read every book on the subject that was available to me, and I loved watching television programs that had an historical theme. Sadly, my knowledge of my own ancestry was limited to the few names and stories that my parents and grandparents could provide, which did not extend far beyond their own lifetimes.

However, with the dawning of the 21st century and the internet, it was suddenly a viable option to be able to trace one's roots online. As more and more people became involved in searching for clues to their past, websites sprang up offering help and allowing members to interact and exchange knowledge. Soon, government agencies followed suit and began releasing documents such as birth, death and marriage certificates, as well as US census and military records. Additionally, many search engines like google.com take you directly to information on specific family trees simply by typing in the name and birth date of a person.

I began my genealogical search in 2005, and it has been one of the most rewarding periods of my life. I have talked online with family members that I did not know existed, and learned more about my family's history than I ever hoped I would. Knowing who my ancestors were and how they lived has given me a sense of self and identity, and in some cases given me insights into why I am the person I have become.

I have compiled the information in this book in order to leave behind a record of my people, and to perhaps provide a clue as to who the pioneers who originally settled the wild and dangerous regions of the Appalachian Mountains over three hundred years ago really were.

Many times, research comes to a dead end in regards with a certain family member. I have included personal pages on all the members of my ancestry where specific information was known and documented. All others are mentioned only on the family tree charts.

Below I have listed a number of genealogy websites for anyone who is interested in researching their ancestors.

The US GenWeb Project: www.usgenweb.org
The West Virginia Division of Culture and Heritage   www.wvculture.org
Ancestry.com   www.ancestry.com
Family Search   www.familysearch.org

Nancy Richmond

DEDICATION

I wrote this book for Victoria, who asked me to tell her about our family.

CHAPTER ONE

A FAMILY HISTORY

THE GEORGE FAMILY

NANCY GEORGE (RICHMOND)

Nancy Kay George was born in a small coal camp in southern West Virginia – Marfrance – named for the two owners of the local mines, on December 13, 1952. Her father, *Aldon George*, was a coal miner and her mother, *Susie Elizabeth Burdiss George*, was a housewife. Nancy had four sisters, *Patsy Sue*, *Mary Margaret*, *Connie Juanita*, and *Janice Rebecca*. She had one brother, *Aldon David*. Their home was a small wood frame house with five rooms that was heated by one coal stove. Her family had no television, telephone or indoor bathroom until she was past four years old.

Nancy and her siblings attended Marfrance Elementary School, where two teachers taught three grades of students per room, and where the children used outside toilets. She graduated from Greenbrier West High School in 1970 at the age of seventeen. She then moved to Sidney Ohio, where she married Marvin J. Murray and had two children — *Tamara Lynn Murray*, born April 17, 1972 and *Misty Dawn Murray*, born April 30, 1974. When Nancy and Marvin divorced in 1975, she and the children moved to Quinwood, WV, where her parents had been living since 1973.

Nancy met *Charles Lee Richmond* at the Quinwood Baptist Church in 1976. They married on September 24, 1977, and had three children together — *Charity Marie Richmond*, born July 10, 1977, *Thor Richmond*, born May 28, 1979, and *Lora Lee Richmond*, born March 12, 1982. The children all attended Crichton Elementary School and Greenbrier West High School.

Nancy was a homemaker, and also served as Town Recorder and Municipal Court Judge in Quinwood. After her children were grown, she attended Bluefield State College as a Business Major.

Nancy was involved in breeding and showing dogs, and authored several dog books, ghost books and historical books. She was also a columnist and wrote regularly for newspapers and magazines.

Nancy's oldest daughter, Tamara, married *Ronnie Joseph Workman* and moved to Lewisburg, WV. Misty, a well known artist, married *James Roy Walkup Jr.* They moved to Crichton, WV and had three children — *James Roy Walkup 3rd* , born August 6, 1993; *Tia Dawn Walkup*, born April 20, 2001; and *Jesse James Walkup*, born November 5, 2008. Charity joined the US Army, where she met and married William Francis. They had a daughter, *Victoria Angelique Francis*, born February 23, 2000, and eventually divorced. Charity and her fiancé, *Reney Allen Cordial 4th*, had a son, *Reney Allen Cordial 5th*, on February 21, 2005. Thor married *Bethany Ellard* on October 10, 2010, and they moved to Alderson, WV. Lora married *Gary Dale Boone*, a descendent of the Daniel Boone pioneer family, and they had two children — *Hope Marie Boone*, born on December 3, 1999 and *Gary Dale Boone Jr*, born May 18, 2005.

Nancy and her husband Charles moved to Lewisburg, WV in 2003.

···

ALDON GEORGE AND SUSIE BURDISS
(Parents of Nancy George Richmond)

Aldon George was born at Hominy Falls, WV on September 16, 1917, the oldest of seven children. His parents were *Walter Greg George* and *Virgie Delta Cales George*. In 1924, his parents received 75 acres of land from Virgie's father Allen Cales, which was located in Nicholas County, WV.

The family built a two story house and farmed the land. Aldon grew up during the depression, and worked ten to twelve hours each day on the farm, but still went to bed hungry many times. He went to school when he was not needed on the farm, but he only achieved a 4th grade education.

When he reached adulthood, Aldon went to work in the coal mines, which was one of the few types of jobs available to unskilled workers in WV at that time. On April 2, 1942, Aldon joined the Army. He was sent to Fort Thomas, Kentucky for basic training. His unit was sent to Oran, Africa, where Aldon served as a cook. Although he did not participate in any regular fighting, the army base was attacked on one occasion and Aldon fought to repel the enemy. Luckily, he was not seriously wounded, but he was hit by shrapnel which remained in his leg for the rest of his life.

Aldon returned to the US in November of 1943 to marry Susie Elizabeth Burdiss. He was discharged from the service on February 2, 1946. He was awarded a Good Conduct Medal, an American Theater Ribbon, a European African Middle Eastern Theater Ribbon, and a World War II Victory Ribbon.

Aldon and Susie moved to Marfrance, WV and had six children. He worked at several local mines, then with his brother Chester at the George Company coal mines until he retired in 1972. In 1973, the family moved to Quinwood, WV, where he spent the rest of his life. Aldon died from a heart attack at the age of 64 on February 16, 1982.

Susie Elizabeth Burdiss was born on July 3, 1923 at Van Wood in Raleigh County, WV. Her parents were *Edward Peter Burdiss* and *Susie Bell Hundley*. Susie was the oldest of three girls in the family, and had nine brothers. Her father and older brothers were all coal miners.

Susie's family did not believe in formal education for their children, but she pleaded to be allowed to go to school. Her parents finally agreed, but were not supportive. Susie had to get up every morning at five o'clock and get dressed without lighting the coal oil lamp, so she wouldn't disturb her sleeping family, and go to school without breakfast or lunch. She had only one dress which she washed and ironed each night to wear the next day. Susie managed to get a third grade education before the family moved too far from a school that was within walking distance for her to attend.

Susie began dating Aldon George before he went into the army, but while he was overseas they broke up, and she was married briefly to another man, but had the marriage annulled and married Aldon George on December 6, 1943. She had six children, the oldest of whom, Patsy Sue, received brain damage from the doctor's forceps during delivery. Patsy never developed mentally beyond the age of three years.

Susie was a homemaker all her life. She always cared for Patsy in her home. Susie died from complications due to lung cancer on March 21, 1998.

....

WALTER GREG GEORGE AND VIRGIE DELTA CALES
(Paternal grandparents of Nancy George Richmond)

Walter Greg George was born in Tucker County, WV, on October 8, 1894. His parents were *George Washington George* and *Ida Belle Smith*. He and his wife had seven children — Aldon, Chester, Trophie, Bob, Frank, Denver and Olive. The family lived at Marfrance for a time, where Walter worked as a coal miner and later as a timber cutter.

Walter and Virgie received 75 acres of land in Nicholas County from Virgie's father in 1924, where they built a home and farmed the land. They sold most of the farm to the Gauley Land Company in 1936. Walter was diagnosed as being a carrier of tuberculosis, and both his wives died of the disease. Walter died on October12, 1972.

Virgie Delta Cales was born in Ronceverte, WV, on April 1, 1897. She was the daughter of *Allen Taylor Cales* and *Amanda Alice McClung*. She married Walter Greg George on June 15, 1916 in Ironton, Ohio. The couple had seven children. She was a

3

homemaker. Virgie died of pulmonary tuberculosis on June 25, 1942, at the age of forty five. She was buried at the Mt Urim Baptist Church Cemetery in Nicholas County, WV.

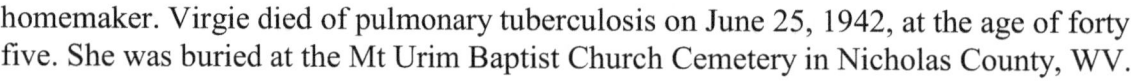

EDWARD PETER BURDISS AND SUSIE BELLE HUNDLEY
(Maternal grandparents of Nancy George Richmond)

Edward Peter Burdiss was born in Jacksonville, Ohio on May 4, 1889. His father was *James Burdiss* and his mother was *Martha Madge Bennett*. Edward moved to WV, where he met and married Susie Belle Hundley in March of 1910. They had twelve children, nine sons and three daughters, all of whom survived to maturity. Edward was a coal miner. During prohibition, he also was a moonshine runner, someone who drove illegal alcohol to various distribution points around the state. He was considered to be the best moonshine runner in Raleigh county.

The family moved to Charmco, WV and lived on Bingham Road. Edward became ill while at work at the Betty Page Coal Company in Rupert, and died of a heart attack while walking to the town physician's office on August 13, 1952.

Susie Belle Hundley (sometimes spelled Hunley) was born in West Virginia on June 25, 1892. (Her death certificate has several mistakes on it, including her date of birth and her father's and mother's names). Her father was *William Hundley* and her mother was *Ellen Cleaver*. Little is known of her early life or parental family, except that she had a brother Samuel and a sister Elizabeth. She married Edward Burdiss in March of 1910, and they produced twelve children. Susie was a homemaker and was a true Appalachian artisan, painting pictures and sculpting wall plaques.

Susie's oldest son Edgar died from injuries in an automobile accident when she was 48, which resulted in a nervous breakdown for her. She recovered, and continued to live at Charmco with her son Cecil for several years after her husband's death, and later moved with him and his family to Kansas, where she died on October 25, 1972.

JAMES BURDISS AND MARTHA MADGE BENNETT
(Maternal great grandparents of Nancy George Richmond)

James Burdiss was born in 1848 in England. At the age of two, he came to America with his father *George Burdiss*,(who was born either in Scotland or Ireland) his mother and his brothers — Henry, George and Alexander. The family departed from Liverpool, England on the ship 'West Point', and arrived in New York, New York on

September 2, 1850. James married Martha Madge Bennett, and was a coal miner. He died in West Virginia.

Martha Madge Bennett was born around 1857 in Kentucky. Her father was born in England and her mother was born in Kentucky. She married James Burdiss and they had at least seven children. In 1900 the family lived in Mount Hope, Fayette County, WV. Martha died in West Virginia.

....

ALLAN TAYLOR CALES AND AMANDA ALICE McCLUNG
(Paternal great grandparents of Nancy George Richmond)

Allen Taylor Cales was born on February 1 of 1848 in a cabin in the Appalachian mountains. His mother was *Mary Polly Cales*, who was born at Stump Lick Hollow near what is now Hinton, WV. It was a very rugged and sparsely settled area, and the Cales family rarely saw outsiders. Mary had five children out of wedlock, called by people in that area 'Children of God' because their father was unknown.
Allen was one of the children, probably fathered by a male relative. Later Mary Polly married and had several more children. Allen met Amanda Alice McClung and they wed on July 29 of 1876. Allen was a farmer in Nicholas County, WV. He died in Bamboo, WV on April 29, 1931. His death certificate listed his cause of death as 'dropsy'.

Amanda Alice McClung was born at Hominy Creek, Virginia (now WV) in January of 1855. Her parents were *Hamilton McClung* and *Susan Moses*. She married Allen T. Cales and they had several children. Amanda died in 1898 at the age of 43.

....

HAMILTON McCLUNG AND SUSAN MOSES
(2nd great grandparents of Nancy George Richmond)

Hamilton McClung was the fourth child of *James and Nancy Williams McClung*. He was born November 23, 1826 in (West) Virginia. He was a farmer in Hominy Falls, Nicholas County. He married Susan Moses on October 13, 1851, and had four children with her.

Susan Moses was born in 1832 in Virginia, and lived in Hominy Falls, where she met Hamilton McClung. Her parents were *James and Mary Moses*. She died in 1897.

....

LABAN SMITH
(3rd great grandfather of Nancy George Richmond)

Laban Smith was born on February 12, 1821. His mother was *Katie Smith* and his father was a young Seneca Indian brave who had been taken in by the Vanmeter family, who lived on a nearby farm. Katie's father forbade them to marry, and Laban was raised by the Smith family. His mother Katie was born in 1799.

....

ISAAC LIPTRAP
(5th great grandfather of Nancy George Richmond)

Isaac Liptrap was born in 1753 in Middlesex, England. He is the founder of the Liptrap family in America. He first appears in the public record in January of 1772, while living in the east end of London. He had been orphaned about 14 years earlier and lived with aunts and uncles until 1771. What he did for a living is unknown, although he was probably an unskilled laborer, which means his wages would not have been enough to pay for food and lodging. London at that time was dirty and overcrowded, and still used a ditch down the middle of the street as a sewer. Many of it's population starved to death.

Around the first of May in 1772, records show that Isaac Liptrap was put on trial at the Old Bailey Justice Hall in London, accused of burglary of the house of Eliezar Pigot of Endfiled, Middlesex, where he allegedly stole several items. His accomplice, Isaac Francis, testified against him. Three cousins testified as to his character (John Liptrap of London, John Allen of Whitechappel, and John Dutton of Ralph's Key). Isaac was sentenced to death, as was the custom, but the sentence was commuted to transportation to the colonies to be an indentured servant.

In July of 1772, Isaac Liptrap, now twenty years old, boarded the ship 'Tayloe' under Captain Dougal McDougal, along with 173 other convicts, to make the two month voyage to Virginia. It is unknown where Isaac Liptrap's indenture was sold. When the American Revolution broke out, the convict trade was ended. The 'Tayloe' was anchored in the Thames River in London and became one of the infamous Prison Hulks that held transportable convicts until transportation to Australia was established.

Isaac's indenture was probably sold to a citizen or company in the Rappahannock River area, and very little is known of him for the next 14 years, which was probably the length of service for his indenture. Isaac was married on July 29, 1785, in Augusta County, to *Mary Bright*, who was born in 1763 and died in 1850. Her father was *George*

Adam Bright. The minister who married the couple was Rev. Archibald Scott of Staunton, Virginia. They had nine children, and purchased land near the town of Moffatts Creek, Virginia. Isaac died around 1820. A complete transcript of Isaac's trial can be found in Chapter Three.

....

JAMES MOSES
(3rd great grandfather of Nancy George Richmond)

James Moses was born in England in the late 1700's and was the son of *William Moses*. He married *Mary Polly Adkins*, also born in England. It is not known exactly when he came to America. He and Mary Polly were farmers in Boutetourt County, Virginia. They later moved to Greenbrier County. They were the parents of eight children. James died sometime in 1867.

....

JAMES McCLUNG AND NANCY WILLIAMS
(3rd great grandparents of Nancy George Richmond)

James McClung (called Limb Jim) was born on May 22, 1798. His parents were *John McClung* and *Jane Bollar*. He married *Nancy Williams* on October 7, 1819. They had five children. James died in January of 1862.

....

JOHN McCLUNG AND JANE BOLLAR
(4th great grandparents of Nancy George Richmond)

John McClung was the first child of *William and Abigail Dickson (Dickinson)*. He was born on January 10, 1768. He married *Jane Bollar* of Bath County, VA, on March 14, 1793. Jane's parents were *John and Margaret Thornton Bollar*. John and Jane McClung lived in a log cabin one mile east of present day Rupert, WV. The couple had a total of ten children. After his first wife's death, John remarried and had five more children.

John was a blacksmith by trade and was called "Black John" by the locals. He served as the postmaster of Rupert, near his home, for several years. Black John was a man of medium height and weight, and was very strong. He enjoyed hunting and outdoor activities. John died on July 20, 1850.

....

WILLIAM McCLUNG AND ABIGAIL DICKSON
(5th great grandparents of Nancy George Richmond)

William McClung was born around 1738 in Somerset, PA. Better known as Captain Billie McClung and in later years as 'Grandfather Billie', he was the first white man to explore the area in what is now Rupert, Greenbrier County, WV. The McClung family was of Scotch-Irish descent. Thomas McClung emigrated from Britain in 1729 and eventually settled in Pennsylvania, where the family flourished.

Around 1742, three McClung brothers, James, William and Hugh moved into what is now Rockbridge County, Va. Their cousin, *John McClung* joined them. Seven of John's sons, including William, moved into Greenbrier County. In 1773, William moved with his wife and three children from Rockbridge to the shores of the Big Clear Creek. He was the first settler on Meadow River (the area was originally called McClung's Meadows, and the river later became the Meadow River). William took a 'tomahawk entry' for ten thousand acres of land. There were no mills or stores for many miles around his first cabin. The local Native Americans were hostile, so that he had to plow his land with his rifle tied to his shoulder, while his wife, *Abigail Dickson*, (sometimes spelled Dickinson) daughter of *Joseph Carpenter* and *Abigail Dickinson*, took the musket with her and the children and hid in the swamp during the day. When the Shawnee raided the area on their second attack of Fort Donnally (twenty miles east of the McClung cabin) spies managed to get through in time to warn them of the raid. The family just made it into the fort before the Indians attacked.

William and his brother-in-law General Andrew Moore patented a forty three thousand acre tract of land between the Meadow and Gauley Rivers, in what is now Nicholas County, WV.

William was tall for a man of his time, and very handsome. He was a good neighbor and citizen. He donated land for what is now the Amwell Baptist Church in Rupert, and was an Elder in the Old Stone Church in Lewisburg, which he would ride 20 miles to attend. He served in the Revolutionary War as an ensign in the Virginia militia.

William and his wife had eleven children, and many grandchildren. William used to say that he could stand in his doorway and blow his bugle and call 200 of his descendants to breakfast. In his old age 'Grandfather Billie' often gave 100 acre tracts of land to his grandchildren as birthday and wedding gifts.

William died on January 18, 1833, at the age of ninety five. He was a true pioneer and a founding father of Greenbrier and Nicholas counties. William is buried in the Old Amwell Cemetery in Greenbrier County.

••

JOHN BOLLAR AND MARGARET THORNTON
(5th great grandparents of Nancy George Richmond)

Major John Bollar (sometimes spelled Bolar) was born on July 23, 1721 in Long Crendon, Buckinghamshire, England, and emigrated to Virginia. He served during the Revolutionary War. He was the son of *Samuel Bolar*. John married *Margaret Thornton* in 1765 at Brandywine Manor, Chester, PA. He died in 1818.

....

THOMAS PRATHER
(9th great grandfather of Nancy George Richmond)

Thomas Prather is listed on 'America's First Families Ancestor Roll of Honor'. He was born in 1604 in Wiltshire, England, at Eton Water House near Salisbury. His name was spelled Prater in England. When he was a young man, England was expanding its control and development of the colonies in America. The King of England knew he could not hold control of the distant land without the allegiance of his subjects there. So, in keeping with the feudal system, he offered property to those 'born of gentry' that would go there to claim it. By doing this he knew that the younger children born to those who held power and property by the grace of the King would go to the Colonies to claim land for themselves. The younger children of gentry in England generally did not receive an inheritance, due to the custom of giving the bulk of the father's property to the first born son, along with the titles. Thus the only way a younger son could gain title, position, or property was by marriage or by the grace of the King.

Thomas came to Virginia on the ship the 'Marie Providence' in 1622. He indentured himself and probably served five years to pay for his passage to the new world. After he was released from his indenture, he was granted fifty acres of land. He married *Mary McKay* and had five sons, several of whom moved to Maryland and were prominent in the State's history. Thomas died in 1666.

....

JOHN NUTHALL
(10th great grandfather of Nancy George Richmond)

John Nuthall is listed on 'America's First Families Ancestor Roll of Honor'. He was born in London, England in 1620, the son of a merchant. He emigrated to America, to Northampton, VA. As a young man, he ran away from his master and lived with the Indians long enough to learn their language, and served later as an interpreter. The

Indians sold John to William Jones, a Chesapeake Bay trader.

By 1640 John had become a prominent man in Northampton, and obtained a commission from the Governor of Maryland to trade with the Indians for furs. In 1651, he signed the Submission to Parliament in Virginia and signed the Instructions to the Virginia House of Burgess in 1652. He was a merchant and a lawyer. He married *Eleanor Holloway* in 1645, and they had four children.

John moved to Maryland in 1661. He bought the Cross Manor and St. Elizabeth's Manor, estates of 200 acres each, and 200 acres on St. Ingoes Creek. There he served as Commissioner and as the Justice of the Peace. He died around 1668.

....

ALEXANDER RAY
(8th great grandfather of Nancy George Richmond)

Alexander Ray is listed on 'America's First Families Ancestor Roll of Honor'. He was born in 1630 in England. Alexander emigrated to America in 1652, on the ship of Captain Augustine Warner. They landed in Virginia on October 26, and little else is known of him until he moved to Maryland in 1664, where he became a prominent citizen. He died on September 15, 1675.

....

ROBERT COLES
(10th great grandfather of Nancy George Richmond)

Robert Coles was born in Sudbury, Suffolk, England in 1597. He came from England in the fleet with Governor Winthrop in 1630 to either Ipswich or the Massachusetts Bay Colony, and in October of that year requested to be a Freeman of Roxbury, Mass. His request was granted in 1631.

Robert was fined by the village several times for public intoxication. He was shamed publicly and forced to sew a red letter 'D' for drunkard on his clothing for a year. The town records state: "March 4, 1663: The court orders that Robert Coles, for drunkenness by him committed at Roxbury, shall be disenfranchised, weare about his necke and so to hange upon his outward garment this for a yeare, and not to leave it off at any time when he comes amongst company, under penalty of XLS, for the first offense, and V (five pounds) the second, and after to be punished by the court as they think meete; also he is to weare the D outwards, and is enjoyned to appear at the next general court, and to contynue until it be ended". The fines against Robert were eventually dropped on the condition that he leave the colony. He moved to Rhode Island in 1637, where he reformed and became one of the town founders. Robert married *Mary Hawkhurst* with whom he had a son Robert. He died around 1658.

••

JOHN POWELL
(10th great grandfather of Nancy George Richmond)

John Powell, born around 1580, was one of the founders of the original Jamestown Colony in Virginia. He came to America from England aboard the ship the 'Swallow' in 1609. He was listed in the passenger muster as 'John Powell, Tailor'. His future wife, *Kathern Burgess*, born in 1602, came to America on the ship 'Flying Hart' in 1622. John survived the "starving time" of the 1609-1610 winter. Land records indicate that he lived in Newport News, where he owned 150 acres, listed on September 10, 1624, and in Elizabeth City (50 acres) on May 2, 1638. He married Kathern in 1623 in Elizabeth City. John died sometime around 1638.

••

THOMAS SPRIGG
(9th great grandfather of Nancy George Richmond)

Thomas Sprigg was born in 1630 in Kettering, Northamptonshire, England. He came first to the Colony of Virginia and lived in Northamptonshire County. There he signed the Submission to Parliament in 1651. From Virginia he moved to Maryland in what later became Prince George County. He received a grant of 1000 acres from Lord Baltimore in that county. He was one of the justices of Calvert County and High Sheriff. He died on December 29, 1704.

••

KING BELA OF HUNGARY
(26th great grandfather of Nancy George Richmond)

Bela was born 1148-died 1196. He was educated in the court of the Byzantine Emperor of Manuel I. He was one of the most powerful rulers of Hungary and he was also one of the most wealthy monarchs of Europe of that age. It was probably he who began to organize the Royal Chancellery in Hungary. Bela was a powerful ruler, and his court was one of the most brilliant in Europe. He was an exceptionally tall man for his time, well over six feet. His remains are interred at the Mathias Church in Budapest, with those of his wife *Agnes*.

Through his mother, Bela descended from ***Harold II of England*** (whose descendants were dispossessed as a result of the Norman Conquest). Through his son, Andrew II, Bela was an ancestor of ***King Edward III of England***. As a result, all subsequent English and British monarchs could claim descent from Harold II.

••

YAROSLAV I THE WISE
(31ˢᵗ great grandfather of Nancy George Richmond)

Yaroslav was born in 978 in Kiev and died there in 1054 (East Slavic). He was thrice Grand Prince of Novgorod and Kiev, uniting the two for a time under his rule. During his reign, Kiev reached the height of its cultural and military power. One of the largest cathedrals in Kiev is dedicated to him. His memory is kept alive by innumerable Russian folk ballads and legends, which refer to him as Krasno Solnyshko, the Fair Son. With him the Varangian periold of Slavic history ends and the Christian period begins.

••

KING WILLIAM I (WILLIAM THE CONQUEROR)
(31th great grandfather of Nancy George Richmond)

William I, better known as William the Conqueror, was the Duke of Normandy from 1035 and King of England from late 1066 until his death in 1087. Before his conquest of England, he was sometimes known as William the Bastard, because of the illegitimacy of his birth.

To press his claim to the English throne, William invaded England in 1066, leading an army of Normans, Bretons, and Frenchmen to victory over the English forces of King Harold Godwinson (who died in the conflict) at the Battle of Hastings, and suppressed subsequent English revolts in what has become known as the Norman Conquest. The impact of that change and the extent of the changes was vast. Besides the change in rulers, William's reign also brought a program of building and fortification, changes to the English language, a shift in the upper levels of society and the church, changes in law, trade, agriculture, women's roles and rights, and education.

William was born in Falaise, Normandy, around 1027, the illegitimate and only son of *Robert I*, Duke of Normandy, who named him as heir of Normandy. His mother was the daughter of the local tanner. William was fair complected, with very powerful arms and a 'magnificent appearance'. He was remarkably healthy and remained so until his death in 1087.

12

···

KING MALCOM I OF SCOTLAND
(36th great grandfather of Nancy George Richmond)

Malcom I, the son of *Donald Dasachtach*, obtained the abdicated throne of his father. He was a ruler of great abilities and prudence, and King Edmund of England sought his alliance by ceding Cumbria, which consisted of Cumberland and part of Westmorland to him in the year 945, on the condition that he would defend that northern county, and become an ally. Edred, the brother and successor of Edmond, obtained the aid of Malcolm against Anlaf, King of Northumberland, whose country he wasted, and carried off the people and cattle. Malcom was later slain by nobles in retaliation, sometime around 1020.

···

QUEEN EALDGYTH OF ENGLAND
(28th great grandmother of Nancy George Richmond)

Ealdgyth was born around 1034 in Mercia, England. She died after 1086. She married *Harold II of Godwinsson* around 1064.

···

LADY GODIVA
(30th great grandmother of Nancy George Richmond)

Lady Godiva, born in 1040,was the wife of *Leofric*, Earl of Mercia. Her name occurs on charters and the Domesday survey, though the spelling varies. Her name means 'Gift of God'. She was a widow when she married Leofric. They were both generous benefactors to the Church.

After Leofric's death in 1057, she lived on until around 1087. Below is the story of Lady Godiva and her famous ride.

Lady Godiva took pity on the people of Coventry, who were suffering terribly under her husband's oppressive taxation. She appealed to him many times to lower the taxes, but he refused. Finally, angered by her entreaties, Leofric said he would grant her request if she would strip naked and ride through the streets of the town. Lady Godiva took him at his word, and after issuing a decree that all persons must stay indoors and shut their windows, she rode though the village, clothed only in her long hair. One villager, a tailor named Tom, disobeyed. He bored a hole in his shutter so that he could watch her pass by, and was arrested for his impudence. This is where the term 'Peeping Tom' originated.

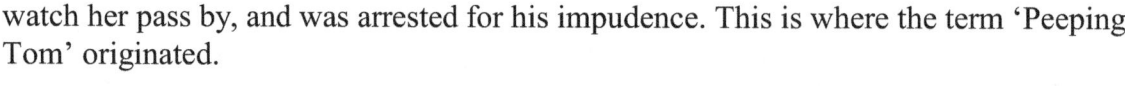

KING ETHELRED 'THE UNREADY' OF ENGLAND
(30th great grandfather of Nancy George Richmond)

King Ethelred was born around 968, in Wessex, England and died on April 23, 1016 in London. He married *Queen Alfgifu* of England around 985. He was born into the royal house of Wessex, which was the ruler of all the Anglo-Saxons. He was a direct descendant of Alfred the Great, and the son of *King Edgar*, who had ruled a peaceful England for 16 years. At Edgar's death in 975, the realm passed to Ethelred's brother Edward, who was still a child. The nobles of the kingdom formed rival parties around the two brothers, and Edward was murdered on March 18, 978, making Ethelred king. Edward became honored as a saint, which gave the noblemen an excuse to make war against Ethelred.

From the time of Ethelred's accession at 10 years of age, his reign was marred by treason and revolts by the nobles. He was an indecisive ruler and tried buying off his enemies, which shamed his subjects, and he was given the name of 'Unready'.

QUEEN ALFGIFU OF ENGLAND
(30th great grandmother of Nancy George Richmond)

Queen Alfgifu was born about 985 in Wessex, England. She was the daughter of *Thorad Gunnarsson*, the wife of King Ethelred, and the mother of Elfgifu of England.

KING EDGAR 'THE PEACEABLE' OF ENGLAND
(31st great grandfather of Nancy George Richmond)

King Edgar was born in 943 and died in July 975. In 955 Edgar's uncle, King Edred, died and his elder brother Edwig became King. Two years later, the kingdom was divided and Edgar was given the northern regions of Merica and Northumbria to reign.

Although he was a good king, Edgar was not overly religious. He had many affairs, which gave rise to numerous stories. One said that he had fallen in love with the beautiful daughter of a nobleman of Andover. While visiting the town, he ordered that she be sent to his chambers for the night. Instead, the family sent a young maid servant in her place. After spending the night with the girl, he discovered the switch, and repaid the nobleman's treachery by confiscating all his lands and giving them to the maidservant.

....

QUEEN AELFTHRYTH OF ENGLAND
(31st great grandmother of Nancy George Richmond)

Queen AElfthryth is considered by many historians to be one of the most ruthless women to ever have lived. She put her own ambitions above everything else, including her family. She caused the death of her first husband and was responsible for the murder of her step son, King Edward the Martyr.

AElfthryth was of royal blood on both sides of her family. She was reputed to be so lovely that *King Edgar* sent his trusted friend, Aethelwald, to go and see for himself how beautiful she was, and if the stories were true, to make an offer for her hand on his behalf. Aethelwald fell in love with AElfthryth himself, and married her. He wrote to the King and told him that the woman was horrible. Edgar was no fool, and he sent word that he would come to console the lady for being so ugly. Aethelwald begged his wife to make herself look as bad as possible for the King, but she did not. King Edgar fell madly in love with her and killed Aethelwald while hunting with him in order to possess her.

King Edgar had been married before. He had children with his first two wives. He and AElfthryth were married around 965. Although Edward, the son of his first wife, was older, the King declared his first son by AElfthryth as his heir. However, the boy died in 970, leaving a little brother, Ethelred, who was born in 968. In 973 Edgar, no doubt to strengthen his claim to being King of England, arranged to be crowned a second time, and he also had AElfthryth crowned and anointed as Queen, the highest honor that could be bestowed upon the wife of a King.

Two years later Edgar died, leaving two sons, Edward by his first wife and the Queen's son Ethelred. Edward had the support of the Archbishops of Canterbury and York and was chosen to be King.

In 978 King Edward visited his stepmother and brother at Corfe Castle. As he rode into sight, he was attacked and killed by men in the Queen's service. Ethelred, just a few years old, became the King of England, with his mother named as regent until he came of age. The Queen's allies deserted her, so she retired from court, but continued to influence her son until her death.

....

KING EDMUND 'THE MAGNIFICENT' OF ENGLAND
(32nd great grandfather of Nancy George Richmond)

King Edmund (922-946) was the eldest son of *King Edward the Elder* by this third wife *Edgiva*. At the age of sixteen, he and his older half-brother, King Aethelstan, fought together to expel the Norsemen from Northern England at the Battle of Brunanburgh. He was the first King to rule a united England upon his brother's death two years later. He was married twice. His first wife, *St. Elgiva*, was the mother of King Edgar the Peaceable.

Edmund was killed by an outlaw during a fight at court in 946, an outrage which shocked the entire country.

••

KING EDWARD 'THE ELDER'
(33rd great grandfather of Nancy George Richmond)

King Edward was born in 874 and died in 924. He became King of England upon the death of his father, *King Alfred the Great*. His court was at Winchester, previously the capital of Wessex. He captured the eastern Midlands and East Anglia from the Danes in 917 and became the ruler of Mercia in 918. He was the second King of the Anglo-Saxons, as this title was created by his father Alfred.

Edward died leading an army against a Welsh-Mercian rebellion on July 17, 924 at Farndon-Upon-Dee and was buried in New Minster in Winchester, Hampshire.

••

KING ALFRED (THE GREAT) OF ENGLAND
(34th great grandfather of Nancy George Richmond)

King Alfred was born in 849 and died October 26, 899. He was the King of the Anglo Saxon Kingdom of Wessex from 871 to 899. He is noted for his defense of the Anglo-Saxon Kingdoms of southern England against the Vikings, and was the only English King to be given the title "the Great". Alfred was a learned man who encouraged education and improved his kingdom's legal system and military structure. Alfred married *Ealhswith*, daughter of *Aethelred Mucil*.

Alfred is venerated as a Saint by the Eastern Orthodox Church and is regarded as the hero of the Christian Church by the Anglican Communion. He had several children with Ealhswith, one of which, Edward the Elder, succeeded him to the throne. Alfred's cause of death is not known.

KING AETHELWULF OF WESSEX
(35th great grandfather of Nancy George Richmond)

King Aethelwulf, whose name means 'Noble Wolf', was born in 795 and died in 858. He was the elder son of *King Egbert of Wessex*. He conquered Kent on behalf of his father in 825. He succeeded his father as King of Wessex, whereupon he became King of Wessex in 839. His father had been a veteran warrior who had fought for survival since his youth, leaving his son a united Kingdom.

Aethelwulf was very religious, but he had little political savvy. One of his first acts as King was to split the kingdom, giving half to his son Athelstan. He and his first wife *Osburga* had five sons and a daughter .Each of his sons succeeded to the throne. Alfred, his youngest son, was one of the greatest Kings ever to rule Britain.

....

KING BERNARD OF ITALY
(37th great grandfather of Nancy George Richmond)

King Bernard (born 795-died 818) was the illegitimate son of *King Pepin* of Italy, who was the second legitimate son of *King Charlemagne*. When Pepin died, Charlemagne allowed Bernard to inherit Italy. Bernard married *Cunigunda* of Laon in 813, and they had one son, Pepin, the Count of Vermandois.

Before 817, Bernard was the trusted agent of his grandfather. His rights in Italy were respected, and he was used to manage events in his sphere of influence. However, when Louis the Pious drew up an Orinatio Imperil, detailing the future of the Frankish Empire, it meant Bernard would get no more territory, and would be a vassal. Bernard began plotting with a group of magnates, Eggideo, Reginhard, and Reginhar, to overthrow Louis.

Louis the Pious reacted swiftly against the plot, marching south to Chalon. Bernard and his associates were taken by surprise, and he and the other ringleaders were forced to surrender. Louis had them taken to Aix-la-Chapelle, where they were condemned to death. Louis 'mercifully' commuted their sentences to blinding, which would end their threat without actually killing them, however, the process of blinding the men (jabbing their eyes with a hot poker) caused the death of Bernard.

....

KING PEPIN OF ITALY
(38th great grandfather of Nancy George Richmond)

King Pepin of Italy(born 777-died July 8, 810) was the second legitimate son of *King Charlemagne*. He was named Carloman, but when his half-brother Pepin the Hunchback betrayed their father, the royal name Pepin passed to him. He was made King of Italy after his father's conquest of the Lombards in 781, and crowned by Pope Hadrian I with the Iron Crown of Lombardy.

Pepin was active as a ruler and worked to expand the Frankish Empire. He held a long but unsuccessful siege of Venice in 810. It lasted six months and the army was ravaged by disease from a nearby swamp and Pepin was forced to withdraw his troops. A few months later, he died.

Pepin married *Bertha*, whose ancestry is not known. They had five daughters. Pepin also had an illegitimate son, Bernard. At Pepin's death, Bernard inherited the Italian Crown, but the empire went to Pepin's younger brother Louis the Pious.

••

KING CHARLEMAGNE (CHARLES THE GREAT) HOLY ROMAN EMPEROR
(39th great grandfather of Nancy George Richmond)

King Charlemagne (born April 742-died January 814) was the King of the Franks from 768 till his death. He expanded the Frankish Kingdom into an Empire that incorporated much of western and central Europe. He conquered Italy and was crowned Imperator Augustus (Holy Roman Emperor) by Pope Leo III on December 25 of 800. His rule is associated with a revival of art, religion and culture. He helped define Western Europe during the Middle Ages. Today, he is regarded as the founding father of both the French and German monarchies, and also as the father of Europe, since his empire united most of Western Europe for the first time since Roman rule.

Charlemagne was six foot four inches tall, and built to scale. He had beautiful hair, animated eyes, a powerful nose and radiated a 'presence' that was always steady and dignified. He was temperate in eating and drinking, hated drunkenness, and kept himself in good health. He married *Hildegard* and they had several children.

Charlemagne learned to read Latin and Greek but never learned to write. He believed that government should benefit the governed. 'By the sword and the cross' Charlemagne became master of Western Europe.

••

THE RICHMOND FAMILY

CHARLES LEE RICHMOND

Charles Lee Richmond was born in Crichton Coal Camp in Crichton, WV on December 30, 1947. His father, *Charles Wyatt Richmond* was a coal miner and his mother *Melva Marie Smith Richmond* was a homemaker. He had a younger brother and sister, *Curtis Roy* and *Trena Ann*.

Their home was within sight of a huge slate dump, a mountain of coal rejected by the mining company as impure. The slate dump burned continually, covering the entire camp with soot. In the winter, the red glow from the fires could be seen even under a blanket of snow.

Charles lost his father in a coal mining accident when he was ten years old. Every summer for the next six years he lived and worked on his great grandmother Phillips' dairy farm in Gallipolis, Ohio, to earn money for school books and school clothes for himself and his siblings.

Charles attended Crichton High School. He graduated in 1965 at the age of seventeen. He joined the US Marine Corp after graduation and asked to serve in Viet Nam, but his request was denied because he was one of the few Marines who had been trained to operate the new IBM punch card system, and was needed stateside.

Charles' mother had three more children who are his half siblings — *Tracy Richmond Jones*, *Russell Loudermilk Jr.* and *Eva Dawn Loudermilk*.

Charles married Margarete Cameron in 1969. They divorced in 1977, and he married *Nancy George Murray* on September 24, 1977. They had three children.

During his working career, Charles was a certified welder, a police officer and a coal miner. In 1996 he attended Bluefield State College as a Business Major.

In 1993, Charles had a heart attack, but recovered and returned to the mines. On December 27, 1996 he was involved in a major roof fall at the Princess Pollyana Coal Company, in which he received 40 fractures on 23 bones. In 1997, while recovering from the accident, Charles began work on a trilogy of books, the Tribulation Series, which was published in 2010. Charles had cancer in 1999, which he recovered from, but which forced him to retire from work permanently. He moved to Lewisburg with his wife in 2003.

···

CHARLES WYATT RICHMOND AND MELVA MARIE SMITH
(Parents of Charles Lee Richmond)

Charles Wyatt Richmond was born in Carl, WV on March 8, 1925. His father was Charley Richmond and his mother was Verna Trout Richmond. He had two brothers, Chestle and Clendenin Andrew. His father was a coal miner and his mother was a homemaker. When Charles was ten years old, his father died in a swimming accident at Hominey Falls in Nicholas County, WV. His mother ran a boarding house in Leslie, WV in order to support the family after her husband's death.

Charles joined the Navy during World War II. He saw service in the Pacific Theater including Pearl Harbor, Saipan, Guam and Okinawa. After the war, he met Melva Marie Smith. They married on February 14, 1947. The couple had three children — Charles, Curtis and Trena.

The family lived in Crichton, WV, where Charles worked as a coal miner. He also ran an electronics shop and managed the Nettie Drive In Theater on the weekends. He died in a mining accident at the Donnegan Coal Company in Richwood on June 25, 1958, at the age of 33.

Melva Marie Smith was born in Beards Fork, WV on August 27, 1931. She was the daughter of Arby Roy Smith and Mary Olive Phillips Smith. She was the oldest of three children. Her brother was Curtis Roy Smith and her sister was Icy Bell Smith. When Melva was six years old, her family moved to the Crichton Coal Camp, where her father was employed as an underground miner. The family lived in a four room house which was divided into two apartments. Each room had one 'drop', which was a bare electric light bulb hanging from the middle of the ceiling. Every house had a pump outside from which the family drew their water. Melva attended the school in Crichton, which was called at that time the Meadow Bluff School Number Two.

When Melva was fourteen, she met Charles Wyatt Richmond, and married him when she was fifteen. She had her oldest child, Charles Lee, at the age of sixteen. After her first husband's death, she worked as a seamstress, and as a waitress to support her family. She married two more times, once to Marshall Johnson, and later to Russell Loudermilk. She had three more children — Tracy, Russell Jr. And Eva Dawn. She continued to live in Crichton until her death on December 24, 2004.

....

CHARLEY RICHMOND AND VERNA TROUT
(Paternal Grandparents of Charles Lee Richmond)

Charley Richmond was born around 1900 in West Virginia. His parents were King Richmond and Nancy Pittsenbarger. He was one of eight children. He lived with his parents in Wilderness, Nicholas County. He met and married Verna Trout. They had three children — Charles Wyatt, Chestle and Clendenin Andrew. Charley drowned at Hominey Falls in 1935, at the age of 33.

Verna Trout was born in 1901 in WV. Her parents were *Ratha Black Trout* and *Elizabeth O'Dell*. Her father was a coal miner and a preacher. She married Charley Richmond and had three children. After her husband's death, she ran a boarding house and later owned and operated a restaurant in Quinwood, WV. She died in 1974.

....

ARBY ROY SMITH AND MARY OLIVE PHILLIPs
(Maternal grandparents of Charles Lee Richmond)

Arby Roy Smith was born on April 6, 1906 in Mudlety, WV. His father was *John Sam Smith* and his mother was *Nancy Casey*. He had one sister, Pearl. His father was a coal miner. He met Mary Phillips in June of 1929, and they were married on December 25 of that year. The couple had three children. Arby moved to the Crichton Coal Camp in Greenbrier County on August 27, 1936. His family joined him there in April 1937. When the Crichton Mines shut down in 1953, Arby worked for the Quinwood Taxi Company. He died on April 4, 1980 during stomach surgery.

Mary Olive Phillips was born on September 6, 1909 in Poca, Putnam County, WV. Her parents were *Webster Phillips* and *Hannah Elizabeth Syner*. She had one sister and three brothers. Her father was a farmer. When Mary was eight, she was kicked in the head by a mule, which resulted in a severe loss of hearing that worsened as she grew, until she became totally deaf. She learned to read lips to communicate. Mary worked long hours on the farm with her siblings as a child, but loved her childhood. The farm she grew up on was sold and eventually became the Yeager Airport in Charleston, WV. Mary was a homemaker her entire life. She suffered a severe stroke in 1991 and was cared for at her home by her granddaughters Trena and Tracy until her death on October 6, 1994.

....

HENRY ADAMS
(10th great grandfather of Charles Lee Richmond)

Henry Adams was born on January 21, 1583, in Barton, Somerset, England. His father was *John Adams* and his mother was *Agnes Stone*. He is believed to have arrived with his wife, eight sons and a daughter in Boston, Mass in 1632 or 1633. The colonial authorities at Boston allotted to him 40 acres of land at the 'Mount'. He was called Henry

Adams of Braintree because he was one of he earliest settlers in the part of Massachusetts Bay named "Mt. Wollasont", which was incorporated in 1640 as the town of Braintree. Henry Adams was the great great grandfather of the second President of the United States, *President John Adams*. He was the great great grandfather of the great orator, *Samuel Adams*. He was the great great great grandfather of *President John Quincy Adams*. During his lifetime he was a farmer and a maltster. He died in Braintree on October 6, 1646.

....

SIR THOMAS PHILLIPS AND JANE DWINN
(13th great grandparents of Charles Lee Richmond)

Sir Thomas Phillips was born in 1456 in Wales. His parents were *Philip Phillips* and *Janet Lloyd*. He married *Jane Dwinn*, the heiress of Picton Castle. Sir Thomas Phillips of Cilsant was the esquire to the body of King Henry VII. The Cilsant family, which held extensive lands in West Carmarthenshire, was descended from a late 11th century magistrate named Cadifor Fawr. His great grandson, Aaron ap Rhys, took part in the Third Crusade, and became a Knight of the Holy Sepulchre, and is said to have added the golden collar and chain to the back of the lion rampart which is the insignia of the Phillips family. The Phillips have held Picton Castle since the days of Sir Thomas, who died in Cilsant in 1550 at the age of 94.

Throughout the 17th and 18th centuries the Phillips of Picton Castle were the most powerful family in Pembrokeshire. The Castle is now owned by the Picton Castle Trust.

Jane Dwinn was the daughter of *Owain Dwinn*, the last in the line of Dwinns to own Picton Castle. She was born in 1475 in Wales, and died in 1520 in Pembrokeshire. She was the wife of Sir Thomas Phillips of Cilsant.

CHAPTER TWO

FAMILY TREE CHARTS

* Highlighted names indicate that person has a second chart in the tree.
* Highlighted lines on the right of a name indicate a person of royalty.
* Highlighted lines on the left of a name indicate an immigrant.
* Stars indicate Kings and Queens.

PART ONE

Charts for Nancy George (Richmond)

Nancy Kay George

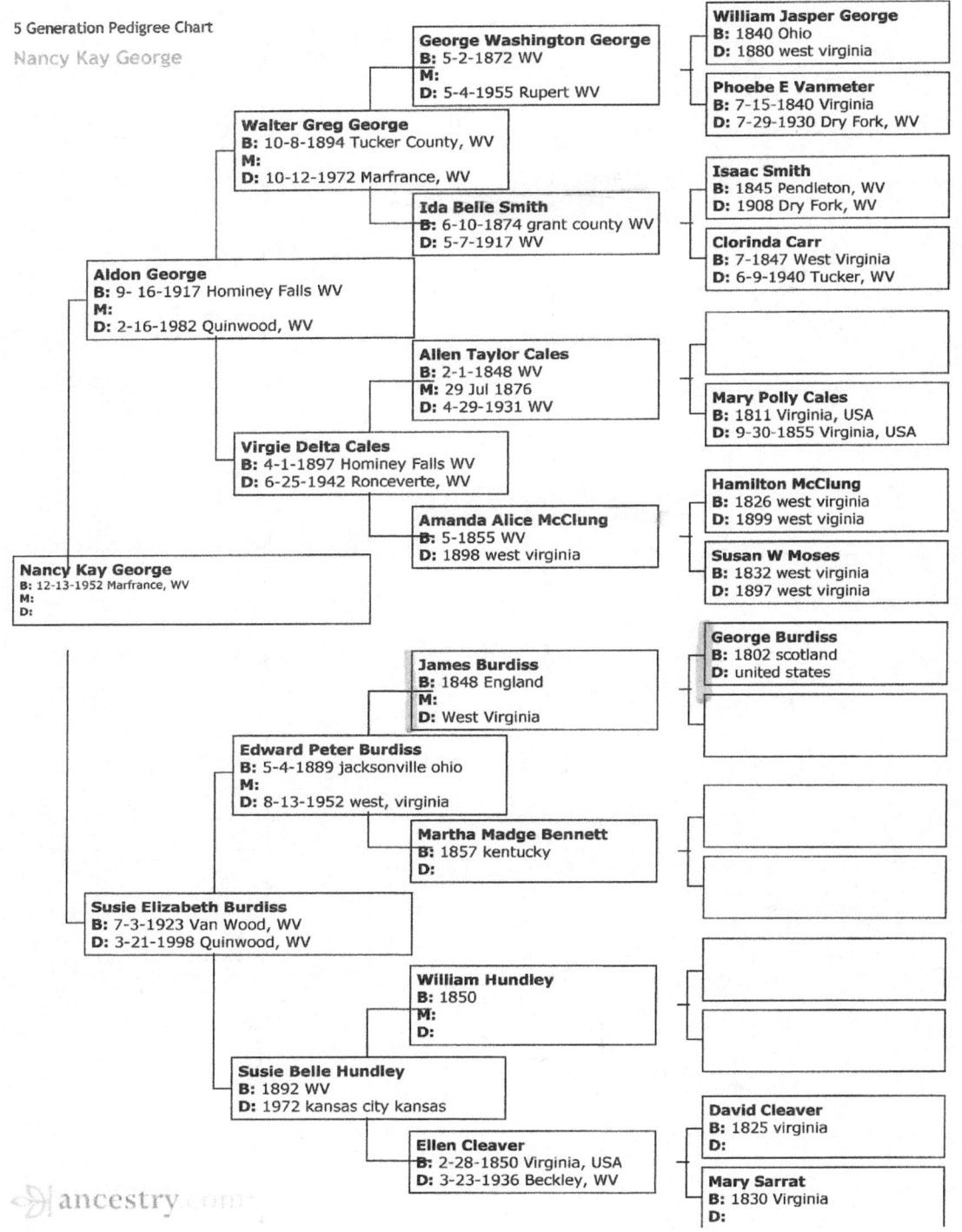

George Washington George
B: 5-2-1872 WV
M:
D: 5-4-1955 Rupert WV

Walter Greg George
B: 10-8-1894 Tucker County, WV
M:
D: 10-12-1972 Marfrance, WV

Ida Belle Smith
B: 6-10-1874 grant county WV
D: 5-7-1917 WV

Aldon George
B: 9- 16-1917 Hominey Falls WV
M:
D: 2-16-1982 Quinwood, WV

Allen Taylor Cales
B: 2-1-1848 WV
M: 29 Jul 1876
D: 4-29-1931 WV

Virgie Delta Cales
B: 4-1-1897 Hominey Falls WV
D: 6-25-1942 Ronceverte, WV

Amanda Alice McClung
B: 5-1855 WV
D: 1898 west virginia

Nancy Kay George
B: 12-13-1952 Marfrance, WV
M:
D:

William Jasper George
B: 1840 Ohio
D: 1880 west virginia

Phoebe E Vanmeter
B: 7-15-1840 Virginia
D: 7-29-1930 Dry Fork, WV

Isaac Smith
B: 1845 Pendleton, WV
D: 1908 Dry Fork, WV

Clorinda Carr
B: 7-1847 West Virginia
D: 6-9-1940 Tucker, WV

Mary Polly Cales
B: 1811 Virginia, USA
D: 9-30-1855 Virginia, USA

Hamilton McClung
B: 1826 west virginia
D: 1899 west viginia

Susan W Moses
B: 1832 west virginia
D: 1897 west virginia

James Burdiss
B: 1848 England
M:
D: West Virginia

Edward Peter Burdiss
B: 5-4-1889 jacksonville ohio
M:
D: 8-13-1952 west, virginia

Martha Madge Bennett
B: 1857 kentucky
D:

Susie Elizabeth Burdiss
B: 7-3-1923 Van Wood, WV
D: 3-21-1998 Quinwood, WV

George Burdiss
B: 1802 scotland
D: united states

William Hundley
B: 1850
M:
D:

Susie Belle Hundley
B: 1892 WV
D: 1972 kansas city kansas

Ellen Cleaver
B: 2-28-1850 Virginia, USA
D: 3-23-1936 Beckley, WV

David Cleaver
B: 1825 virginia
D:

Mary Sarrat
B: 1830 Virginia
D:

25

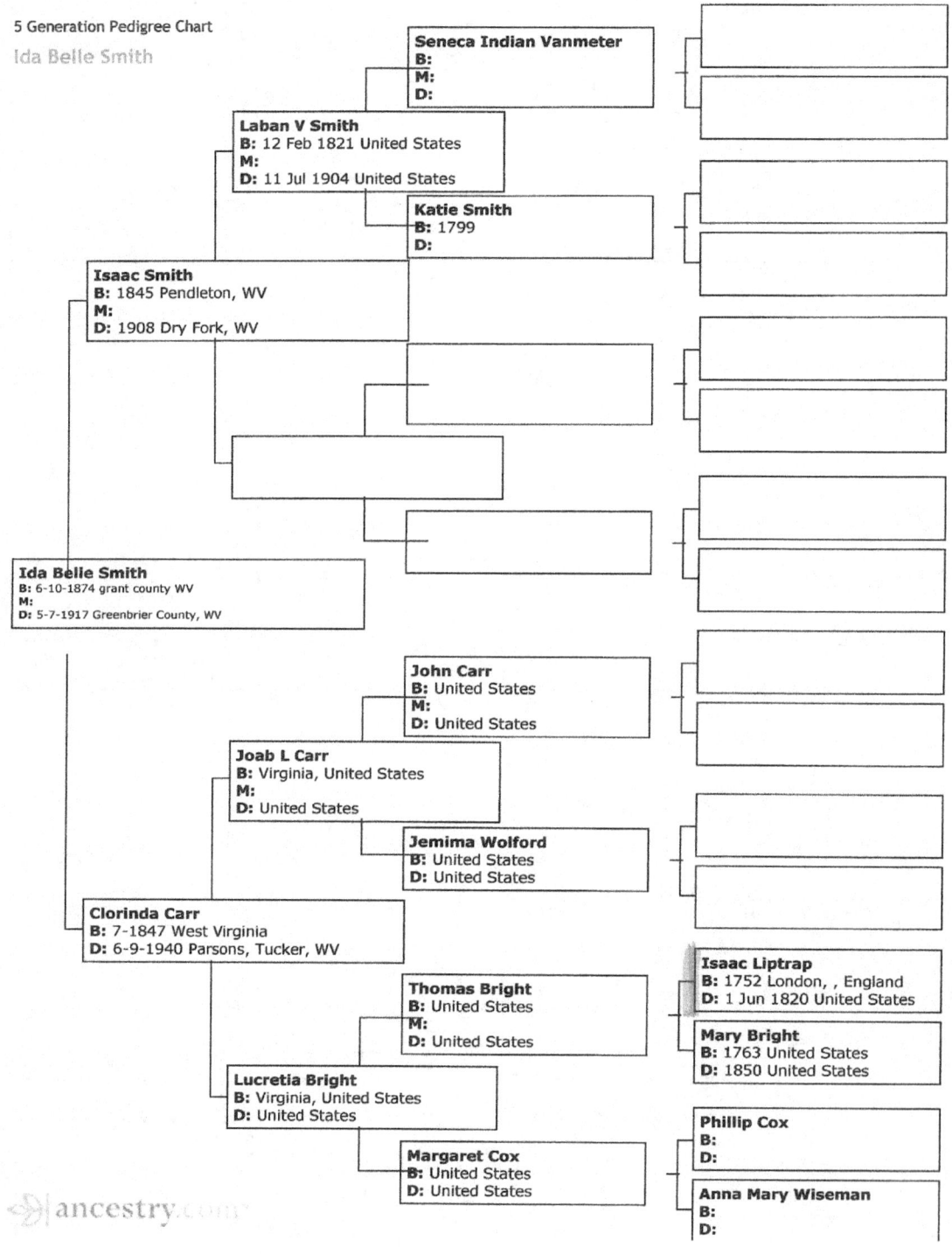

5 Generation Pedigree Chart

Ida Belle Smith

Seneca Indian Vanmeter
B:
M:
D:

Laban V Smith
B: 12 Feb 1821 United States
M:
D: 11 Jul 1904 United States

Katie Smith
B: 1799
D:

Isaac Smith
B: 1845 Pendleton, WV
M:
D: 1908 Dry Fork, WV

Ida Belle Smith
B: 6-10-1874 grant county WV
M:
D: 5-7-1917 Greenbrier County, WV

John Carr
B: United States
M:
D: United States

Joab L Carr
B: Virginia, United States
M:
D: United States

Jemima Wolford
B: United States
D: United States

Clorinda Carr
B: 7-1847 West Virginia
D: 6-9-1940 Parsons, Tucker, WV

Thomas Bright
B: United States
M:
D: United States

Lucretia Bright
B: Virginia, United States
D: United States

Margaret Cox
B: United States
D: United States

Isaac Liptrap
B: 1752 London, , England
D: 1 Jun 1820 United States

Mary Bright
B: 1763 United States
D: 1850 United States

Phillip Cox
B:
D:

Anna Mary Wiseman
B:
D:

ancestry.com

26

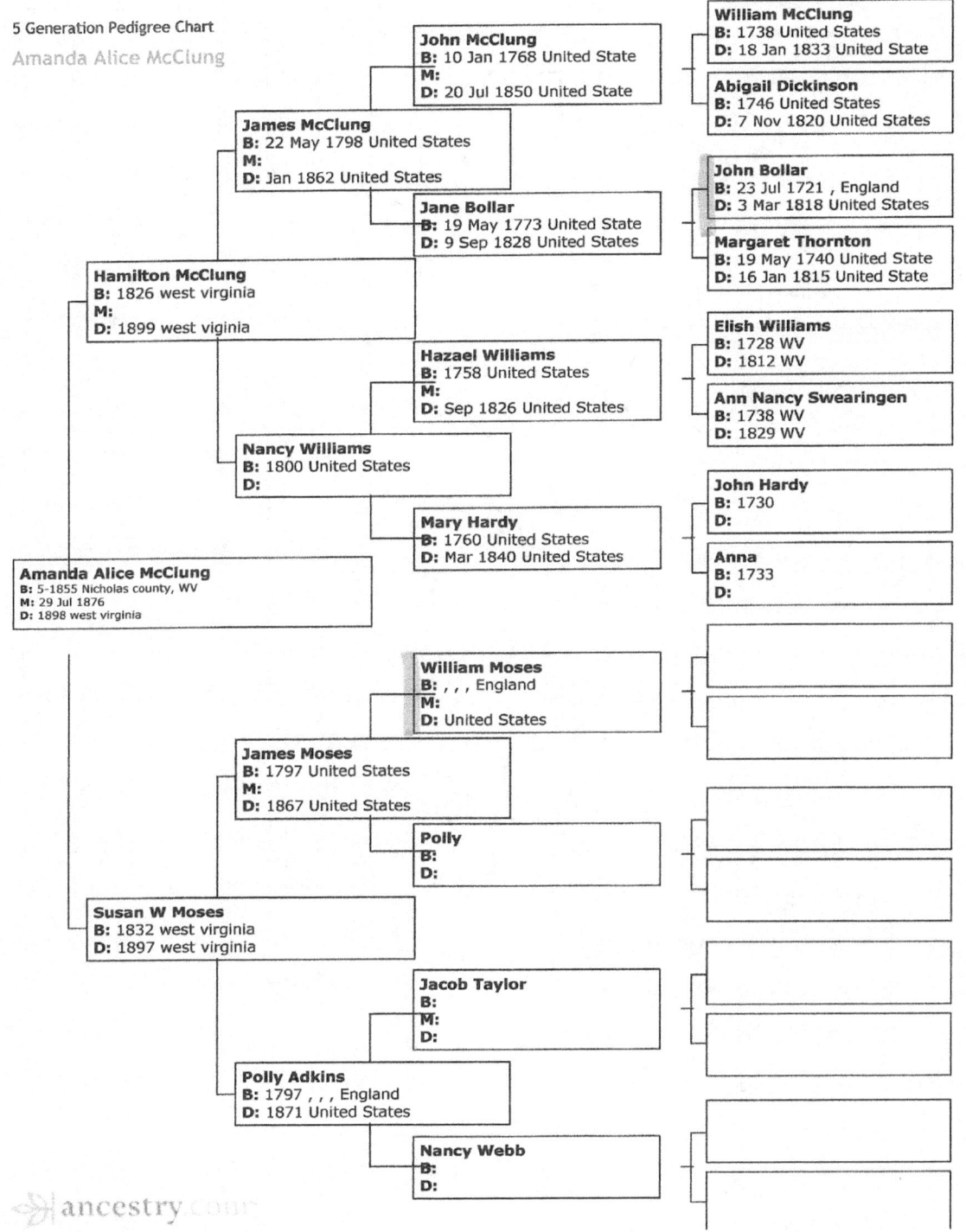

John McClung
B: 10 Jan 1768 United State
M:
D: 20 Jul 1850 United State

James McClung
B: 22 May 1798 United States
M:
D: Jan 1862 United States

Jane Bollar
B: 19 May 1773 United State
D: 9 Sep 1828 United States

Hamilton McClung
B: 1826 west virginia
M:
D: 1899 west viginia

Hazael Williams
B: 1758 United States
M:
D: Sep 1826 United States

Nancy Williams
B: 1800 United States
D:

Mary Hardy
B: 1760 United States
D: Mar 1840 United States

Amanda Alice McClung
B: 5-1855 Nicholas county, WV
M: 29 Jul 1876
D: 1898 west virginia

William McClung
B: 1738 United States
D: 18 Jan 1833 United State

Abigail Dickinson
B: 1746 United States
D: 7 Nov 1820 United States

John Bollar
B: 23 Jul 1721 , England
D: 3 Mar 1818 United States

Margaret Thornton
B: 19 May 1740 United State
D: 16 Jan 1815 United State

Elish Williams
B: 1728 WV
D: 1812 WV

Ann Nancy Swearingen
B: 1738 WV
D: 1829 WV

John Hardy
B: 1730
D:

Anna
B: 1733
D:

William Moses
B: , , , England
M:
D: United States

James Moses
B: 1797 United States
M:
D: 1867 United States

Polly
B:
D:

Susan W Moses
B: 1832 west virginia
D: 1897 west virginia

Jacob Taylor
B:
M:
D:

Polly Adkins
B: 1797 , , , England
D: 1871 United States

Nancy Webb
B:
D:

27

5 Generation Pedigree Chart

William McClung

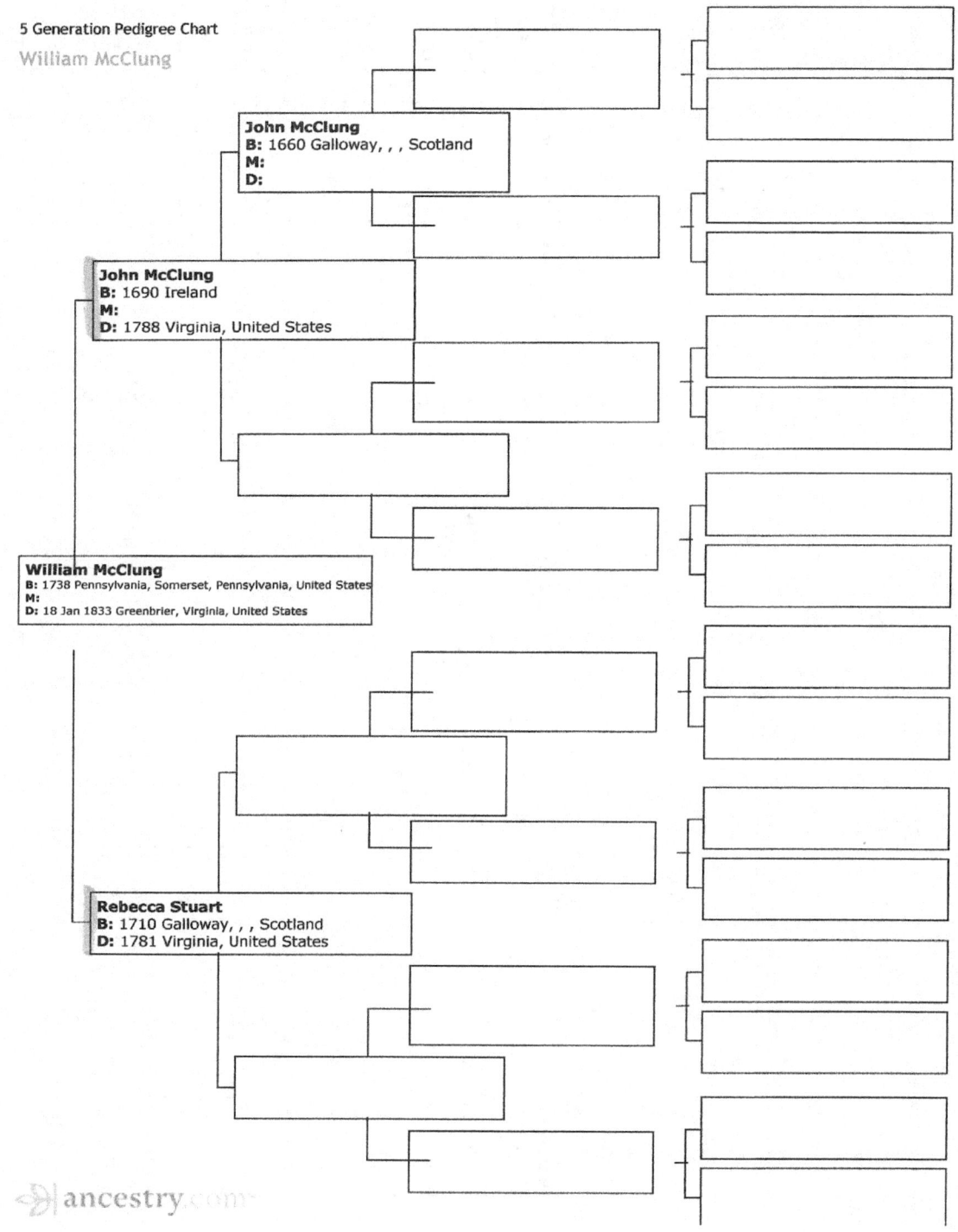

John McClung
B: 1660 Galloway, , , Scotland
M:
D:

John McClung
B: 1690 Ireland
M:
D: 1788 Virginia, United States

William McClung
B: 1738 Pennsylvania, Somerset, Pennsylvania, United States
M:
D: 18 Jan 1833 Greenbrier, Virginia, United States

Rebecca Stuart
B: 1710 Galloway, , , Scotland
D: 1781 Virginia, United States

ancestry.com

28

Abigail Dickson

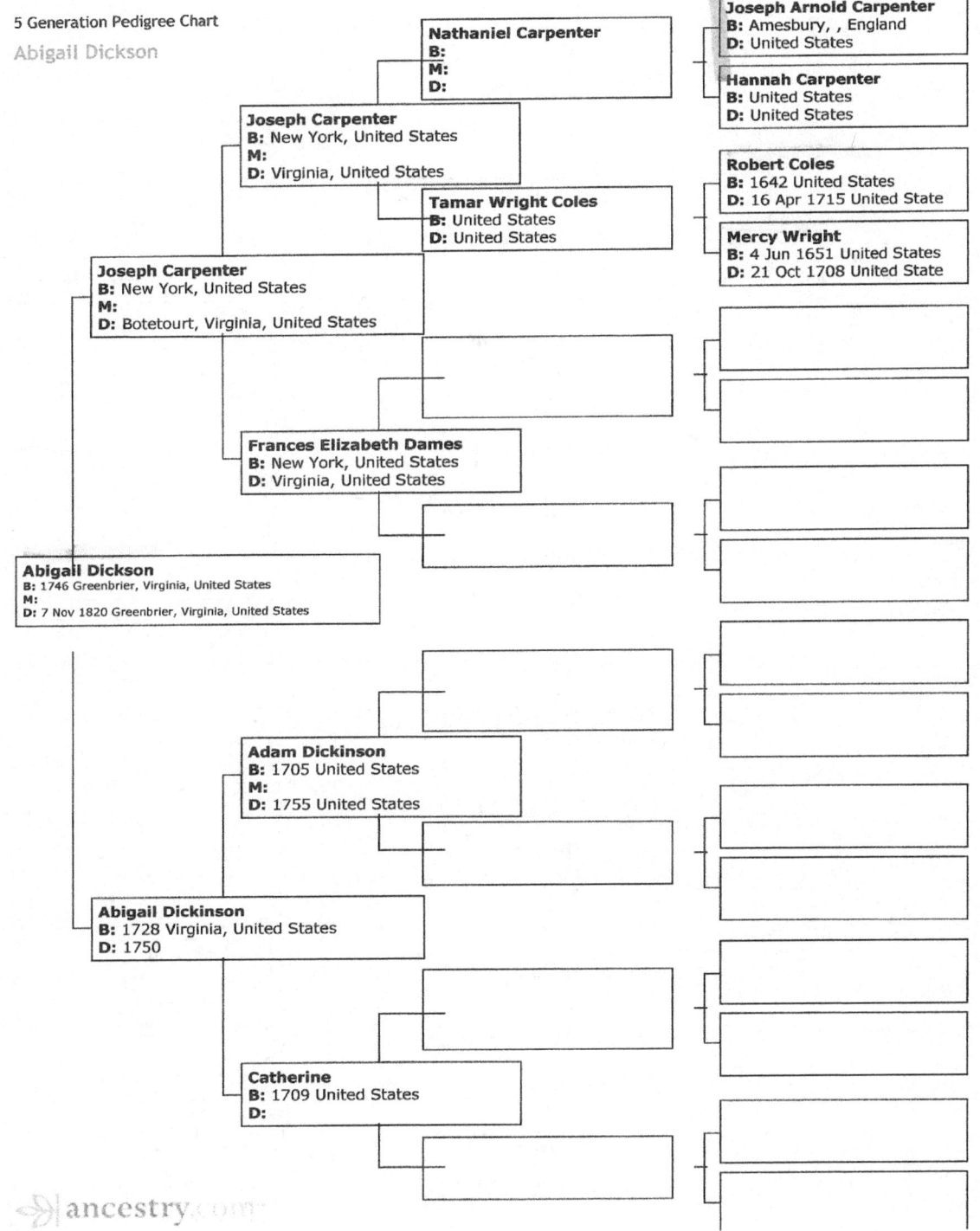

Nathaniel Carpenter
B:
M:
D:

Joseph Carpenter
B: New York, United States
M:
D: Virginia, United States

Tamar Wright Coles
B: United States
D: United States

Joseph Carpenter
B: New York, United States
M:
D: Botetourt, Virginia, United States

Frances Elizabeth Dames
B: New York, United States
D: Virginia, United States

Abigail Dickson
B: 1746 Greenbrier, Virginia, United States
M:
D: 7 Nov 1820 Greenbrier, Virginia, United States

Adam Dickinson
B: 1705 United States
M:
D: 1755 United States

Abigail Dickinson
B: 1728 Virginia, United States
D: 1750

Catherine
B: 1709 United States
D:

Joseph Arnold Carpenter
B: Amesbury, , England
D: United States

Hannah Carpenter
B: United States
D: United States

Robert Coles
B: 1642 United States
D: 16 Apr 1715 United State

Mercy Wright
B: 4 Jun 1651 United States
D: 21 Oct 1708 United State

Elish Williams

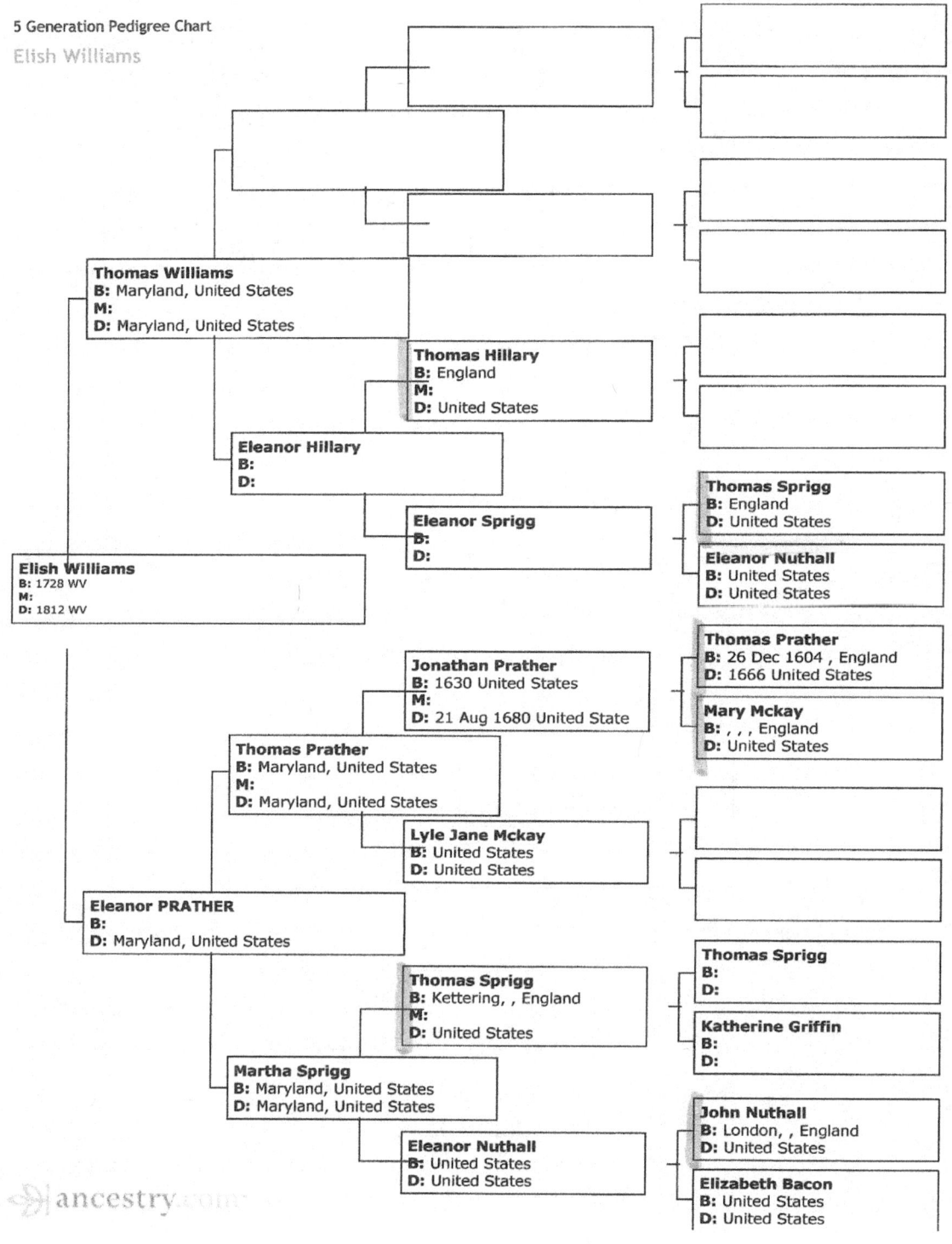

Thomas Williams
B: Maryland, United States
M:
D: Maryland, United States

Thomas Hillary
B: England
M:
D: United States

Eleanor Hillary
B:
D:

Eleanor Sprigg
B:
D:

Elish Williams
B: 1728 WV
M:
D: 1812 WV

Thomas Sprigg
B: England
D: United States

Eleanor Nuthall
B: United States
D: United States

Jonathan Prather
B: 1630 United States
M:
D: 21 Aug 1680 United State

Thomas Prather
B: 26 Dec 1604 , England
D: 1666 United States

Mary Mckay
B: , , , England
D: United States

Thomas Prather
B: Maryland, United States
M:
D: Maryland, United States

Lyle Jane Mckay
B: United States
D: United States

Eleanor PRATHER
B:
D: Maryland, United States

Thomas Sprigg
B: Kettering, , England
M:
D: United States

Thomas Sprigg
B:
D:

Katherine Griffin
B:
D:

Martha Sprigg
B: Maryland, United States
D: Maryland, United States

Eleanor Nuthall
B: United States
D: United States

John Nuthall
B: London, , England
D: United States

Elizabeth Bacon
B: United States
D: United States

30

Ann Nancy Swearingen

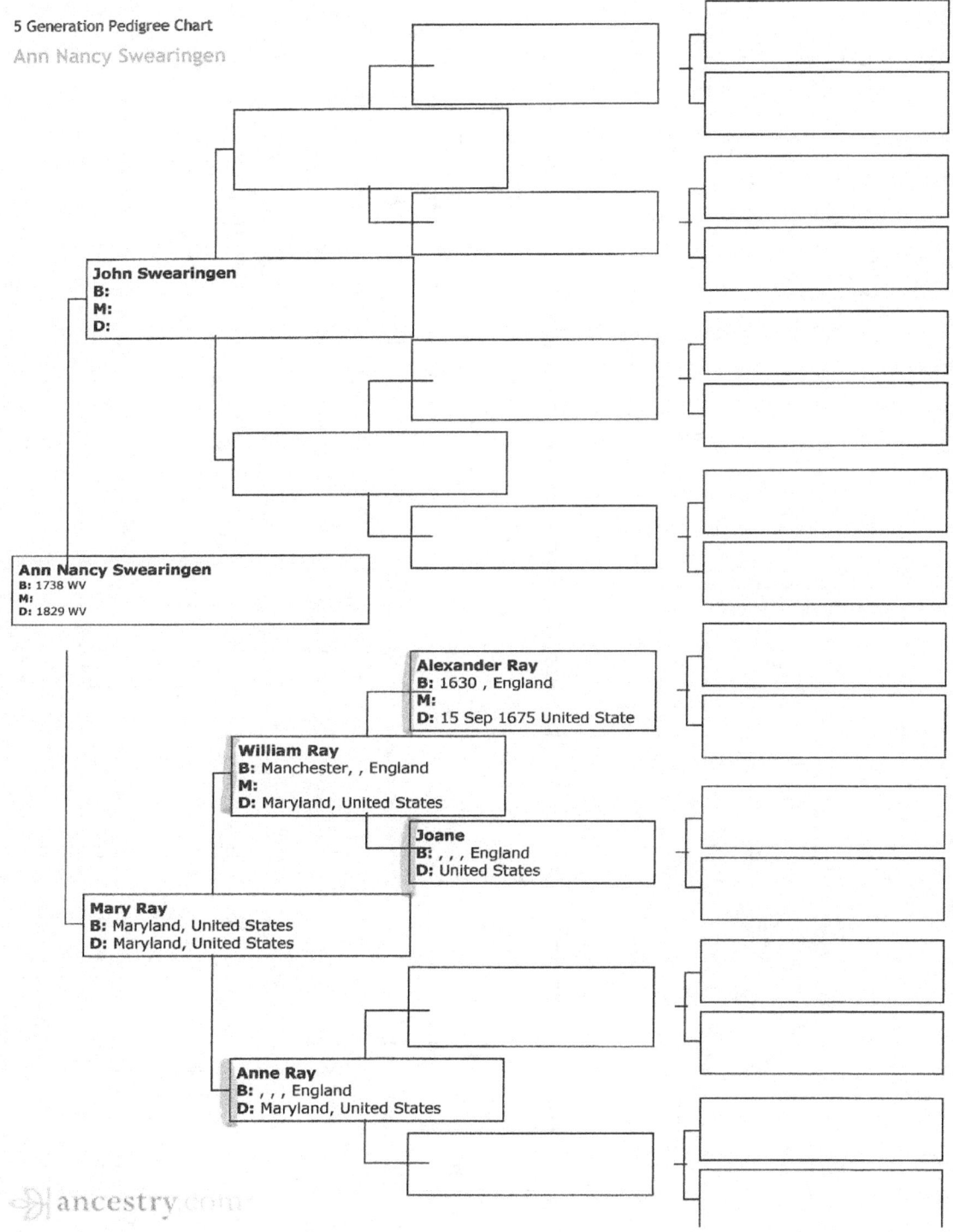

John Swearingen
B:
M:
D:

Ann Nancy Swearingen
B: 1738 WV
M:
D: 1829 WV

Alexander Ray
B: 1630 , England
M:
D: 15 Sep 1675 United State

William Ray
B: Manchester, , England
M:
D: Maryland, United States

Joane
B: , , , England
D: United States

Mary Ray
B: Maryland, United States
D: Maryland, United States

Anne Ray
B: , , , England
D: Maryland, United States

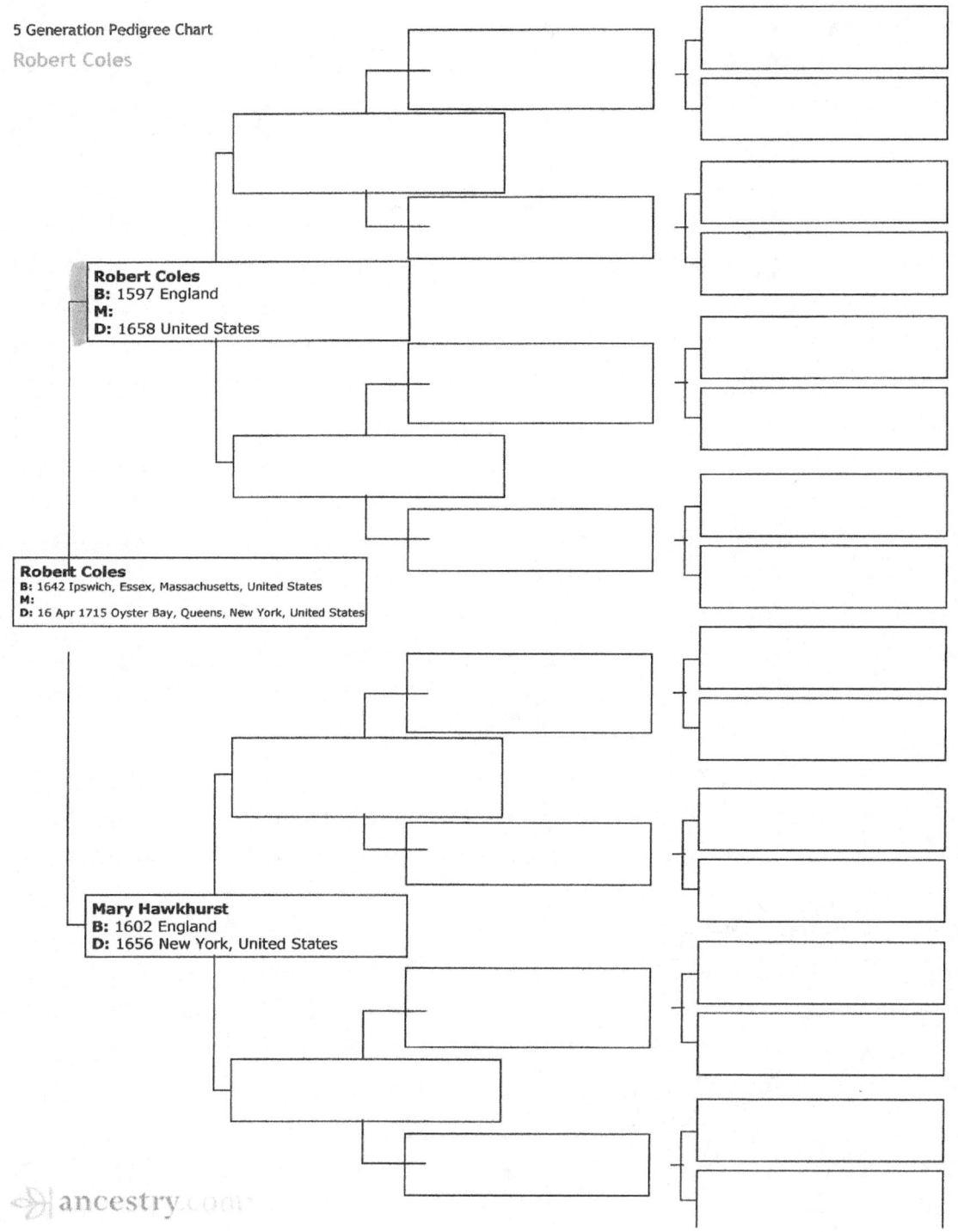

5 Generation Pedigree Chart

Robert Coles

Robert Coles
B: 1597 England
M:
D: 1658 United States

Robert Coles
B: 1642 Ipswich, Essex, Massachusetts, United States
M:
D: 16 Apr 1715 Oyster Bay, Queens, New York, United States

Mary Hawkhurst
B: 1602 England
D: 1656 New York, United States

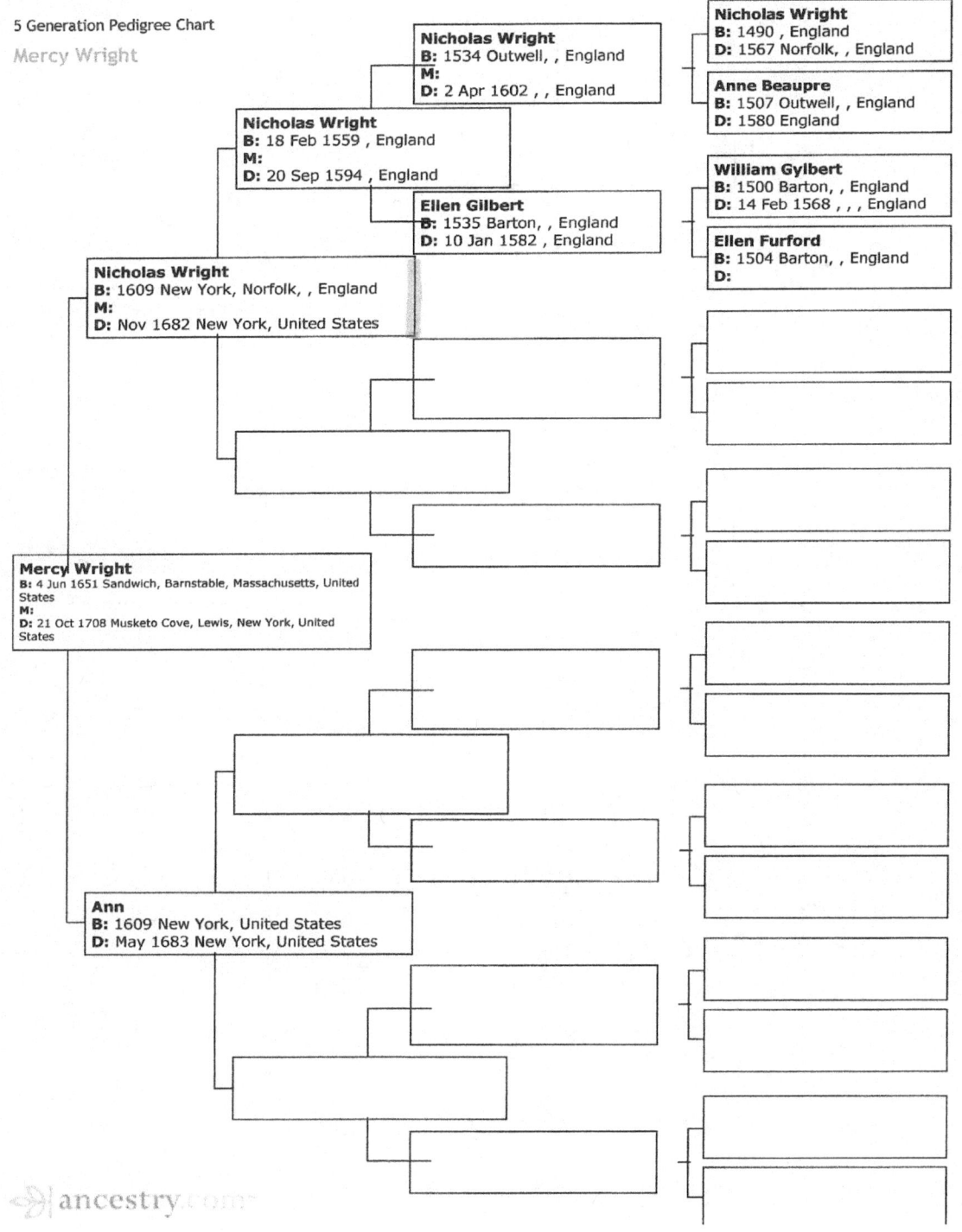

5 Generation Pedigree Chart

Mercy Wright

Nicholas Wright
B: 1490 , England
D: 1567 Norfolk, , England

Anne Beaupre
B: 1507 Outwell, , England
D: 1580 England

Nicholas Wright
B: 1534 Outwell, , England
M:
D: 2 Apr 1602 , , England

William Gylbert
B: 1500 Barton, , England
D: 14 Feb 1568 , , , England

Ellen Furford
B: 1504 Barton, , England
D:

Nicholas Wright
B: 18 Feb 1559 , England
M:
D: 20 Sep 1594 , England

Ellen Gilbert
B: 1535 Barton, , England
D: 10 Jan 1582 , England

Nicholas Wright
B: 1609 New York, Norfolk, , England
M:
D: Nov 1682 New York, United States

Mercy Wright
B: 4 Jun 1651 Sandwich, Barnstable, Massachusetts, United States
M:
D: 21 Oct 1708 Musketo Cove, Lewis, New York, United States

Ann
B: 1609 New York, United States
D: May 1683 New York, United States

33

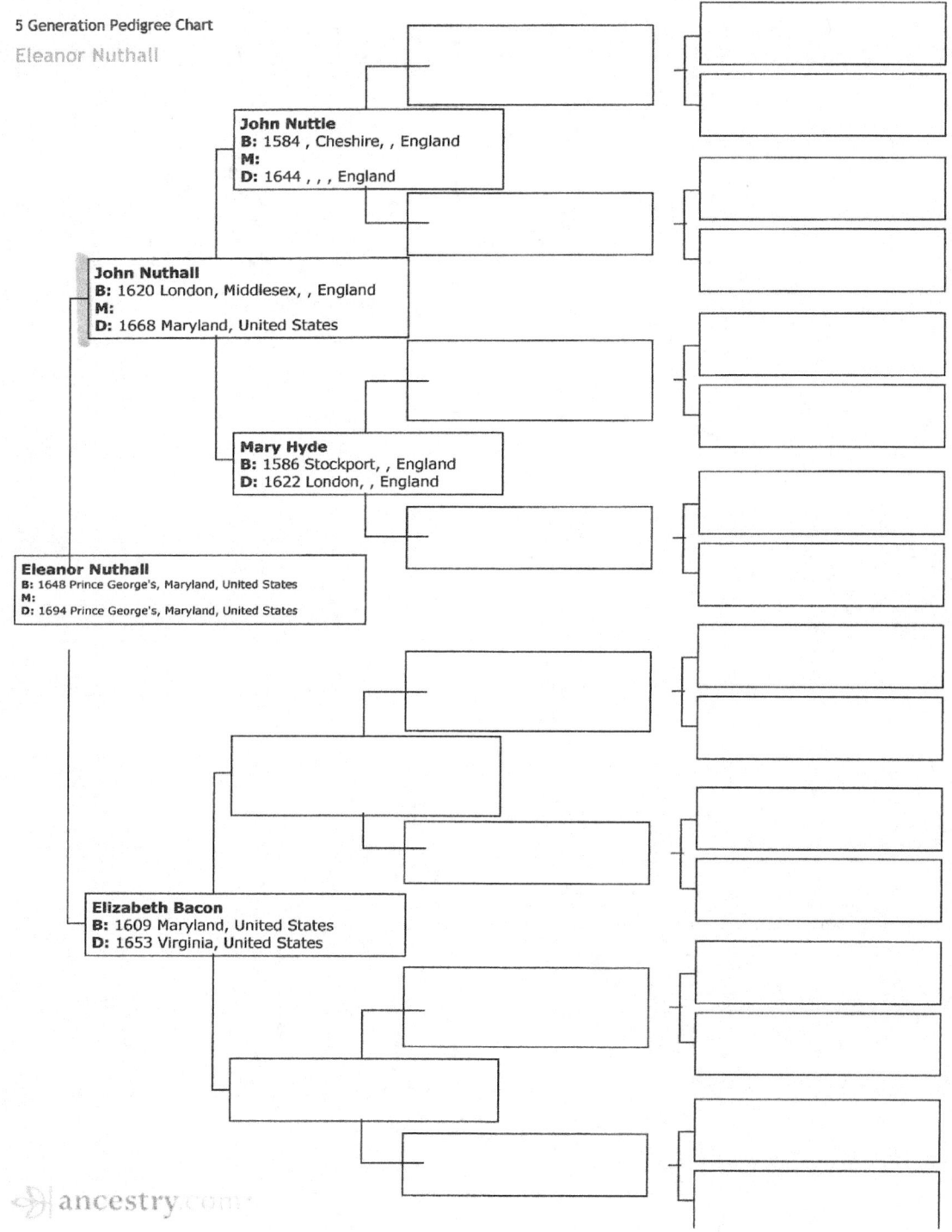

5 Generation Pedigree Chart

Eleanor Nuthall

John Nuttle
B: 1584 , Cheshire, , England
M:
D: 1644 , , , England

John Nuthall
B: 1620 London, Middlesex, , England
M:
D: 1668 Maryland, United States

Mary Hyde
B: 1586 Stockport, , England
D: 1622 London, , England

Eleanor Nuthall
B: 1648 Prince George's, Maryland, United States
M:
D: 1694 Prince George's, Maryland, United States

Elizabeth Bacon
B: 1609 Maryland, United States
D: 1653 Virginia, United States

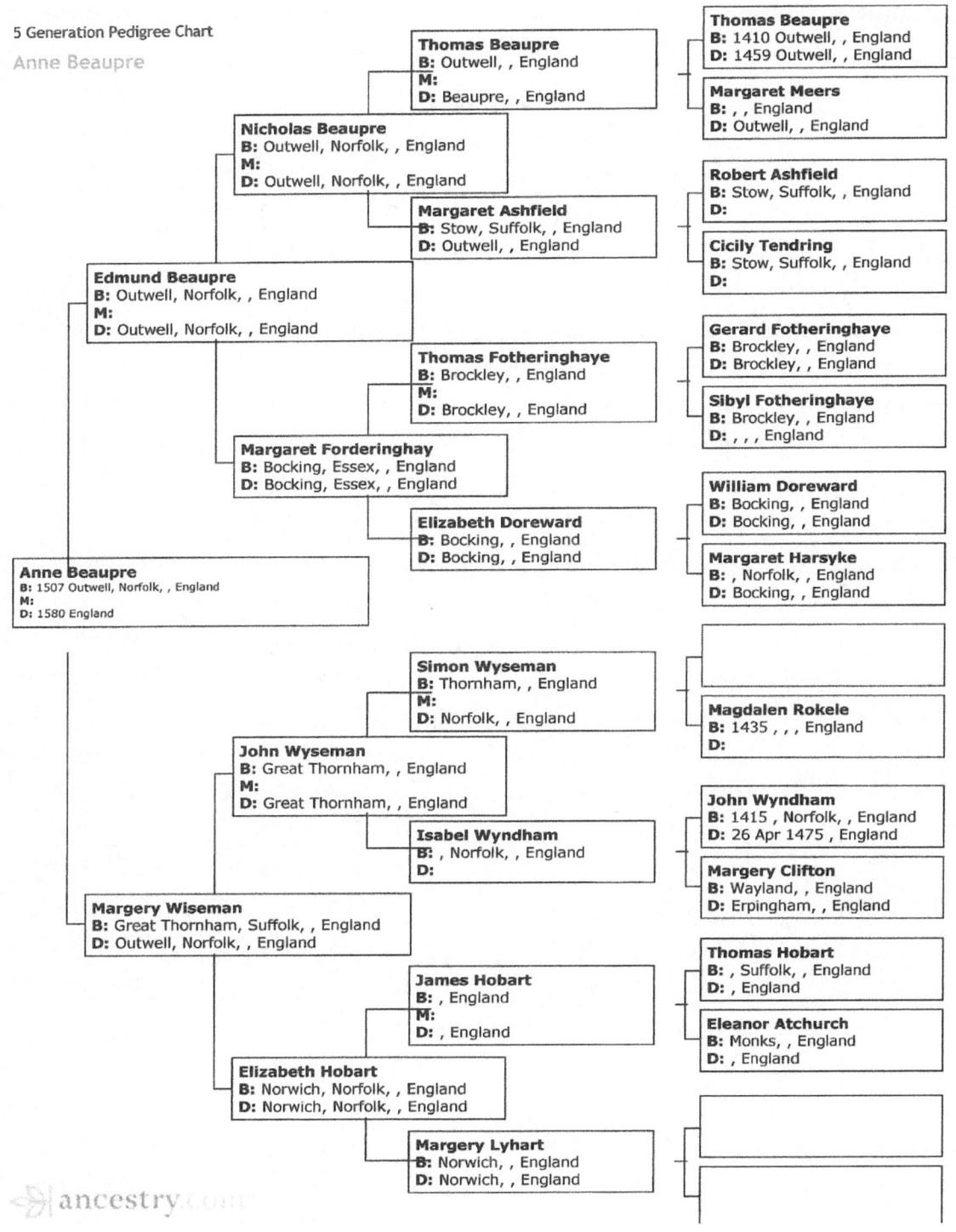

5 Generation Pedigree Chart

Anne Beaupre

Thomas Beaupre
B: Outwell, , England
M:
D: Beaupre, , England

Nicholas Beaupre
B: Outwell, Norfolk, , England
M:
D: Outwell, Norfolk, , England

Margaret Ashfield
B: Stow, Suffolk, , England
D: Outwell, , England

Edmund Beaupre
B: Outwell, Norfolk, , England
M:
D: Outwell, Norfolk, , England

Thomas Fotheringhaye
B: Brockley, , England
M:
D: Brockley, , England

Margaret Forderinghay
B: Bocking, Essex, , England
D: Bocking, Essex, , England

Elizabeth Doreward
B: Bocking, , England
D: Bocking, , England

Anne Beaupre
B: 1507 Outwell, Norfolk, , England
M:
D: 1580 England

Simon Wyseman
B: Thornham, , England
M:
D: Norfolk, , England

John Wyseman
B: Great Thornham, , England
M:
D: Great Thornham, , England

Isabel Wyndham
B: , Norfolk, , England
D:

Margery Wiseman
B: Great Thornham, Suffolk, , England
D: Outwell, Norfolk, , England

James Hobart
B: , England
M:
D: , England

Elizabeth Hobart
B: Norwich, Norfolk, , England
D: Norwich, Norfolk, , England

Margery Lyhart
B: Norwich, , England
D: Norwich, , England

Thomas Beaupre
B: 1410 Outwell, , England
D: 1459 Outwell, , England

Margaret Meers
B: , , England
D: Outwell, , England

Robert Ashfield
B: Stow, Suffolk, , England
D:

Cicily Tendring
B: Stow, Suffolk, , England
D:

Gerard Fotheringhaye
B: Brockley, , England
D: Brockley, , England

Sibyl Fotheringhaye
B: Brockley, , England
D: , , , England

William Doreward
B: Bocking, , England
D: Bocking, , England

Margaret Harsyke
B: , Norfolk, , England
D: Bocking, , England

Magdalen Rokele
B: 1435 , , , England
D:

John Wyndham
B: 1415 , Norfolk, , England
D: 26 Apr 1475 , England

Margery Clifton
B: Wayland, , England
D: Erpingham, , England

Thomas Hobart
B: , Suffolk, , England
D: , England

Eleanor Atchurch
B: Monks, , England
D: , England

ancestry.com

35

Thomas Beaupre

Richard Beaupre
B: Wellingham, , England
M:
D: Wellingham, , England

Thomas DeBeaupre
B: Outwell, Norfolk, , England
M:
D: Outwell, Norfolk, , England

Katherine Mountfort
B: 1301 , England
D:

John Fitzgilbert
B: 1296 , England
D: 1313 , England

Christian SaintOmer
B: 1298 , England
D:

Osbert DeMundeford
B: 1401 , Norfolk, , England
D: , Norfolk, , England

Nicholas Beaupre
B: Wellingham, Norfolk, , England
M:
D: Outwell, Norfolk, , England

Joan Holbeach
B: , Lincolnshire, , England
D: , Lincolnshire, , England

Richard Holbeach
B: , , England
D:

Thomas Beaupre
B: Outwell, Norfolk, , England
M:
D: Outwell, Norfolk, , England

Richard Holdich
B: Didlington, , England
M:
D: Didlington, , England

Margaret Holdich
B: Didlington, Norfolk, , England
D: Didlington, Norfolk, , England

36

Jonathan Prather

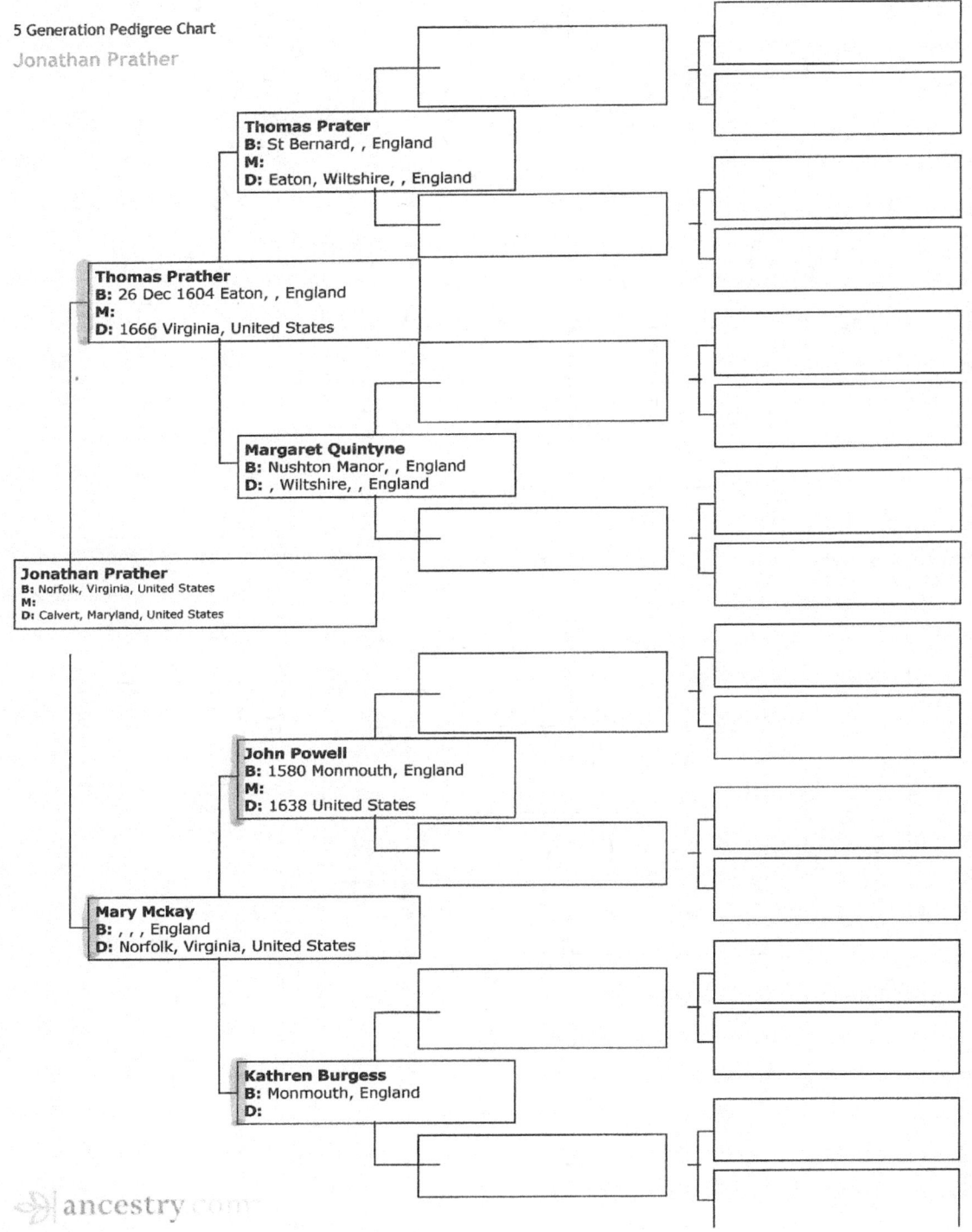

Thomas Prater
B: St Bernard, , England
M:
D: Eaton, Wiltshire, , England

Thomas Prather
B: 26 Dec 1604 Eaton, , England
M:
D: 1666 Virginia, United States

Margaret Quintyne
B: Nushton Manor, , England
D: , Wiltshire, , England

Jonathan Prather
B: Norfolk, Virginia, United States
M:
D: Calvert, Maryland, United States

John Powell
B: 1580 Monmouth, England
M:
D: 1638 United States

Mary Mckay
B: , , , England
D: Norfolk, Virginia, United States

Kathren Burgess
B: Monmouth, England
D:

Christian SaintOmer

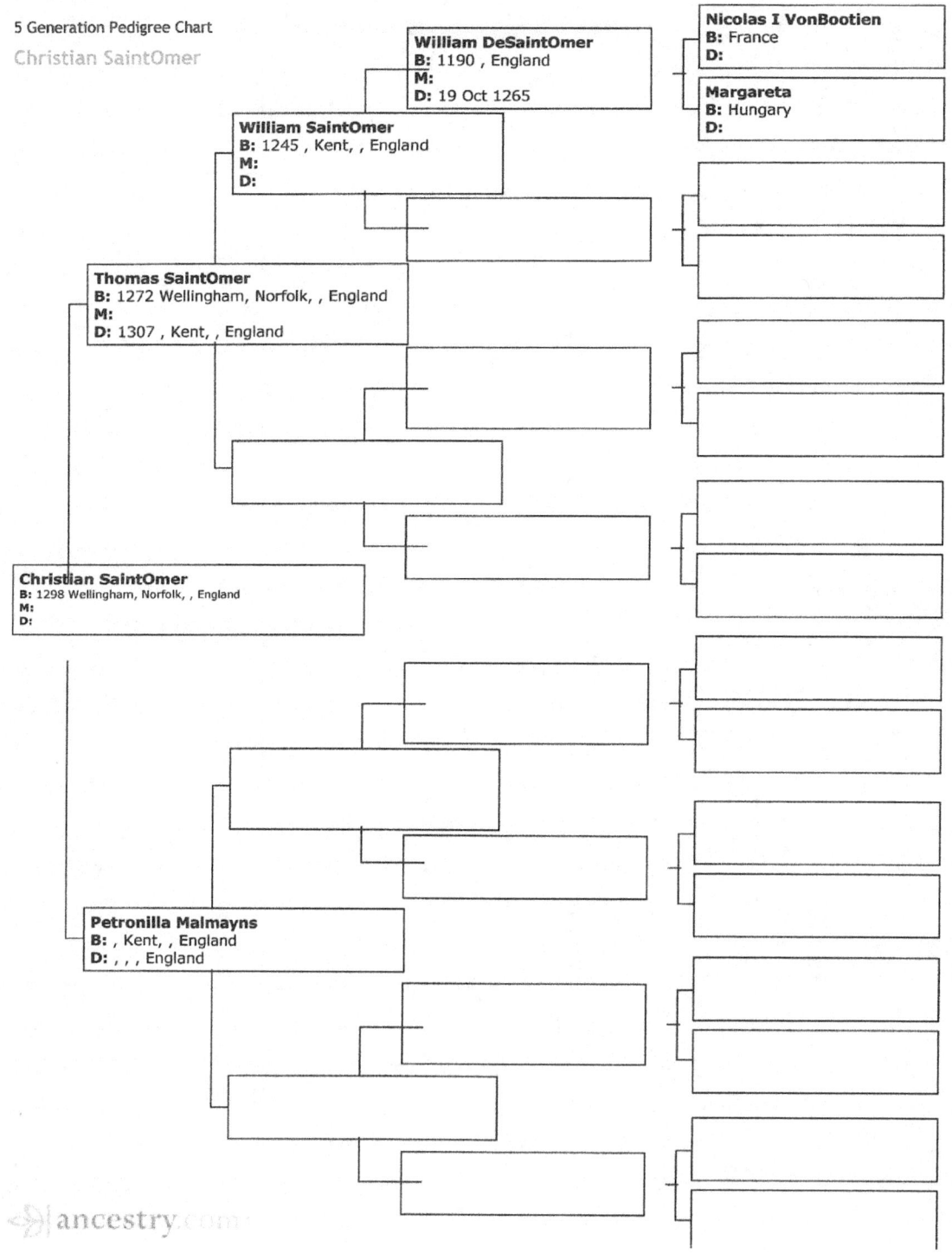

William DeSaintOmer
B: 1190 , England
M:
D: 19 Oct 1265

Nicolas I VonBootien
B: France
D:

Margareta
B: Hungary
D:

William SaintOmer
B: 1245 , Kent, , England
M:
D:

Thomas SaintOmer
B: 1272 Wellingham, Norfolk, , England
M:
D: 1307 , Kent, , England

Christian SaintOmer
B: 1298 Wellingham, Norfolk, , England
M:
D:

Petronilla Malmayns
B: , Kent, , England
D: , , , England

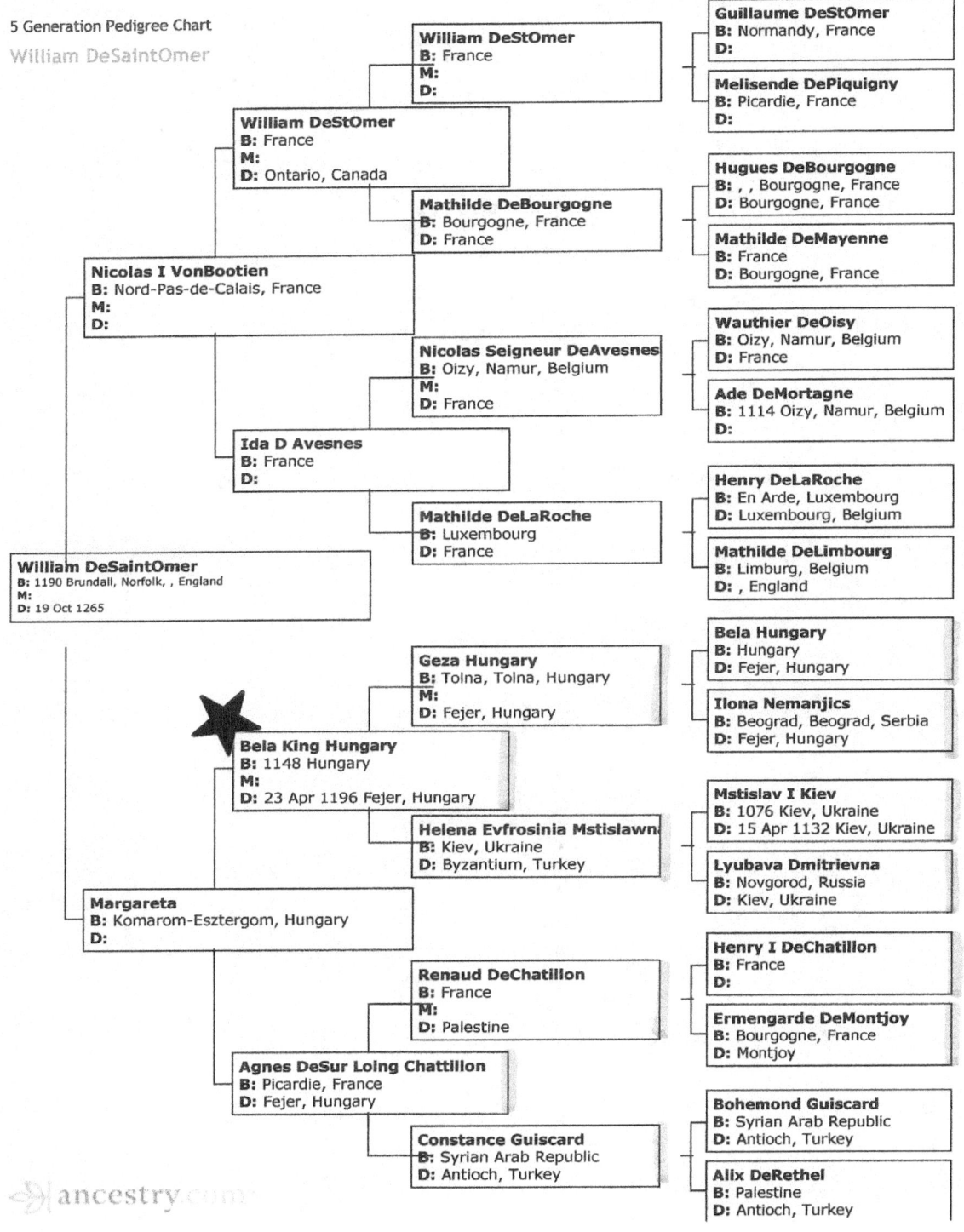

William DeStOmer
B: France
M:
D:

Guillaume DeStOmer
B: Normandy, France
D:

Melisende DePiquigny
B: Picardie, France
D:

William DeStOmer
B: France
M:
D: Ontario, Canada

Mathilde DeBourgogne
B: Bourgogne, France
D: France

Hugues DeBourgogne
B: , , Bourgogne, France
D: Bourgogne, France

Mathilde DeMayenne
B: France
D: Bourgogne, France

Nicolas I VonBootien
B: Nord-Pas-de-Calais, France
M:
D:

Nicolas Seigneur DeAvesnes
B: Oizy, Namur, Belgium
M:
D: France

Wauthier DeOisy
B: Oizy, Namur, Belgium
D: France

Ade DeMortagne
B: 1114 Oizy, Namur, Belgium
D:

Ida D Avesnes
B: France
D:

Mathilde DeLaRoche
B: Luxembourg
D: France

Henry DeLaRoche
B: En Arde, Luxembourg
D: Luxembourg, Belgium

Mathilde DeLimbourg
B: Limburg, Belgium
D: , England

William DeSaintOmer
B: 1190 Brundall, Norfolk, , England
M:
D: 19 Oct 1265

Geza Hungary
B: Tolna, Tolna, Hungary
M:
D: Fejer, Hungary

Bela Hungary
B: Hungary
D: Fejer, Hungary

Ilona Nemanjics
B: Beograd, Beograd, Serbia
D: Fejer, Hungary

Bela King Hungary
B: 1148 Hungary
M:
D: 23 Apr 1196 Fejer, Hungary

Helena Evfrosinia Mstislawna
B: Kiev, Ukraine
D: Byzantium, Turkey

Mstislav I Kiev
B: 1076 Kiev, Ukraine
D: 15 Apr 1132 Kiev, Ukraine

Lyubava Dmitrievna
B: Novgorod, Russia
D: Kiev, Ukraine

Margareta
B: Komarom-Esztergom, Hungary
D:

Renaud DeChatillon
B: France
M:
D: Palestine

Henry I DeChatillon
B: France
D:

Ermengarde DeMontjoy
B: Bourgogne, France
D: Montjoy

Agnes DeSur Loing Chattillon
B: Picardie, France
D: Fejer, Hungary

Constance Guiscard
B: Syrian Arab Republic
D: Antioch, Turkey

Bohemond Guiscard
B: Syrian Arab Republic
D: Antioch, Turkey

Alix DeRethel
B: Palestine
D: Antioch, Turkey

ancestry.com

39

Helena Evfrosinia Mstislawna

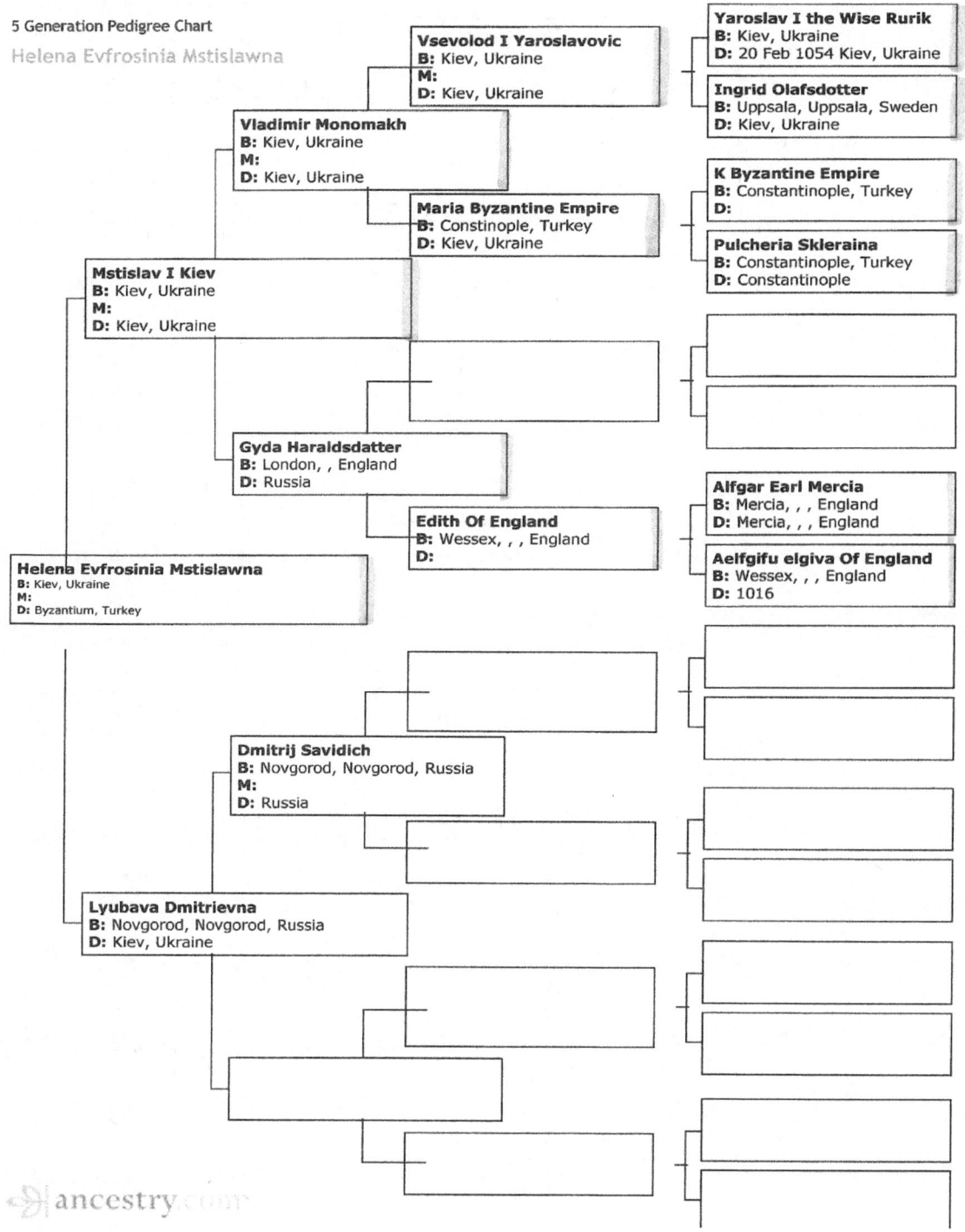

Vsevolod I Yaroslavovic
B: Kiev, Ukraine
M:
D: Kiev, Ukraine

Yaroslav I the Wise Rurik
B: Kiev, Ukraine
D: 20 Feb 1054 Kiev, Ukraine

Ingrid Olafsdotter
B: Uppsala, Uppsala, Sweden
D: Kiev, Ukraine

Vladimir Monomakh
B: Kiev, Ukraine
M:
D: Kiev, Ukraine

K Byzantine Empire
B: Constantinople, Turkey
D:

Maria Byzantine Empire
B: Constinople, Turkey
D: Kiev, Ukraine

Pulcheria Skleraina
B: Constantinople, Turkey
D: Constantinople

Mstislav I Kiev
B: Kiev, Ukraine
M:
D: Kiev, Ukraine

Gyda Haraldsdatter
B: London, , England
D: Russia

Alfgar Earl Mercia
B: Mercia, , , England
D: Mercia, , , England

Edith Of England
B: Wessex, , , England
D:

Aelfgifu elgiva Of England
B: Wessex, , , England
D: 1016

Helena Evfrosinia Mstislawna
B: Kiev, Ukraine
M:
D: Byzantium, Turkey

Dmitrij Savidich
B: Novgorod, Novgorod, Russia
M:
D: Russia

Lyubava Dmitrievna
B: Novgorod, Novgorod, Russia
D: Kiev, Ukraine

John Wyndham

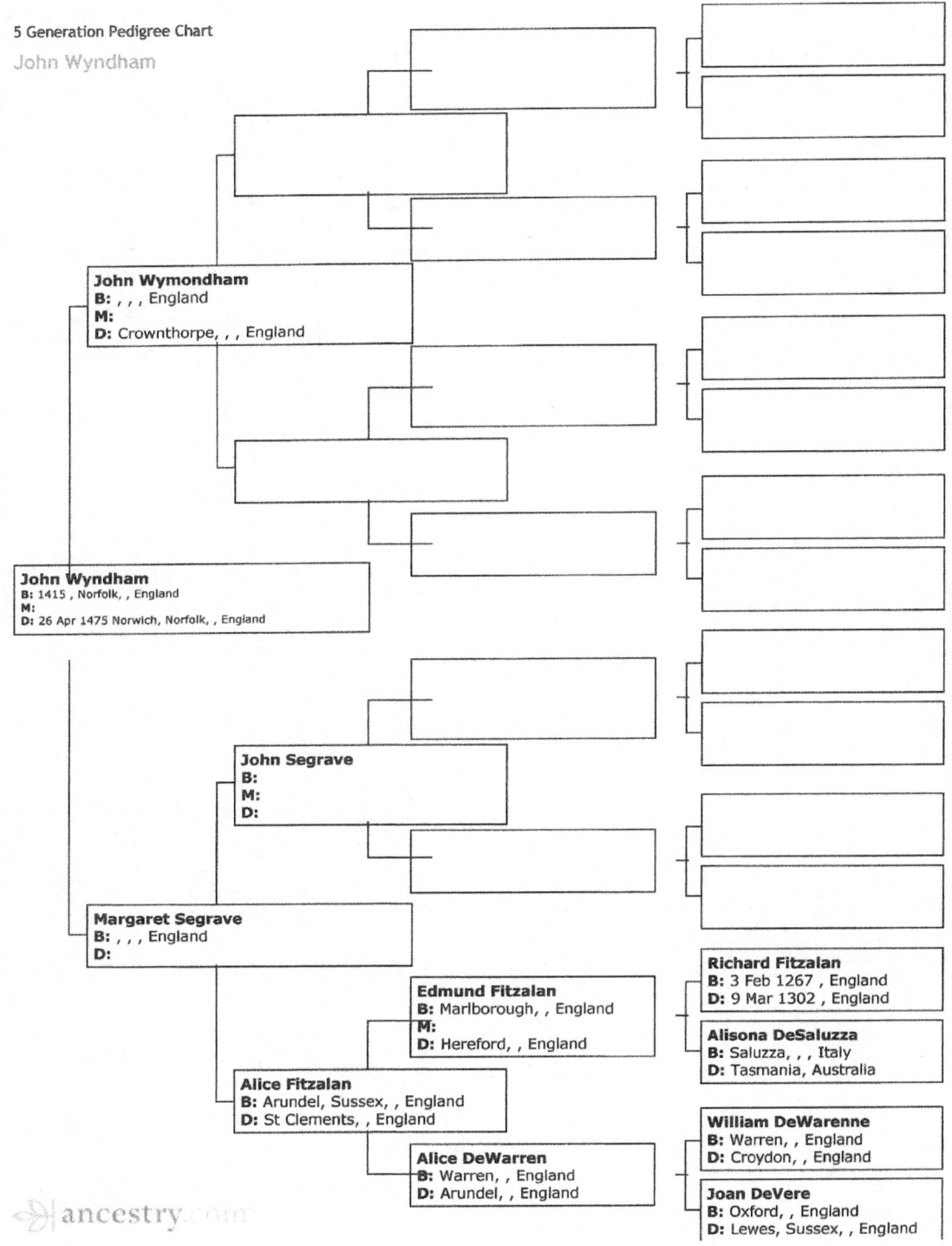

John Wymondham
B: , , , England
M:
D: Crownthorpe, , , England

John Wyndham
B: 1415 , Norfolk, , England
M:
D: 26 Apr 1475 Norwich, Norfolk, , England

John Segrave
B:
M:
D:

Margaret Segrave
B: , , , England
D:

Edmund Fitzalan
B: Marlborough, , England
M:
D: Hereford, , England

Alice Fitzalan
B: Arundel, Sussex, , England
D: St Clements, , England

Alice DeWarren
B: Warren, , England
D: Arundel, , England

Richard Fitzalan
B: 3 Feb 1267 , England
D: 9 Mar 1302 , England

Alisona DeSaluzza
B: Saluzza, , , Italy
D: Tasmania, Australia

William DeWarenne
B: Warren, , England
D: Croydon, , England

Joan DeVere
B: Oxford, , England
D: Lewes, Sussex, , England

Richard Fitzalan

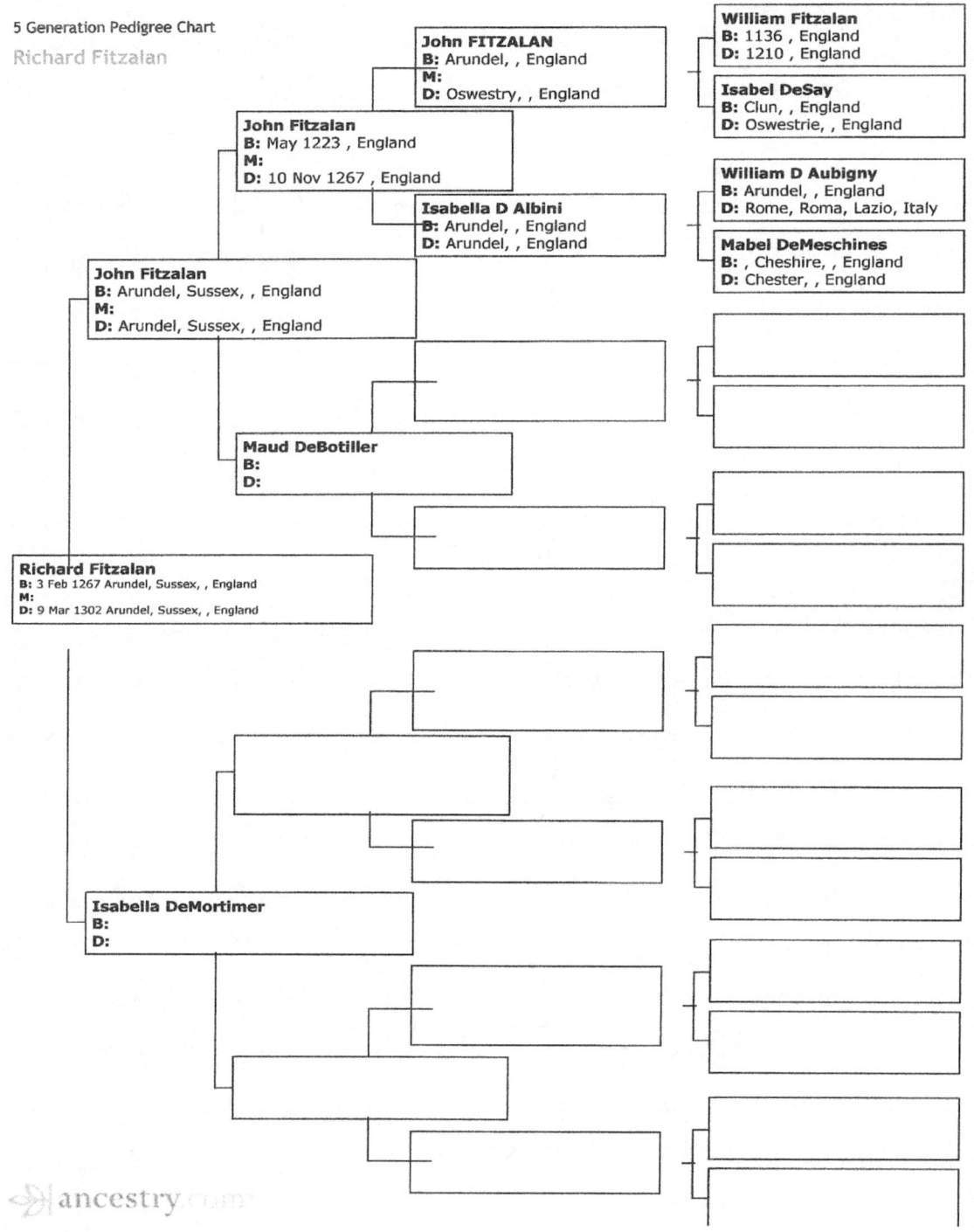

John FITZALAN
B: Arundel, , England
M:
D: Oswestry, , England

John Fitzalan
B: May 1223 , England
M:
D: 10 Nov 1267 , England

Isabella D Albini
B: Arundel, , England
D: Arundel, , England

John Fitzalan
B: Arundel, Sussex, , England
M:
D: Arundel, Sussex, , England

Maud DeBotiller
B:
D:

Richard Fitzalan
B: 3 Feb 1267 Arundel, Sussex, , England
M:
D: 9 Mar 1302 Arundel, Sussex, , England

Isabella DeMortimer
B:
D:

William Fitzalan
B: 1136 , England
D: 1210 , England

Isabel DeSay
B: Clun, , England
D: Oswestrie, , England

William D Aubigny
B: Arundel, , England
D: Rome, Roma, Lazio, Italy

Mabel DeMeschines
B: , Cheshire, , England
D: Chester, , England

William Fitzalan

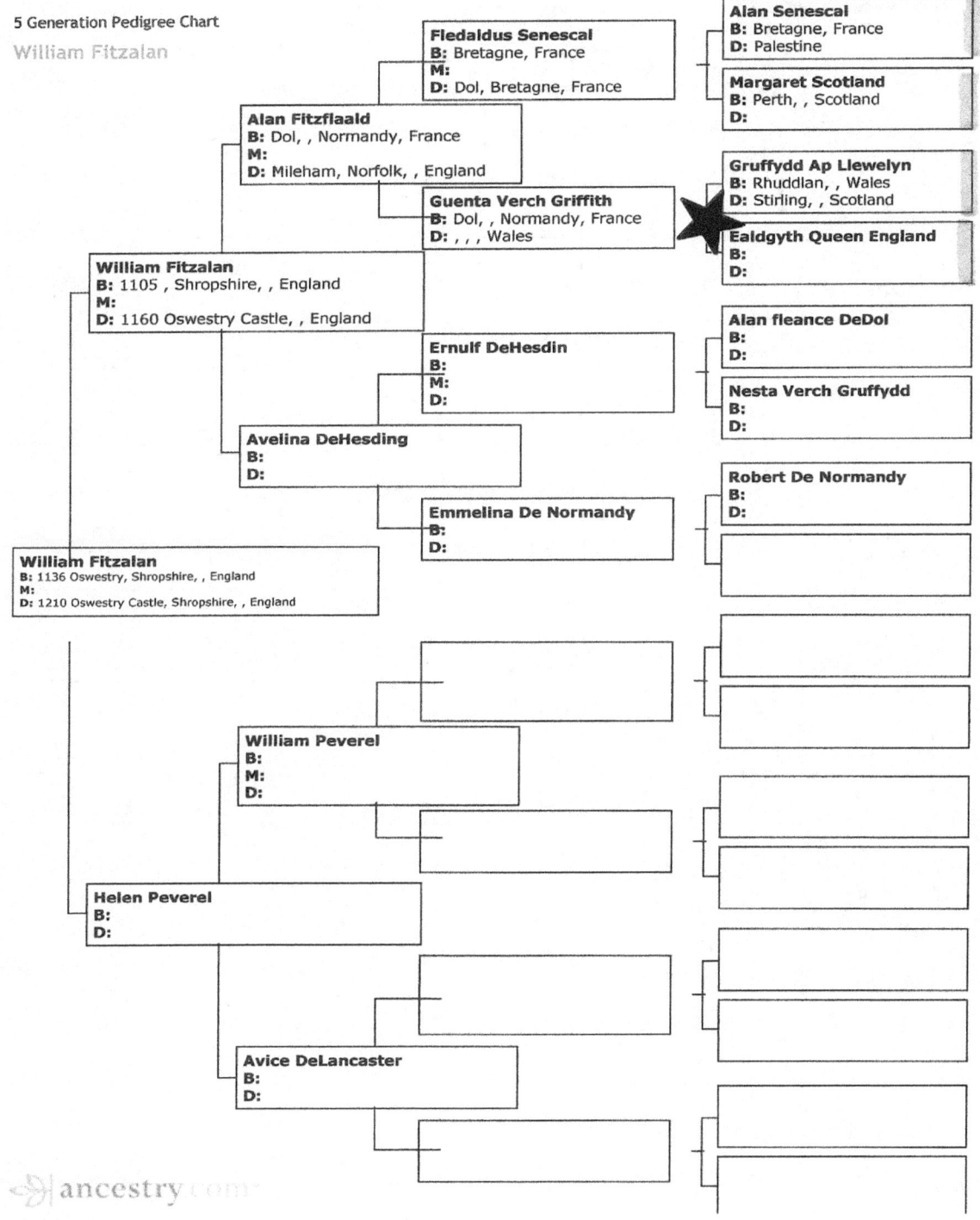

Fiedaldus Senescal
B: Bretagne, France
M:
D: Dol, Bretagne, France

Alan Fitzflaald
B: Dol, , Normandy, France
M:
D: Mileham, Norfolk, , England

Guenta Verch Griffith
B: Dol, , Normandy, France
D: , , , Wales

William Fitzalan
B: 1105 , Shropshire, , England
M:
D: 1160 Oswestry Castle, , England

Ernulf DeHesdin
B:
M:
D:

Avelina DeHesding
B:
D:

Emmelina De Normandy
B:
D:

William Fitzalan
B: 1136 Oswestry, Shropshire, , England
M:
D: 1210 Oswestry Castle, Shropshire, , England

William Peverel
B:
M:
D:

Helen Peverel
B:
D:

Avice DeLancaster
B:
D:

Alan Senescal
B: Bretagne, France
D: Palestine

Margaret Scotland
B: Perth, , Scotland
D:

Gruffydd Ap Llewelyn
B: Rhuddlan, , Wales
D: Stirling, , Scotland

Ealdgyth Queen England
B:
D:

Alan fleance DeDol
B:
D:

Nesta Verch Gruffydd
B:
D:

Robert De Normandy
B:
D:

Alan Senescal

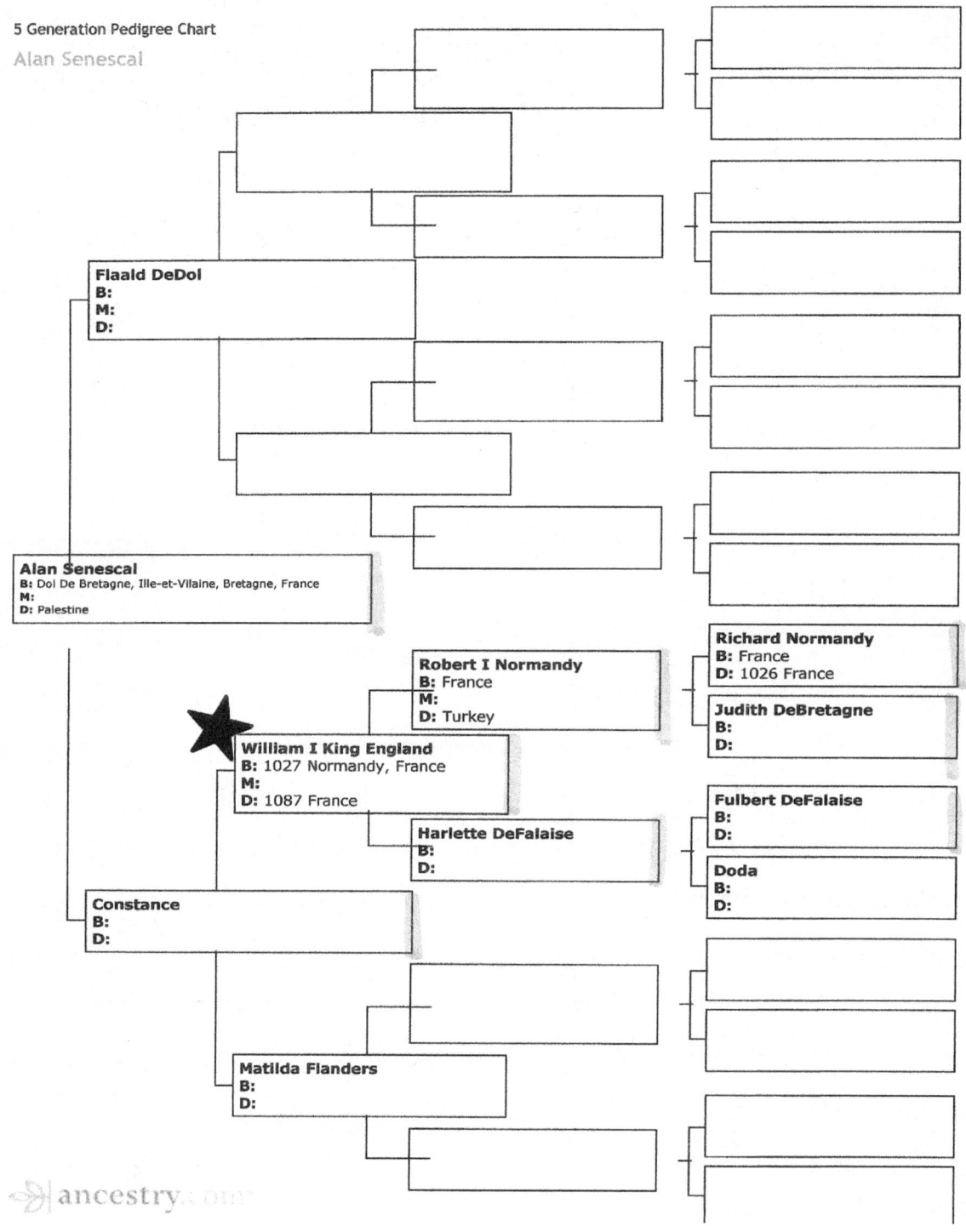

Flaald DeDol
B:
M:
D:

Alan Senescal
B: Dol De Bretagne, Ille-et-Vilaine, Bretagne, France
M:
D: Palestine

Robert I Normandy
B: France
M:
D: Turkey

William I King England
B: 1027 Normandy, France
M:
D: 1087 France

Harlette DeFalaise
B:
D:

Constance
B:
D:

Matilda Flanders
B:
D:

Richard Normandy
B: France
D: 1026 France

Judith DeBretagne
B:
D:

Fulbert DeFalaise
B:
D:

Doda
B:
D:

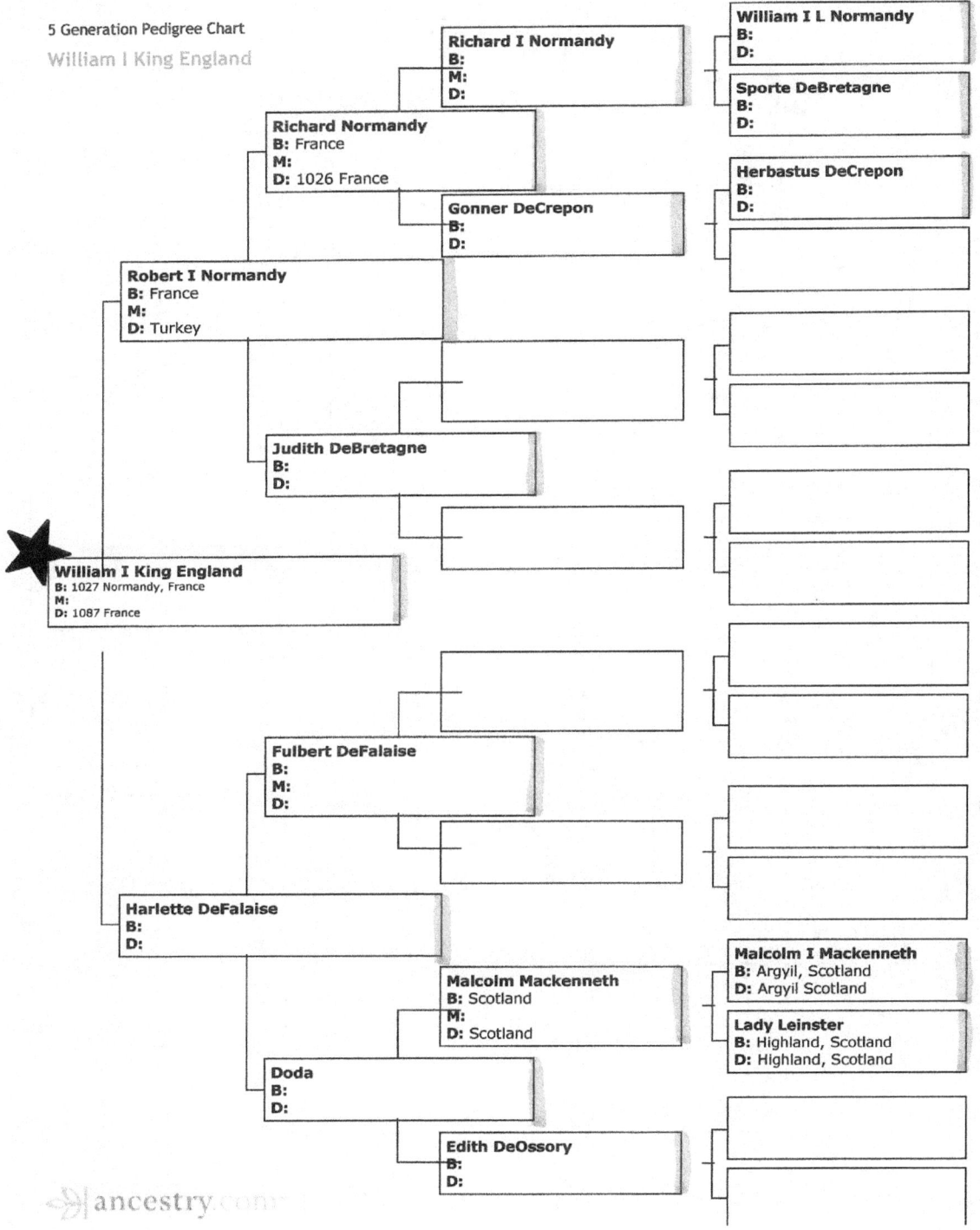

Richard I Normandy
B:
M:
D:

William I L Normandy
B:
D:

Sporte DeBretagne
B:
D:

Richard Normandy
B: France
M:
D: 1026 France

Gonner DeCrepon
B:
D:

Herbastus DeCrepon
B:
D:

Robert I Normandy
B: France
M:
D: Turkey

Judith DeBretagne
B:
D:

William I King England
B: 1027 Normandy, France
M:
D: 1087 France

Fulbert DeFalaise
B:
M:
D:

Harlette DeFalaise
B:
D:

Malcolm Mackenneth
B: Scotland
M:
D: Scotland

Malcolm I Mackenneth
B: Argyil, Scotland
D: Argyil Scotland

Lady Leinster
B: Highland, Scotland
D: Highland, Scotland

Doda
B:
D:

Edith DeOssory
B:
D:

45

Malcolm Mackenneth

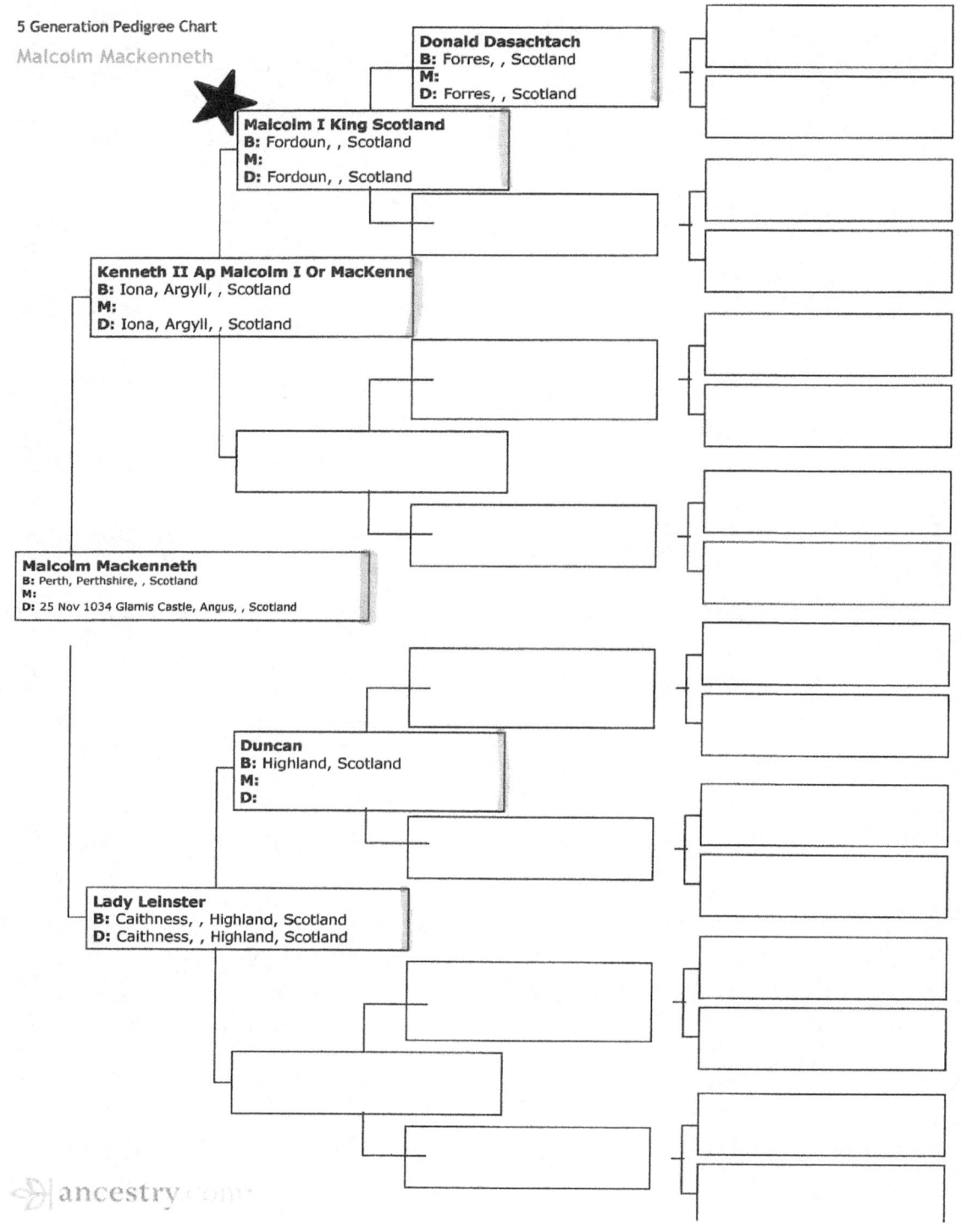

Donald Dasachtach
B: Forres, , Scotland
M:
D: Forres, , Scotland

Malcolm I King Scotland
B: Fordoun, , Scotland
M:
D: Fordoun, , Scotland

Kenneth II Ap Malcolm I Or MacKenne
B: Iona, Argyll, , Scotland
M:
D: Iona, Argyll, , Scotland

Malcolm Mackenneth
B: Perth, Perthshire, , Scotland
M:
D: 25 Nov 1034 Glamis Castle, Angus, , Scotland

Duncan
B: Highland, Scotland
M:
D:

Lady Leinster
B: Caithness, , Highland, Scotland
D: Caithness, , Highland, Scotland

ancestry.com

Richard Normandy

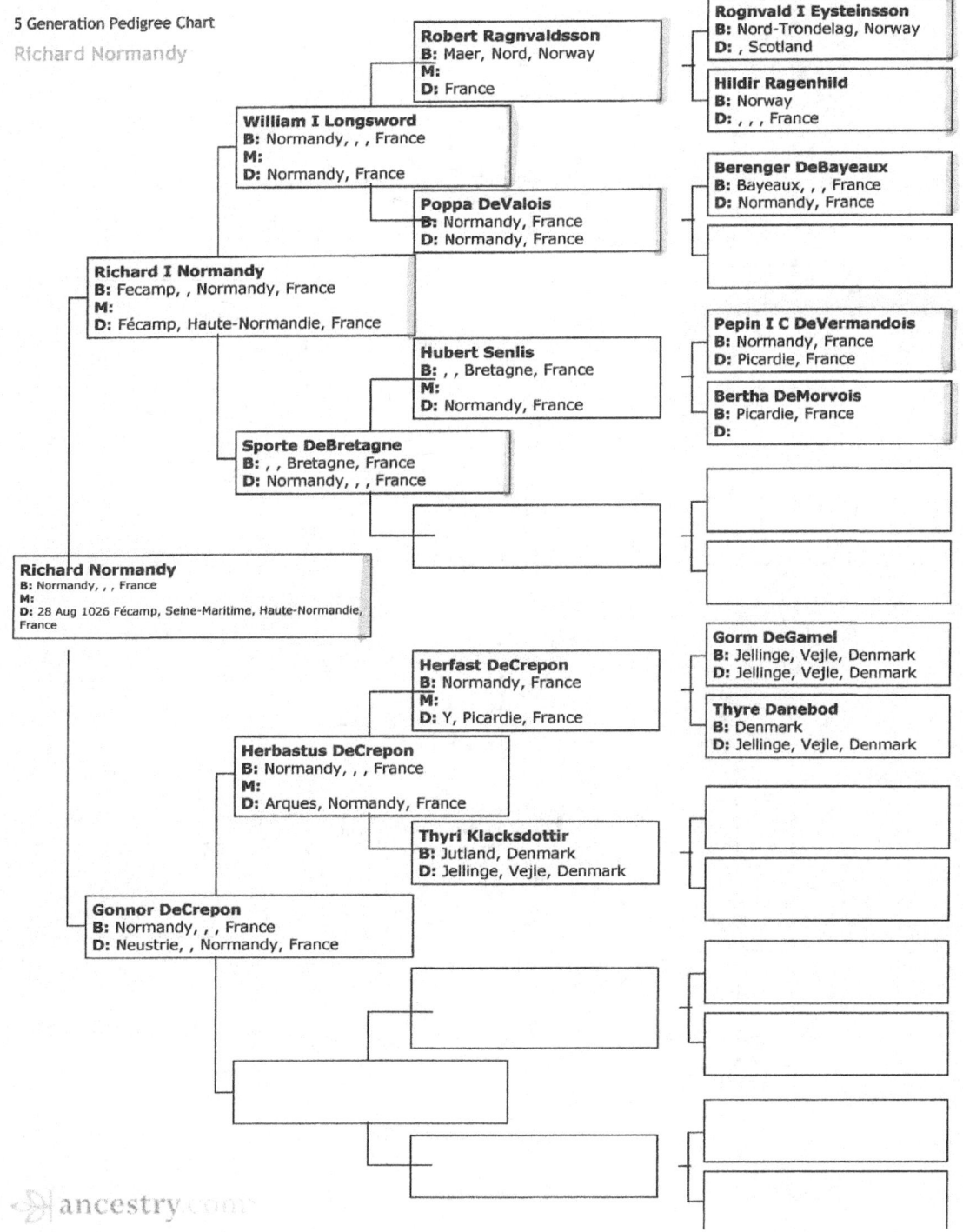

Robert Ragnvaldsson
B: Maer, Nord, Norway
M:
D: France

Rognvald I Eysteinsson
B: Nord-Trondelag, Norway
D: , Scotland

Hildir Ragenhild
B: Norway
D: , , , France

William I Longsword
B: Normandy, , , France
M:
D: Normandy, France

Poppa DeValois
B: Normandy, France
D: Normandy, France

Berenger DeBayeaux
B: Bayeaux, , , France
D: Normandy, France

Richard I Normandy
B: Fecamp, , Normandy, France
M:
D: Fécamp, Haute-Normandie, France

Hubert Senlis
B: , , Bretagne, France
M:
D: Normandy, France

Pepin I C DeVermandois
B: Normandy, France
D: Picardie, France

Bertha DeMorvois
B: Picardie, France
D:

Sporte DeBretagne
B: , , Bretagne, France
D: Normandy, , , France

Richard Normandy
B: Normandy, , , France
M:
D: 28 Aug 1026 Fécamp, Seine-Maritime, Haute-Normandie, France

Herfast DeCrepon
B: Normandy, France
M:
D: Y, Picardie, France

Gorm DeGamel
B: Jellinge, Vejle, Denmark
D: Jellinge, Vejle, Denmark

Thyre Danebod
B: Denmark
D: Jellinge, Vejle, Denmark

Herbastus DeCrepon
B: Normandy, , , France
M:
D: Arques, Normandy, France

Thyri Klacksdottir
B: Jutland, Denmark
D: Jellinge, Vejle, Denmark

Gonnor DeCrepon
B: Normandy, , , France
D: Neustrie, , Normandy, France

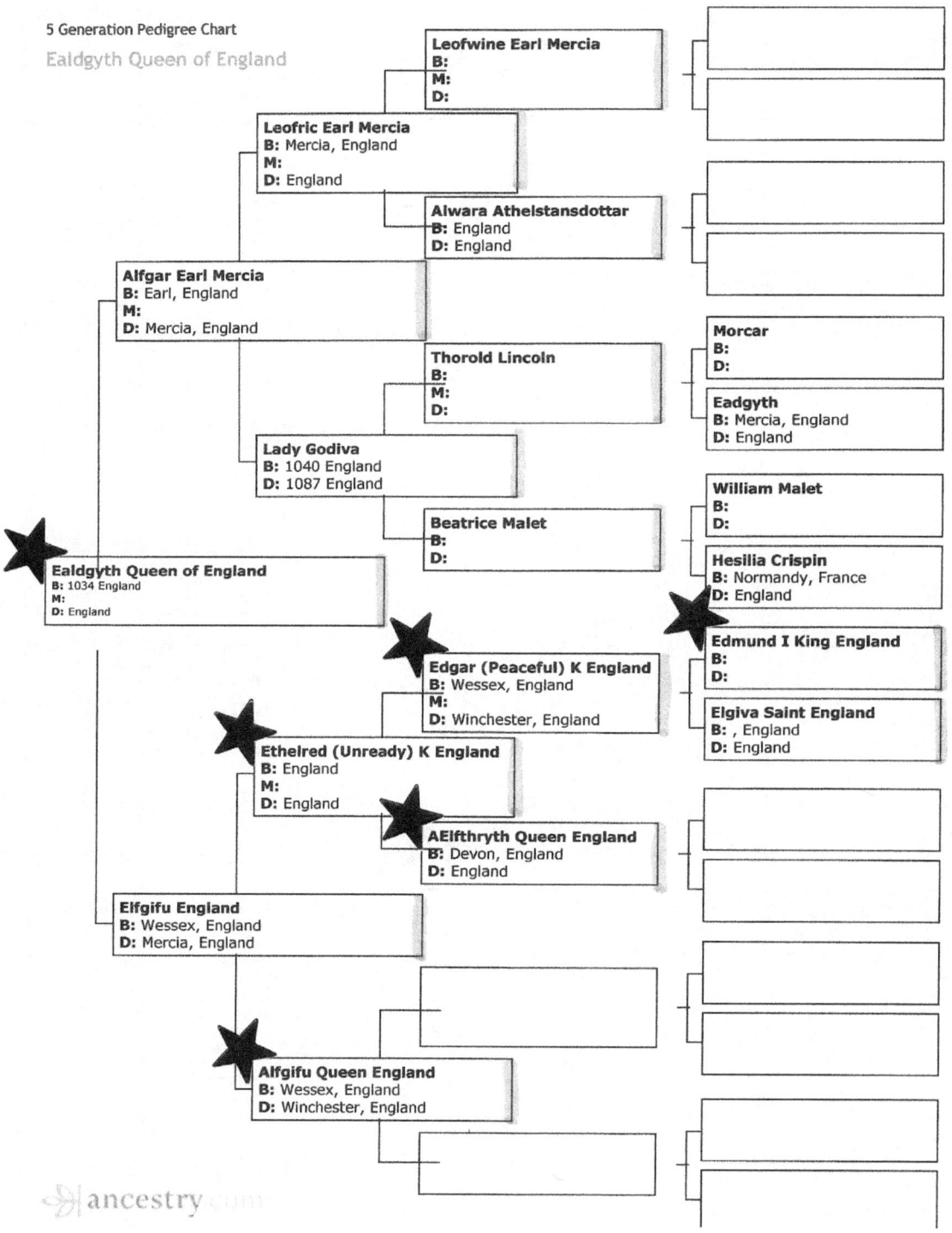

5 Generation Pedigree Chart

Ealdgyth Queen of England

Leofwine Earl Mercia
B:
M:
D:

Leofric Earl Mercia
B: Mercia, England
M:
D: England

Alwara Athelstansdottar
B: England
D: England

Alfgar Earl Mercia
B: Earl, England
M:
D: Mercia, England

Thorold Lincoln
B:
M:
D:

Morcar
B:
D:

Eadgyth
B: Mercia, England
D: England

Lady Godiva
B: 1040 England
D: 1087 England

Beatrice Malet
B:
D:

William Malet
B:
D:

Hesilia Crispin
B: Normandy, France
D: England

Ealdgyth Queen of England
B: 1034 England
M:
D: England

Edgar (Peaceful) K England
B: Wessex, England
M:
D: Winchester, England

Edmund I King England
B:
D:

Elgiva Saint England
B: , England
D: England

Ethelred (Unready) K England
B: England
M:
D: England

AElfthryth Queen England
B: Devon, England
D: England

Elfgifu England
B: Wessex, England
D: Mercia, England

Alfgifu Queen England
B: Wessex, England
D: Winchester, England

ancestry.com

48

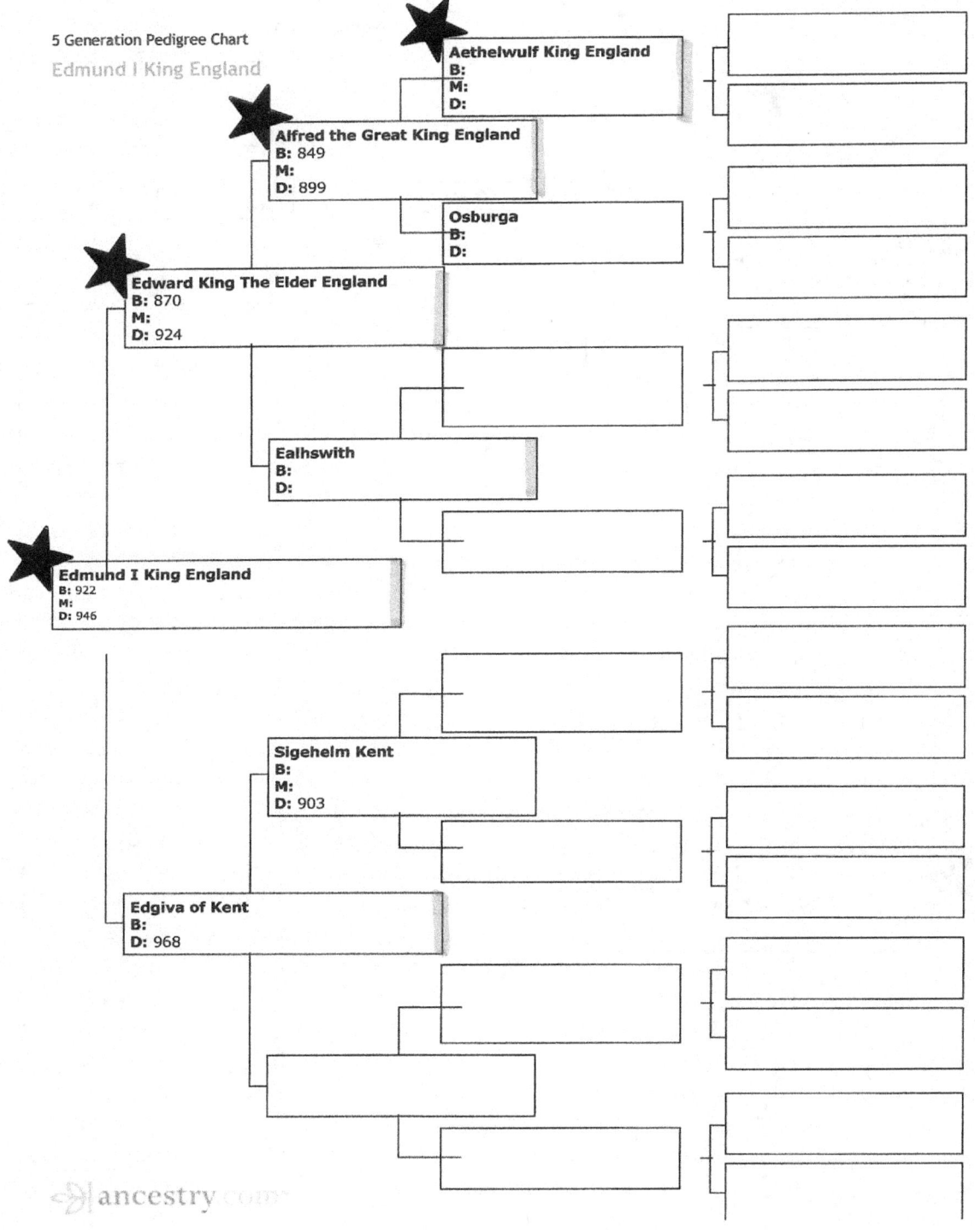

Edmund I King England

Aethelwulf King England
B:
M:
D:

Alfred the Great King England
B: 849
M:
D: 899

Osburga
B:
D:

Edward King The Elder England
B: 870
M:
D: 924

Ealhswith
B:
D:

Edmund I King England
B: 922
M:
D: 946

Sigehelm Kent
B:
M:
D: 903

Edgiva of Kent
B:
D: 968

Pepin I Count DeVermandois

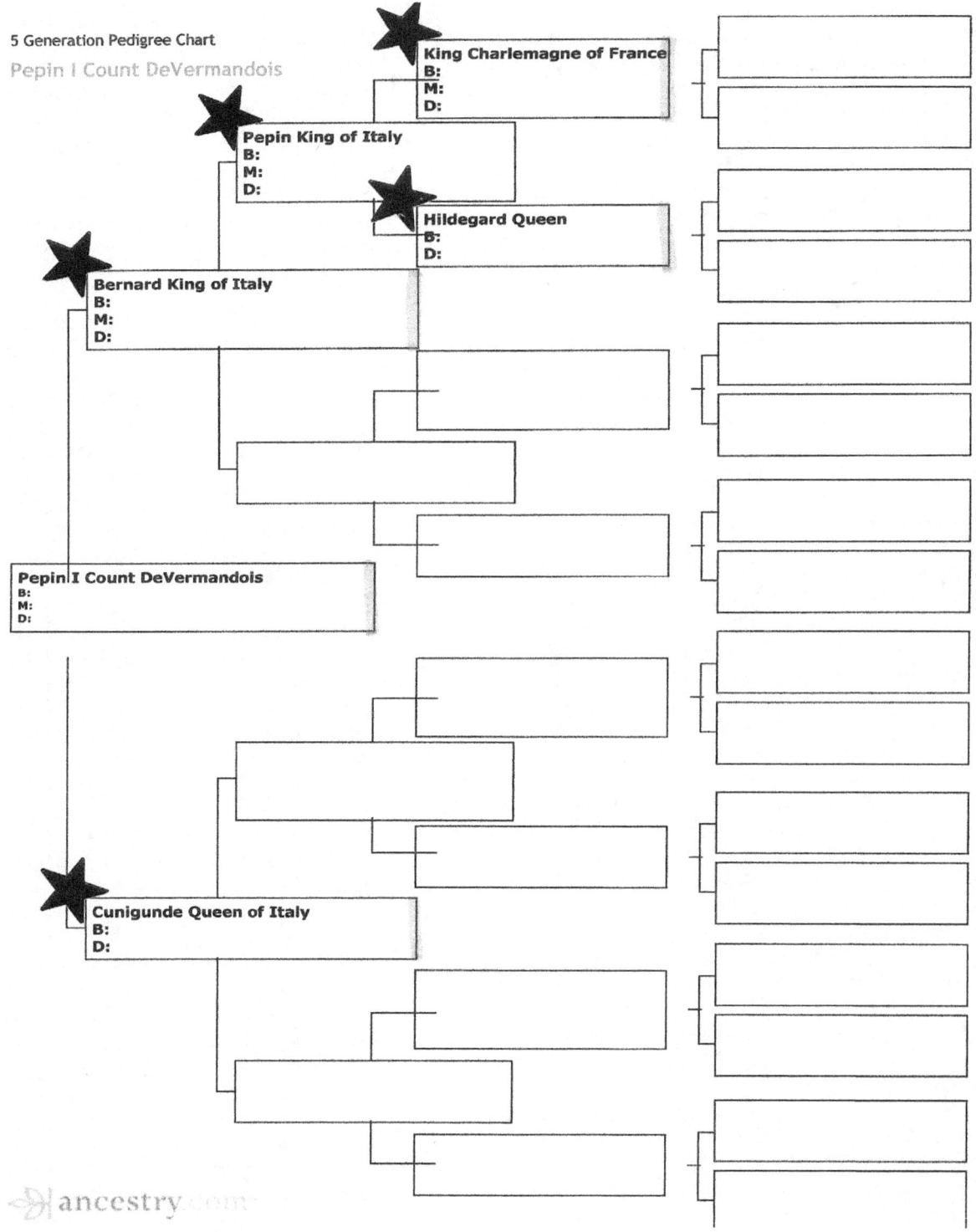

King Charlemagne of France
B:
M:
D:

Pepin King of Italy
B:
M:
D:

Hildegard Queen
B:
D:

Bernard King of Italy
B:
M:
D:

Pepin I Count DeVermandois
B:
M:
D:

Cunigunde Queen of Italy
B:
D:

PART TWO

Charts for Charles Lee Richmond

Charles Lee Richmond

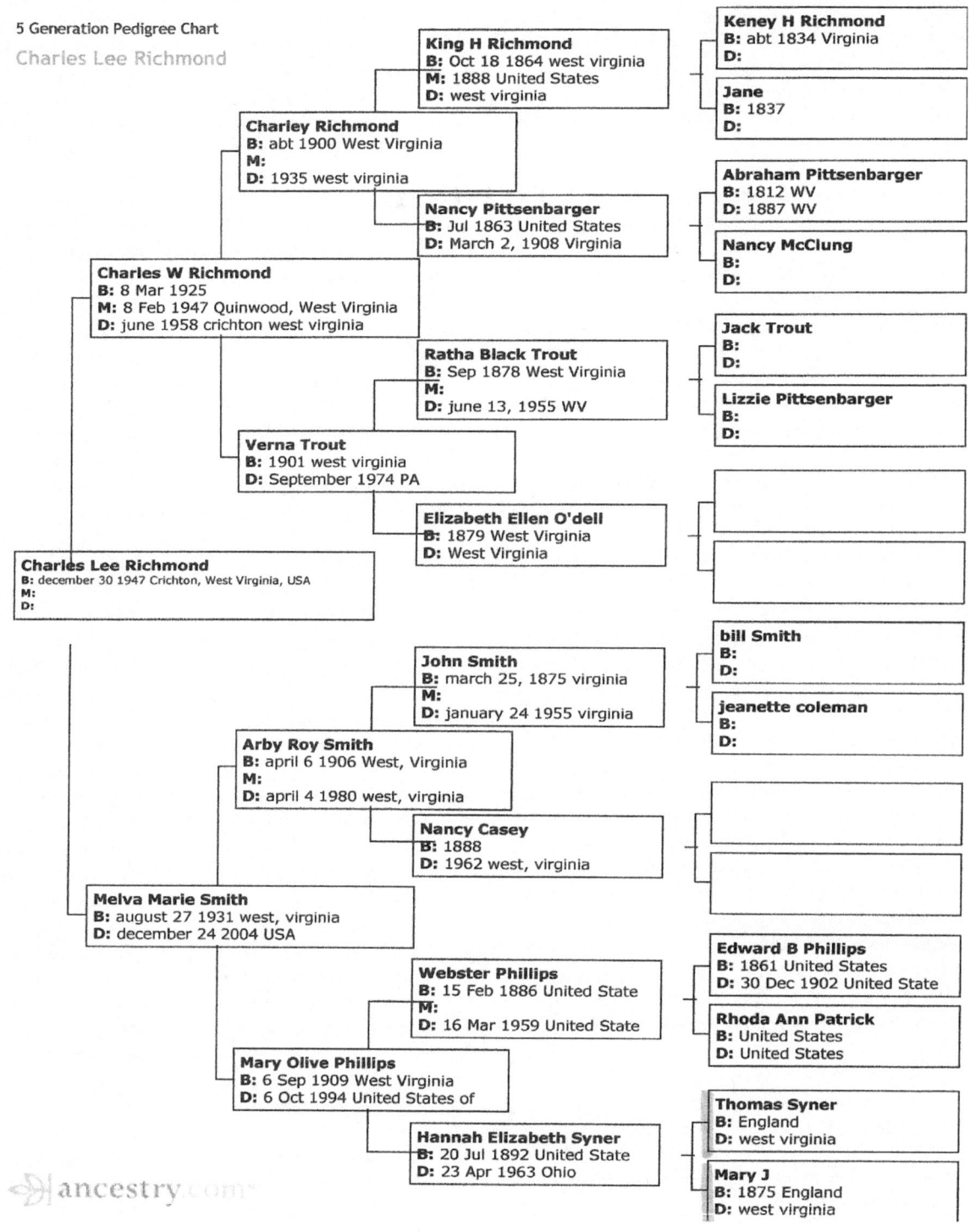

Keney H Richmond
B: abt 1834 Virginia
D:

Jane
B: 1837
D:

King H Richmond
B: Oct 18 1864 west virginia
M: 1888 United States
D: west virginia

Charley Richmond
B: abt 1900 West Virginia
M:
D: 1935 west virginia

Abraham Pittsenbarger
B: 1812 WV
D: 1887 WV

Nancy McClung
B:
D:

Nancy Pittsenbarger
B: Jul 1863 United States
D: March 2, 1908 Virginia

Charles W Richmond
B: 8 Mar 1925
M: 8 Feb 1947 Quinwood, West Virginia
D: june 1958 crichton west virginia

Jack Trout
B:
D:

Lizzie Pittsenbarger
B:
D:

Ratha Black Trout
B: Sep 1878 West Virginia
M:
D: june 13, 1955 WV

Verna Trout
B: 1901 west virginia
D: September 1974 PA

Elizabeth Ellen O'dell
B: 1879 West Virginia
D: West Virginia

Charles Lee Richmond
B: december 30 1947 Crichton, West Virginia, USA
M:
D:

bill Smith
B:
D:

jeanette coleman
B:
D:

John Smith
B: march 25, 1875 virginia
M:
D: january 24 1955 virginia

Arby Roy Smith
B: april 6 1906 West, Virginia
M:
D: april 4 1980 west, virginia

Nancy Casey
B: 1888
D: 1962 west, virginia

Melva Marie Smith
B: august 27 1931 west, virginia
D: december 24 2004 USA

Edward B Phillips
B: 1861 United States
D: 30 Dec 1902 United State

Rhoda Ann Patrick
B: United States
D: United States

Webster Phillips
B: 15 Feb 1886 United State
M:
D: 16 Mar 1959 United State

Mary Olive Phillips
B: 6 Sep 1909 West Virginia
D: 6 Oct 1994 United States of

Thomas Syner
B: England
D: west virginia

Mary J
B: 1875 England
D: west virginia

Hannah Elizabeth Syner
B: 20 Jul 1892 United State
D: 23 Apr 1963 Ohio

52

Edward B Phillips

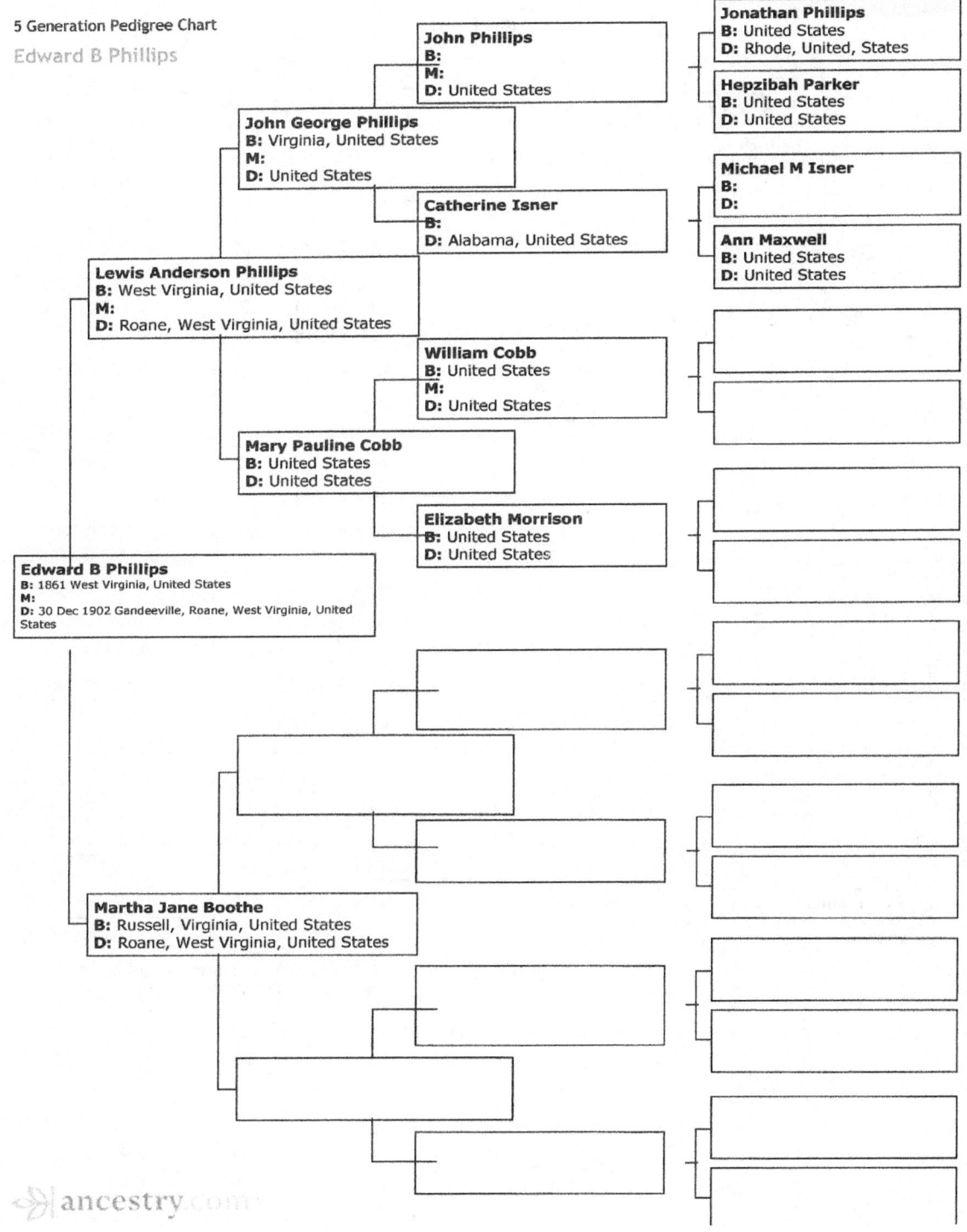

John Phillips
B:
M:
D: United States

John George Phillips
B: Virginia, United States
M:
D: United States

Catherine Isner
B:
D: Alabama, United States

Lewis Anderson Phillips
B: West Virginia, United States
M:
D: Roane, West Virginia, United States

William Cobb
B: United States
M:
D: United States

Mary Pauline Cobb
B: United States
D: United States

Elizabeth Morrison
B: United States
D: United States

Edward B Phillips
B: 1861 West Virginia, United States
M:
D: 30 Dec 1902 Gandeeville, Roane, West Virginia, United States

Jonathan Phillips
B: United States
D: Rhode, United, States

Hepzibah Parker
B: United States
D: United States

Michael M Isner
B:
D:

Ann Maxwell
B: United States
D: United States

Martha Jane Boothe
B: Russell, Virginia, United States
D: Roane, West Virginia, United States

53

Jonathan Phillips

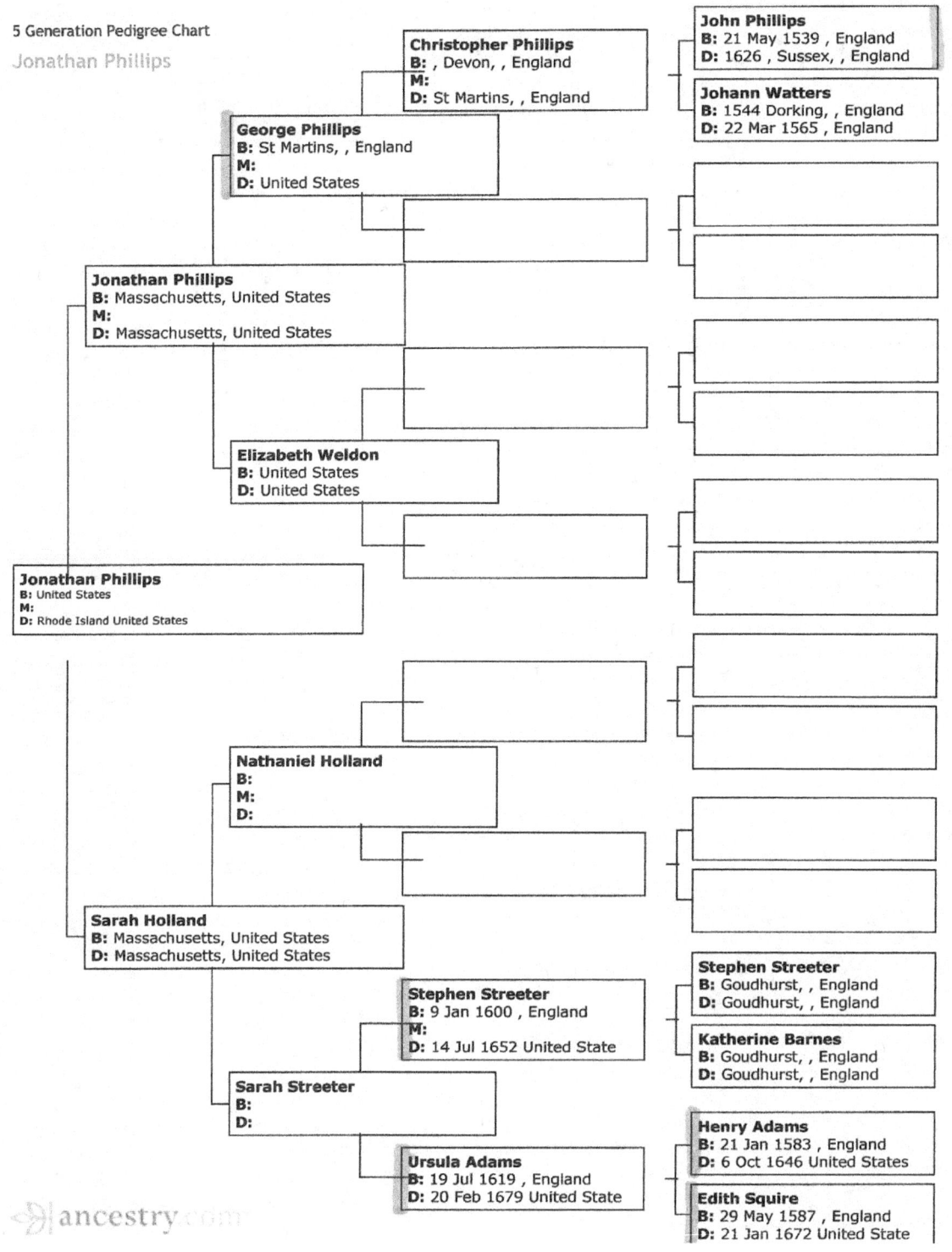

Christopher Phillips
B: , Devon, , England
M:
D: St Martins, , England

George Phillips
B: St Martins, , England
M:
D: United States

Jonathan Phillips
B: Massachusetts, United States
M:
D: Massachusetts, United States

Elizabeth Weldon
B: United States
D: United States

Jonathan Phillips
B: United States
M:
D: Rhode Island United States

Nathaniel Holland
B:
M:
D:

Sarah Holland
B: Massachusetts, United States
D: Massachusetts, United States

Stephen Streeter
B: 9 Jan 1600 , England
M:
D: 14 Jul 1652 United State

Sarah Streeter
B:
D:

Ursula Adams
B: 19 Jul 1619 , England
D: 20 Feb 1679 United State

John Phillips
B: 21 May 1539 , England
D: 1626 , Sussex, , England

Johann Watters
B: 1544 Dorking, , England
D: 22 Mar 1565 , England

Stephen Streeter
B: Goudhurst, , England
D: Goudhurst, , England

Katherine Barnes
B: Goudhurst, , England
D: Goudhurst, , England

Henry Adams
B: 21 Jan 1583 , England
D: 6 Oct 1646 United States

Edith Squire
B: 29 May 1587 , England
D: 21 Jan 1672 United State

54

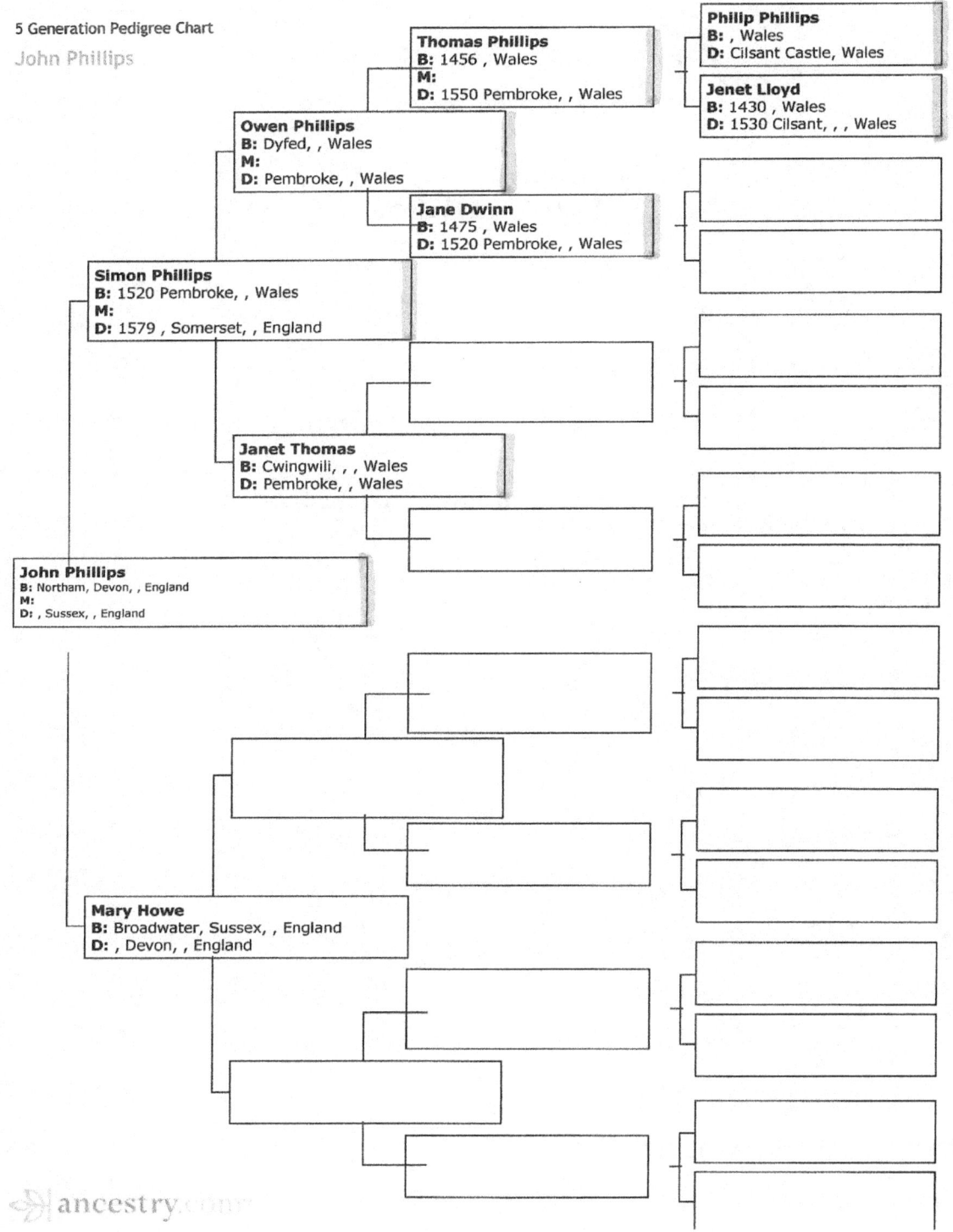

5 Generation Pedigree Chart

John Phillips

Philip Phillips
B: , Wales
D: Cilsant Castle, Wales

Jenet Lloyd
B: 1430 , Wales
D: 1530 Cilsant, , , Wales

Thomas Phillips
B: 1456 , Wales
M:
D: 1550 Pembroke, , Wales

Owen Phillips
B: Dyfed, , Wales
M:
D: Pembroke, , Wales

Jane Dwinn
B: 1475 , Wales
D: 1520 Pembroke, , Wales

Simon Phillips
B: 1520 Pembroke, , Wales
M:
D: 1579 , Somerset, , England

Janet Thomas
B: Cwingwili, , , Wales
D: Pembroke, , Wales

John Phillips
B: Northam, Devon, , England
M:
D: , Sussex, , England

Mary Howe
B: Broadwater, Sussex, , England
D: , Devon, , England

PART THREE

Charts for Children and Grandchildren

Tamara Lynn Murray

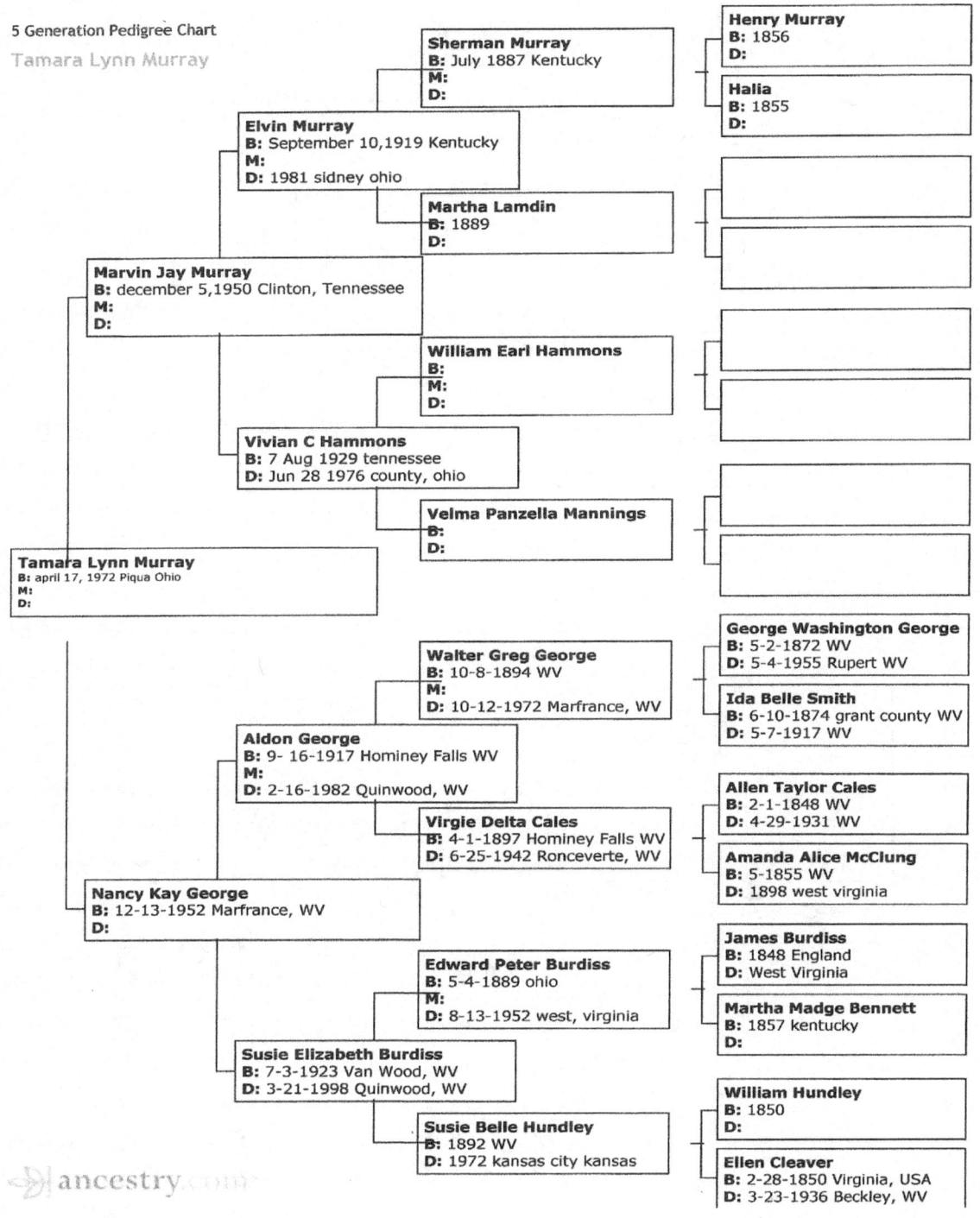

Sherman Murray
B: July 1887 Kentucky
M:
D:

Henry Murray
B: 1856
D:

Halia
B: 1855
D:

Elvin Murray
B: September 10,1919 Kentucky
M:
D: 1981 sidney ohio

Martha Lamdin
B: 1889
D:

Marvin Jay Murray
B: december 5,1950 Clinton, Tennessee
M:
D:

William Earl Hammons
B:
M:
D:

Vivian C Hammons
B: 7 Aug 1929 tennessee
D: Jun 28 1976 county, ohio

Velma Panzella Mannings
B:
D:

Tamara Lynn Murray
B: april 17, 1972 Piqua Ohio
M:
D:

Walter Greg George
B: 10-8-1894 WV
M:
D: 10-12-1972 Marfrance, WV

George Washington George
B: 5-2-1872 WV
D: 5-4-1955 Rupert WV

Ida Belle Smith
B: 6-10-1874 grant county WV
D: 5-7-1917 WV

Aldon George
B: 9- 16-1917 Hominey Falls WV
M:
D: 2-16-1982 Quinwood, WV

Virgie Delta Cales
B: 4-1-1897 Hominey Falls WV
D: 6-25-1942 Ronceverte, WV

Allen Taylor Cales
B: 2-1-1848 WV
D: 4-29-1931 WV

Amanda Alice McClung
B: 5-1855 WV
D: 1898 west virginia

Nancy Kay George
B: 12-13-1952 Marfrance, WV
D:

Edward Peter Burdiss
B: 5-4-1889 ohio
M:
D: 8-13-1952 west, virginia

James Burdiss
B: 1848 England
D: West Virginia

Martha Madge Bennett
B: 1857 kentucky
D:

Susie Elizabeth Burdiss
B: 7-3-1923 Van Wood, WV
D: 3-21-1998 Quinwood, WV

Susie Belle Hundley
B: 1892 WV
D: 1972 kansas city kansas

William Hundley
B: 1850
D:

Ellen Cleaver
B: 2-28-1850 Virginia, USA
D: 3-23-1936 Beckley, WV

ancestry.com

57

5 Generation Pedigree Chart

Misty Dawn Murray

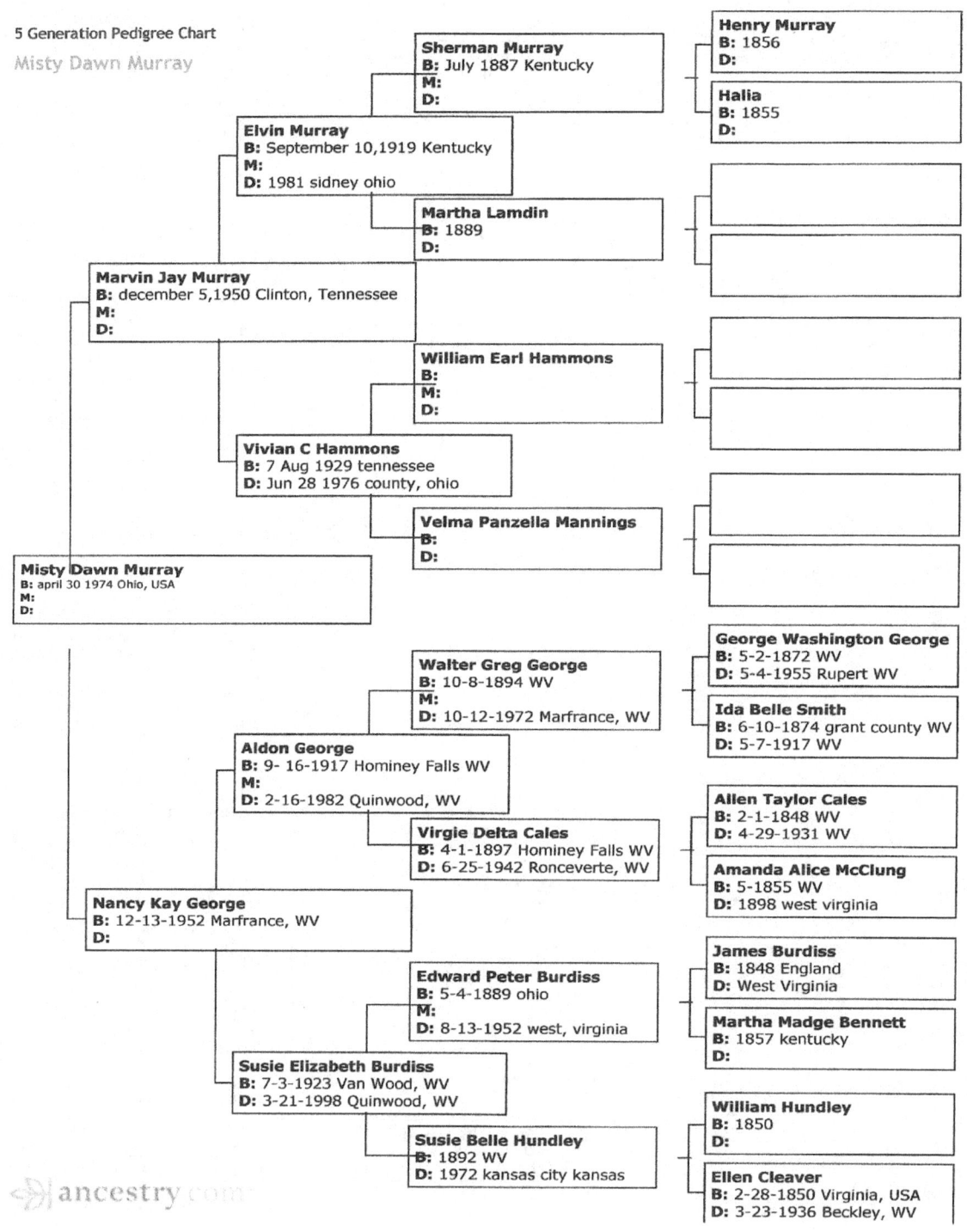

Henry Murray
B: 1856
D:

Halia
B: 1855
D:

Sherman Murray
B: July 1887 Kentucky
M:
D:

Elvin Murray
B: September 10,1919 Kentucky
M:
D: 1981 sidney ohio

Martha Lamdin
B: 1889
D:

Marvin Jay Murray
B: december 5,1950 Clinton, Tennessee
M:
D:

William Earl Hammons
B:
M:
D:

Vivian C Hammons
B: 7 Aug 1929 tennessee
D: Jun 28 1976 county, ohio

Velma Panzella Mannings
B:
D:

Misty Dawn Murray
B: april 30 1974 Ohio, USA
M:
D:

George Washington George
B: 5-2-1872 WV
D: 5-4-1955 Rupert WV

Ida Belle Smith
B: 6-10-1874 grant county WV
D: 5-7-1917 WV

Walter Greg George
B: 10-8-1894 WV
M:
D: 10-12-1972 Marfrance, WV

Aldon George
B: 9- 16-1917 Hominey Falls WV
M:
D: 2-16-1982 Quinwood, WV

Virgie Delta Cales
B: 4-1-1897 Hominey Falls WV
D: 6-25-1942 Ronceverte, WV

Allen Taylor Cales
B: 2-1-1848 WV
D: 4-29-1931 WV

Amanda Alice McClung
B: 5-1855 WV
D: 1898 west virginia

Nancy Kay George
B: 12-13-1952 Marfrance, WV
D:

James Burdiss
B: 1848 England
D: West Virginia

Martha Madge Bennett
B: 1857 kentucky
D:

Edward Peter Burdiss
B: 5-4-1889 ohio
M:
D: 8-13-1952 west, virginia

Susie Elizabeth Burdiss
B: 7-3-1923 Van Wood, WV
D: 3-21-1998 Quinwood, WV

Susie Belle Hundley
B: 1892 WV
D: 1972 kansas city kansas

William Hundley
B: 1850
D:

Ellen Cleaver
B: 2-28-1850 Virginia, USA
D: 3-23-1936 Beckley, WV

ancestry.com

58

Charity Marie Richmond

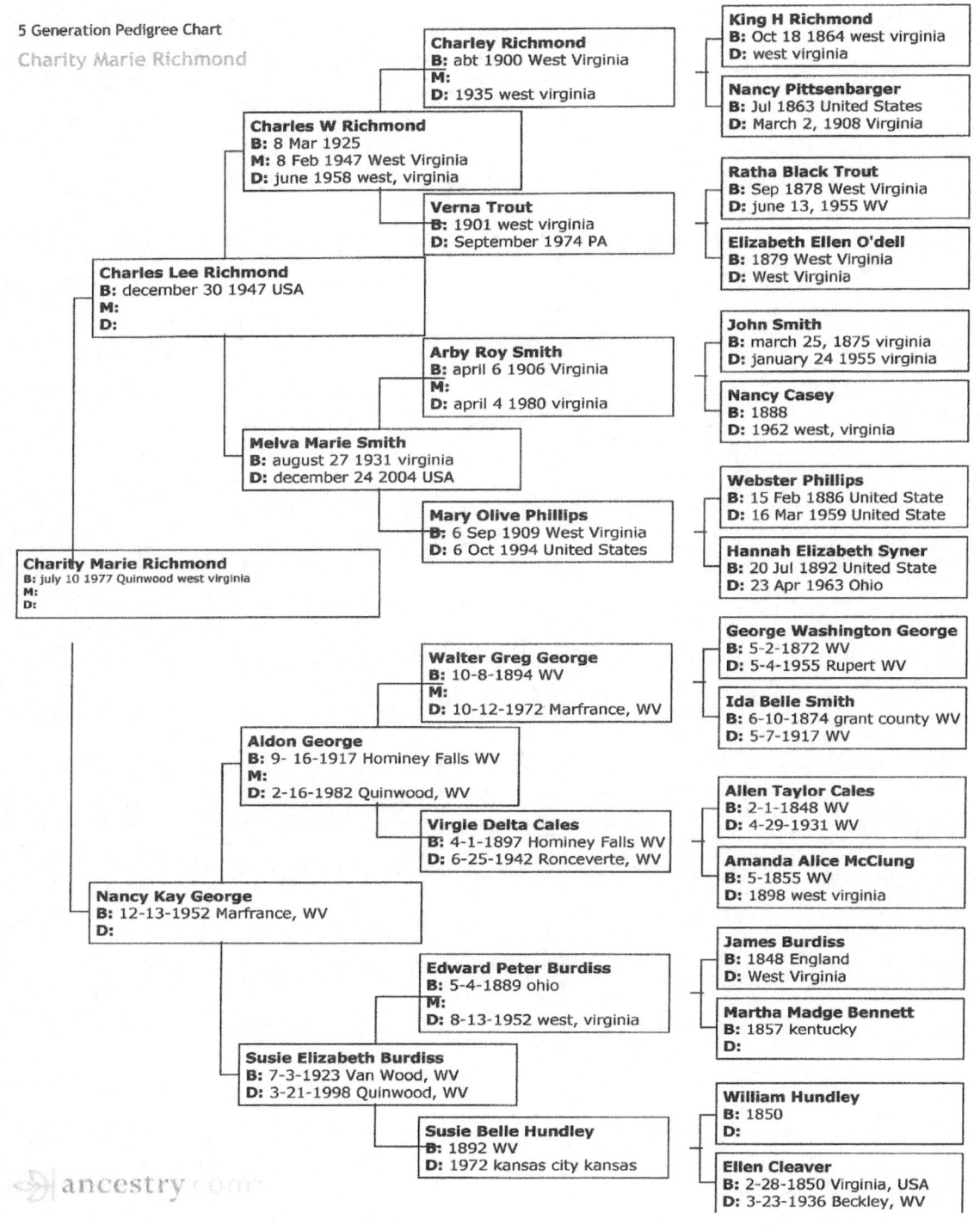

Charley Richmond
B: abt 1900 West Virginia
M:
D: 1935 west virginia

King H Richmond
B: Oct 18 1864 west virginia
D: west virginia

Nancy Pittsenbarger
B: Jul 1863 United States
D: March 2, 1908 Virginia

Charles W Richmond
B: 8 Mar 1925
M: 8 Feb 1947 West Virginia
D: june 1958 west, virginia

Verna Trout
B: 1901 west virginia
D: September 1974 PA

Ratha Black Trout
B: Sep 1878 West Virginia
D: june 13, 1955 WV

Elizabeth Ellen O'dell
B: 1879 West Virginia
D: West Virginia

Charles Lee Richmond
B: december 30 1947 USA
M:
D:

Arby Roy Smith
B: april 6 1906 Virginia
M:
D: april 4 1980 virginia

John Smith
B: march 25, 1875 virginia
D: january 24 1955 virginia

Nancy Casey
B: 1888
D: 1962 west, virginia

Melva Marie Smith
B: august 27 1931 virginia
D: december 24 2004 USA

Mary Olive Phillips
B: 6 Sep 1909 West Virginia
D: 6 Oct 1994 United States

Webster Phillips
B: 15 Feb 1886 United State
D: 16 Mar 1959 United State

Hannah Elizabeth Syner
B: 20 Jul 1892 United State
D: 23 Apr 1963 Ohio

Charity Marie Richmond
B: july 10 1977 Quinwood west virginia
M:
D:

Walter Greg George
B: 10-8-1894 WV
M:
D: 10-12-1972 Marfrance, WV

George Washington George
B: 5-2-1872 WV
D: 5-4-1955 Rupert WV

Ida Belle Smith
B: 6-10-1874 grant county WV
D: 5-7-1917 WV

Aldon George
B: 9- 16-1917 Hominey Falls WV
M:
D: 2-16-1982 Quinwood, WV

Virgie Delta Cales
B: 4-1-1897 Hominey Falls WV
D: 6-25-1942 Ronceverte, WV

Allen Taylor Cales
B: 2-1-1848 WV
D: 4-29-1931 WV

Amanda Alice McClung
B: 5-1855 WV
D: 1898 west virginia

Nancy Kay George
B: 12-13-1952 Marfrance, WV
D:

Edward Peter Burdiss
B: 5-4-1889 ohio
M:
D: 8-13-1952 west, virginia

James Burdiss
B: 1848 England
D: West Virginia

Martha Madge Bennett
B: 1857 kentucky
D:

Susie Elizabeth Burdiss
B: 7-3-1923 Van Wood, WV
D: 3-21-1998 Quinwood, WV

Susie Belle Hundley
B: 1892 WV
D: 1972 kansas city kansas

William Hundley
B: 1850
D:

Ellen Cleaver
B: 2-28-1850 Virginia, USA
D: 3-23-1936 Beckley, WV

ancestry.com

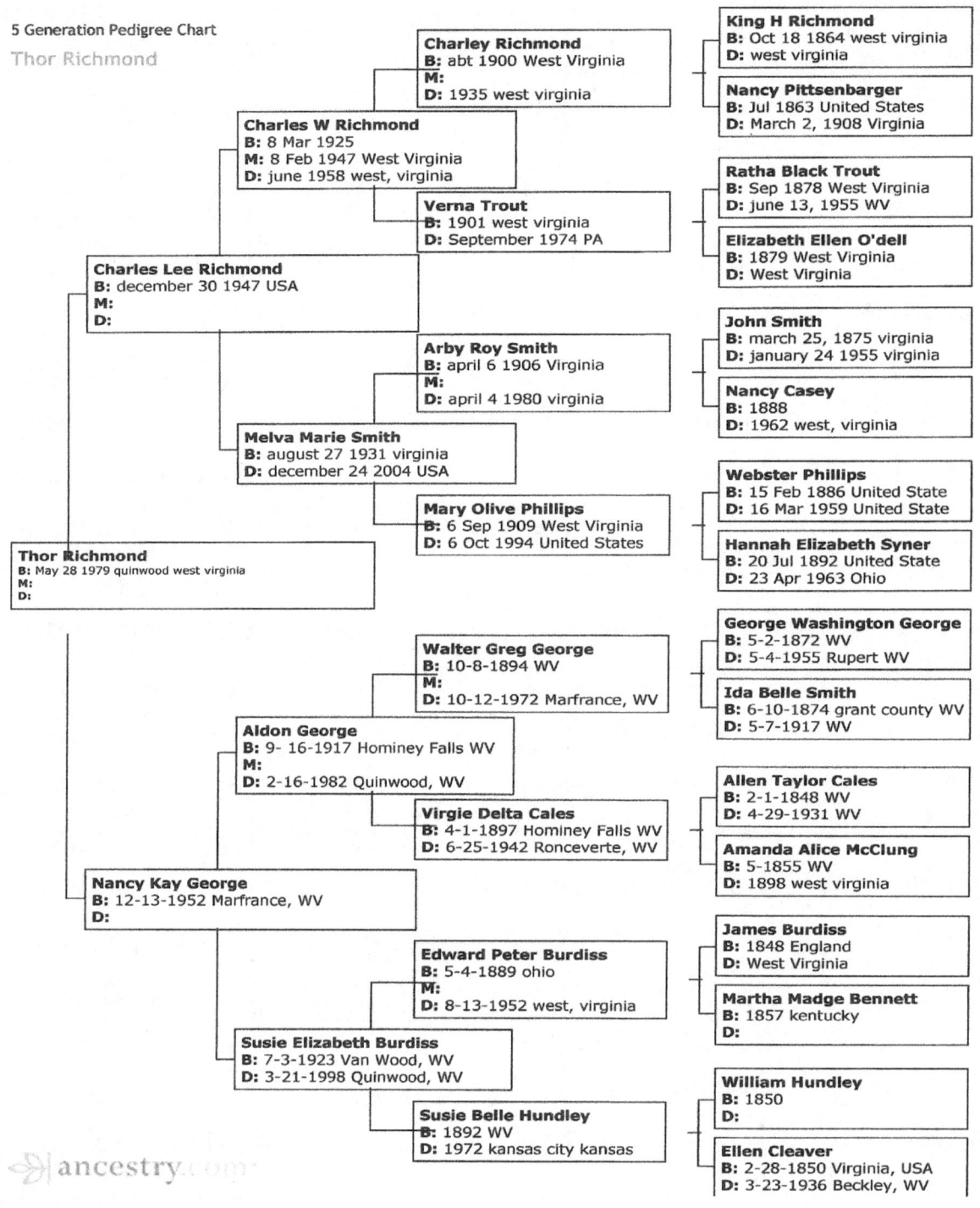

Charley Richmond
B: abt 1900 West Virginia
M:
D: 1935 west virginia

Charles W Richmond
B: 8 Mar 1925
M: 8 Feb 1947 West Virginia
D: june 1958 west, virginia

Verna Trout
B: 1901 west virginia
D: September 1974 PA

Charles Lee Richmond
B: december 30 1947 USA
M:
D:

Arby Roy Smith
B: april 6 1906 Virginia
M:
D: april 4 1980 virginia

Melva Marie Smith
B: august 27 1931 virginia
D: december 24 2004 USA

Mary Olive Phillips
B: 6 Sep 1909 West Virginia
D: 6 Oct 1994 United States

Thor Richmond
B: May 28 1979 quinwood west virginia
M:
D:

King H Richmond
B: Oct 18 1864 west virginia
D: west virginia

Nancy Pittsenbarger
B: Jul 1863 United States
D: March 2, 1908 Virginia

Ratha Black Trout
B: Sep 1878 West Virginia
D: june 13, 1955 WV

Elizabeth Ellen O'dell
B: 1879 West Virginia
D: West Virginia

John Smith
B: march 25, 1875 virginia
D: january 24 1955 virginia

Nancy Casey
B: 1888
D: 1962 west, virginia

Webster Phillips
B: 15 Feb 1886 United State
D: 16 Mar 1959 United State

Hannah Elizabeth Syner
B: 20 Jul 1892 United State
D: 23 Apr 1963 Ohio

Walter Greg George
B: 10-8-1894 WV
M:
D: 10-12-1972 Marfrance, WV

Aldon George
B: 9- 16-1917 Hominey Falls WV
M:
D: 2-16-1982 Quinwood, WV

Virgie Delta Cales
B: 4-1-1897 Hominey Falls WV
D: 6-25-1942 Ronceverte, WV

Nancy Kay George
B: 12-13-1952 Marfrance, WV
D:

Edward Peter Burdiss
B: 5-4-1889 ohio
M:
D: 8-13-1952 west, virginia

Susie Elizabeth Burdiss
B: 7-3-1923 Van Wood, WV
D: 3-21-1998 Quinwood, WV

Susie Belle Hundley
B: 1892 WV
D: 1972 kansas city kansas

George Washington George
B: 5-2-1872 WV
D: 5-4-1955 Rupert WV

Ida Belle Smith
B: 6-10-1874 grant county WV
D: 5-7-1917 WV

Allen Taylor Cales
B: 2-1-1848 WV
D: 4-29-1931 WV

Amanda Alice McClung
B: 5-1855 WV
D: 1898 west virginia

James Burdiss
B: 1848 England
D: West Virginia

Martha Madge Bennett
B: 1857 kentucky
D:

William Hundley
B: 1850
D:

Ellen Cleaver
B: 2-28-1850 Virginia, USA
D: 3-23-1936 Beckley, WV

Lora Lee Richmond

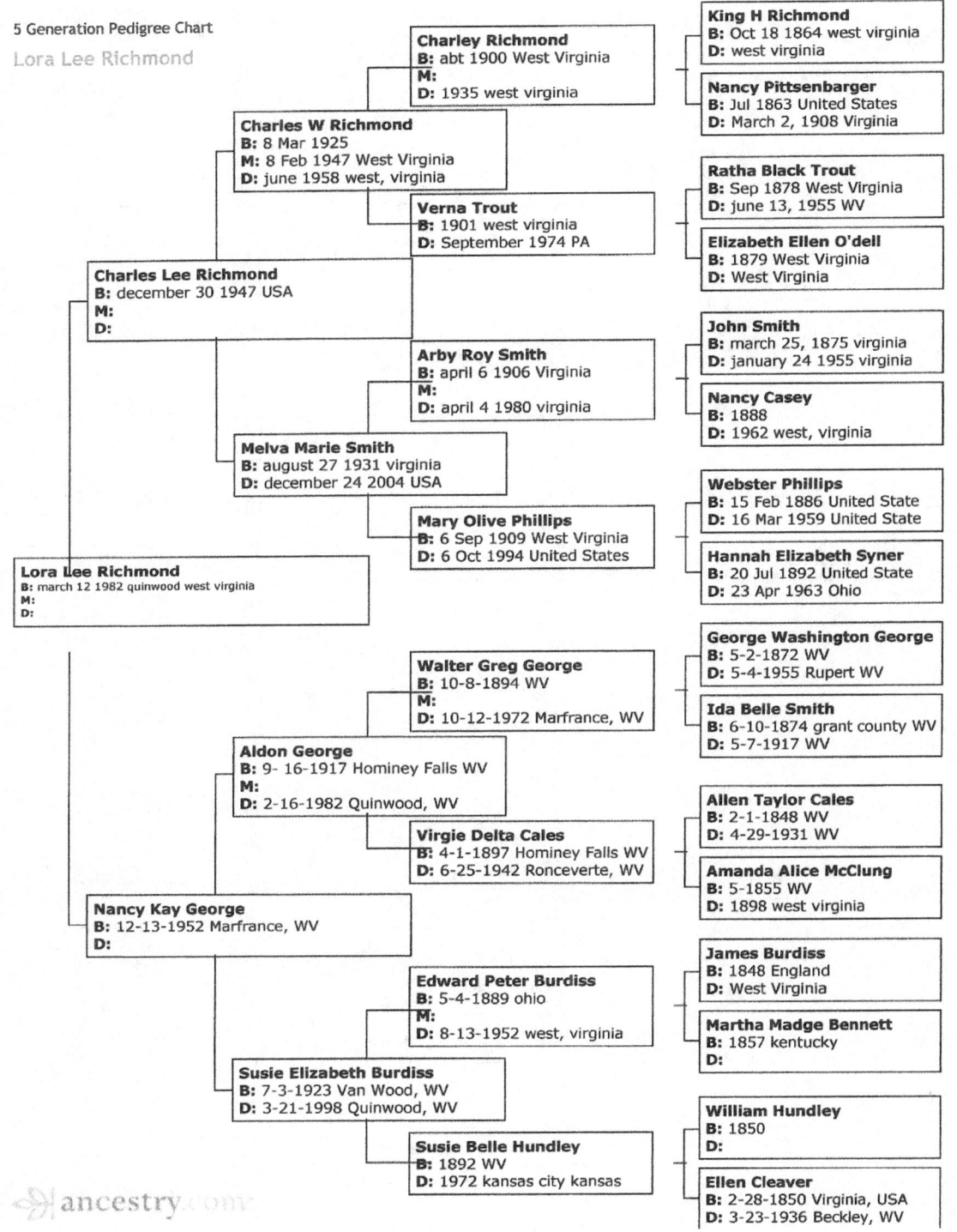

Charley Richmond
B: abt 1900 West Virginia
M:
D: 1935 west virginia

Charles W Richmond
B: 8 Mar 1925
M: 8 Feb 1947 West Virginia
D: june 1958 west, virginia

Verna Trout
B: 1901 west virginia
D: September 1974 PA

Charles Lee Richmond
B: december 30 1947 USA
M:
D:

Arby Roy Smith
B: april 6 1906 Virginia
M:
D: april 4 1980 virginia

Melva Marie Smith
B: august 27 1931 virginia
D: december 24 2004 USA

Mary Olive Phillips
B: 6 Sep 1909 West Virginia
D: 6 Oct 1994 United States

Lora Lee Richmond
B: march 12 1982 quinwood west virginia
M:
D:

King H Richmond
B: Oct 18 1864 west virginia
D: west virginia

Nancy Pittsenbarger
B: Jul 1863 United States
D: March 2, 1908 Virginia

Ratha Black Trout
B: Sep 1878 West Virginia
D: june 13, 1955 WV

Elizabeth Ellen O'dell
B: 1879 West Virginia
D: West Virginia

John Smith
B: march 25, 1875 virginia
D: january 24 1955 virginia

Nancy Casey
B: 1888
D: 1962 west, virginia

Webster Phillips
B: 15 Feb 1886 United State
D: 16 Mar 1959 United State

Hannah Elizabeth Syner
B: 20 Jul 1892 United State
D: 23 Apr 1963 Ohio

Walter Greg George
B: 10-8-1894 WV
M:
D: 10-12-1972 Marfrance, WV

Aldon George
B: 9- 16-1917 Hominey Falls WV
M:
D: 2-16-1982 Quinwood, WV

Virgie Delta Cales
B: 4-1-1897 Hominey Falls WV
D: 6-25-1942 Ronceverte, WV

Nancy Kay George
B: 12-13-1952 Marfrance, WV
D:

Edward Peter Burdiss
B: 5-4-1889 ohio
M:
D: 8-13-1952 west, virginia

Susie Elizabeth Burdiss
B: 7-3-1923 Van Wood, WV
D: 3-21-1998 Quinwood, WV

Susie Belle Hundley
B: 1892 WV
D: 1972 kansas city kansas

George Washington George
B: 5-2-1872 WV
D: 5-4-1955 Rupert WV

Ida Belle Smith
B: 6-10-1874 grant county WV
D: 5-7-1917 WV

Allen Taylor Cales
B: 2-1-1848 WV
D: 4-29-1931 WV

Amanda Alice McClung
B: 5-1855 WV
D: 1898 west virginia

James Burdiss
B: 1848 England
D: West Virginia

Martha Madge Bennett
B: 1857 kentucky
D:

William Hundley
B: 1850
D:

Ellen Cleaver
B: 2-28-1850 Virginia, USA
D: 3-23-1936 Beckley, WV

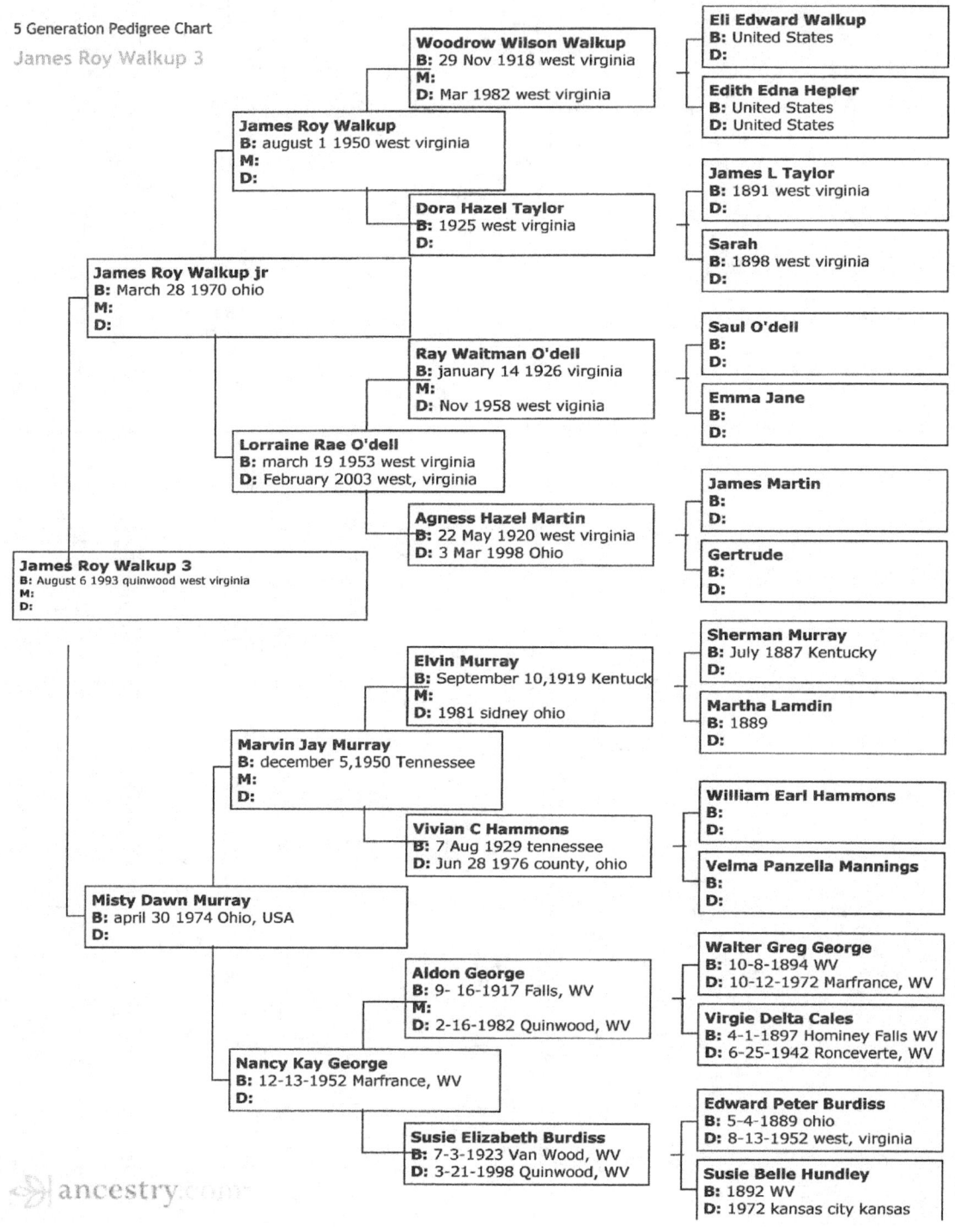

5 Generation Pedigree Chart

James Roy Walkup 3

James Roy Walkup jr
B: March 28 1970 ohio
M:
D:

James Roy Walkup
B: august 1 1950 west virginia
M:
D:

Woodrow Wilson Walkup
B: 29 Nov 1918 west virginia
M:
D: Mar 1982 west virginia

Eli Edward Walkup
B: United States
D:

Edith Edna Hepler
B: United States
D: United States

Dora Hazel Taylor
B: 1925 west virginia
D:

James L Taylor
B: 1891 west virginia
D:

Sarah
B: 1898 west virginia
D:

Lorraine Rae O'dell
B: march 19 1953 west virginia
D: February 2003 west, virginia

Ray Waitman O'dell
B: january 14 1926 virginia
M:
D: Nov 1958 west viginia

Saul O'dell
B:
D:

Emma Jane
B:
D:

Agness Hazel Martin
B: 22 May 1920 west virginia
D: 3 Mar 1998 Ohio

James Martin
B:
D:

Gertrude
B:
D:

James Roy Walkup 3
B: August 6 1993 quinwood west virginia
M:
D:

Misty Dawn Murray
B: april 30 1974 Ohio, USA
D:

Marvin Jay Murray
B: december 5,1950 Tennessee
M:
D:

Elvin Murray
B: September 10,1919 Kentuck
M:
D: 1981 sidney ohio

Sherman Murray
B: July 1887 Kentucky
D:

Martha Lamdin
B: 1889
D:

Vivian C Hammons
B: 7 Aug 1929 tennessee
D: Jun 28 1976 county, ohio

William Earl Hammons
B:
D:

Velma Panzella Mannings
B:
D:

Nancy Kay George
B: 12-13-1952 Marfrance, WV
D:

Aldon George
B: 9- 16-1917 Falls, WV
M:
D: 2-16-1982 Quinwood, WV

Walter Greg George
B: 10-8-1894 WV
D: 10-12-1972 Marfrance, WV

Virgie Delta Cales
B: 4-1-1897 Hominey Falls WV
D: 6-25-1942 Ronceverte, WV

Susie Elizabeth Burdiss
B: 7-3-1923 Van Wood, WV
D: 3-21-1998 Quinwood, WV

Edward Peter Burdiss
B: 5-4-1889 ohio
D: 8-13-1952 west, virginia

Susie Belle Hundley
B: 1892 WV
D: 1972 kansas city kansas

Tia Dawn Walkup

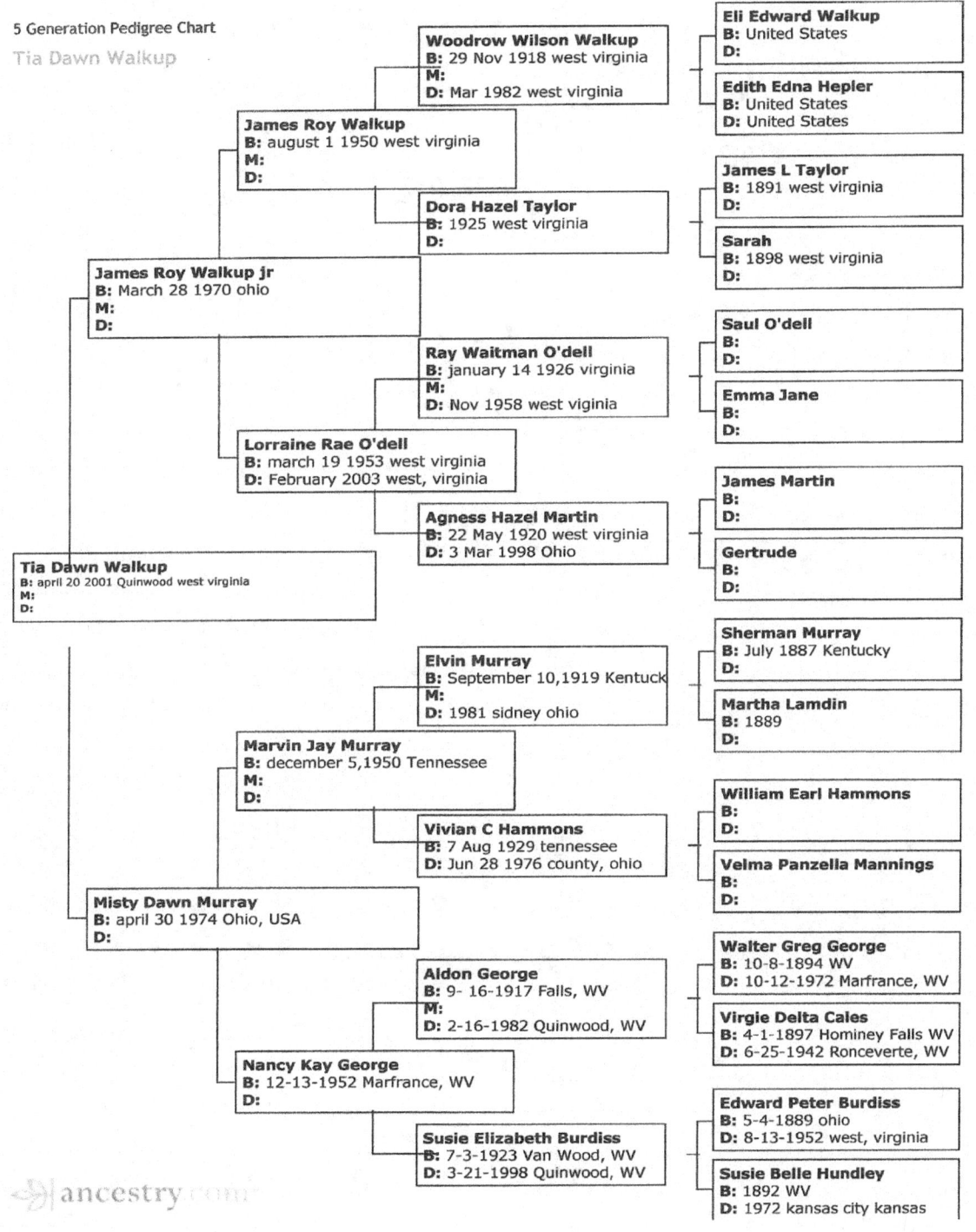

Woodrow Wilson Walkup
B: 29 Nov 1918 west virginia
M:
D: Mar 1982 west virginia

James Roy Walkup
B: august 1 1950 west virginia
M:
D:

Dora Hazel Taylor
B: 1925 west virginia
D:

James Roy Walkup jr
B: March 28 1970 ohio
M:
D:

Ray Waitman O'dell
B: january 14 1926 virginia
M:
D: Nov 1958 west viginia

Lorraine Rae O'dell
B: march 19 1953 west virginia
D: February 2003 west, virginia

Agness Hazel Martin
B: 22 May 1920 west virginia
D: 3 Mar 1998 Ohio

Tia Dawn Walkup
B: april 20 2001 Quinwood west virginia
M:
D:

Elvin Murray
B: September 10,1919 Kentuck
M:
D: 1981 sidney ohio

Marvin Jay Murray
B: december 5,1950 Tennessee
M:
D:

Vivian C Hammons
B: 7 Aug 1929 tennessee
D: Jun 28 1976 county, ohio

Misty Dawn Murray
B: april 30 1974 Ohio, USA
D:

Aldon George
B: 9- 16-1917 Falls, WV
M:
D: 2-16-1982 Quinwood, WV

Nancy Kay George
B: 12-13-1952 Marfrance, WV
D:

Susie Elizabeth Burdiss
B: 7-3-1923 Van Wood, WV
D: 3-21-1998 Quinwood, WV

Eli Edward Walkup
B: United States
D:

Edith Edna Hepler
B: United States
D: United States

James L Taylor
B: 1891 west virginia
D:

Sarah
B: 1898 west virginia
D:

Saul O'dell
B:
D:

Emma Jane
B:
D:

James Martin
B:
D:

Gertrude
B:
D:

Sherman Murray
B: July 1887 Kentucky
D:

Martha Lamdin
B: 1889
D:

William Earl Hammons
B:
D:

Velma Panzella Mannings
B:
D:

Walter Greg George
B: 10-8-1894 WV
D: 10-12-1972 Marfrance, WV

Virgie Delta Cales
B: 4-1-1897 Hominey Falls WV
D: 6-25-1942 Ronceverte, WV

Edward Peter Burdiss
B: 5-4-1889 ohio
D: 8-13-1952 west, virginia

Susie Belle Hundley
B: 1892 WV
D: 1972 kansas city kansas

Jesse James Walkup

Woodrow Wilson Walkup
B: 29 Nov 1918 west virginia
M:
D: Mar 1982 west virginia

Eli Edward Walkup
B: United States
D:

Edith Edna Hepler
B: United States
D: United States

James Roy Walkup
B: august 1 1950 west virginia
M:
D:

Dora Hazel Taylor
B: 1925 west virginia
D:

James L Taylor
B: 1891 west virginia
D:

Sarah
B: 1898 west virginia
D:

James Roy Walkup jr
B: March 28 1970 ohio
M:
D:

Ray Waitman O'dell
B: january 14 1926 virginia
M:
D: Nov 1958 west viginia

Saul O'dell
B:
D:

Emma Jane
B:
D:

Lorraine Rae O'dell
B: march 19 1953 west virginia
D: February 2003 west, virginia

Agness Hazel Martin
B: 22 May 1920 west virginia
D: 3 Mar 1998 Ohio

James Martin
B:
D:

Gertrude
B:
D:

Jesse James Walkup
B: november 5 2008 Quinwood west virginia
M:
D:

Elvin Murray
B: September 10,1919 Kentuck
M:
D: 1981 sidney ohio

Sherman Murray
B: July 1887 Kentucky
D:

Martha Lamdin
B: 1889
D:

Marvin Jay Murray
B: december 5,1950 Tennessee
M:
D:

Vivian C Hammons
B: 7 Aug 1929 tennessee
D: Jun 28 1976 county, ohio

William Earl Hammons
B:
D:

Velma Panzella Mannings
B:
D:

Misty Dawn Murray
B: april 30 1974 Ohio, USA
D:

Aldon George
B: 9- 16-1917 Falls, WV
M:
D: 2-16-1982 Quinwood, WV

Walter Greg George
B: 10-8-1894 WV
D: 10-12-1972 Marfrance, WV

Virgie Delta Cales
B: 4-1-1897 Hominey Falls WV
D: 6-25-1942 Ronceverte, WV

Nancy Kay George
B: 12-13-1952 Marfrance, WV
D:

Susie Elizabeth Burdiss
B: 7-3-1923 Van Wood, WV
D: 3-21-1998 Quinwood, WV

Edward Peter Burdiss
B: 5-4-1889 ohio
D: 8-13-1952 west, virginia

Susie Belle Hundley
B: 1892 WV
D: 1972 kansas city kansas

Victoria Angelique Francis

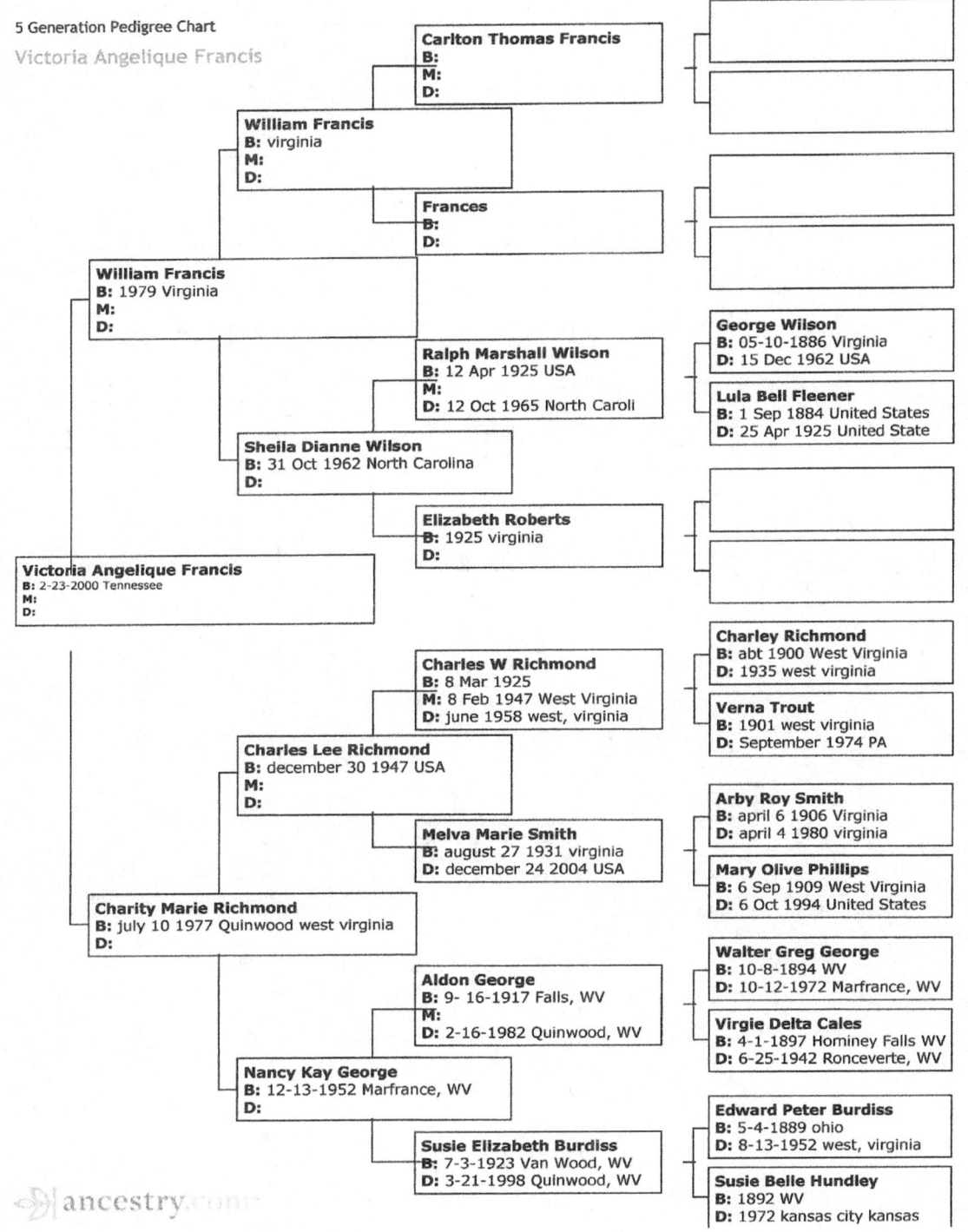

Carlton Thomas Francis
B:
M:
D:

William Francis
B: virginia
M:
D:

Frances
B:
D:

William Francis
B: 1979 Virginia
M:
D:

Ralph Marshall Wilson
B: 12 Apr 1925 USA
M:
D: 12 Oct 1965 North Caroli

George Wilson
B: 05-10-1886 Virginia
D: 15 Dec 1962 USA

Lula Bell Fleener
B: 1 Sep 1884 United States
D: 25 Apr 1925 United State

Sheila Dianne Wilson
B: 31 Oct 1962 North Carolina
D:

Elizabeth Roberts
B: 1925 virginia
D:

Victoria Angelique Francis
B: 2-23-2000 Tennessee
M:
D:

Charles W Richmond
B: 8 Mar 1925
M: 8 Feb 1947 West Virginia
D: June 1958 west, virginia

Charley Richmond
B: abt 1900 West Virginia
D: 1935 west virginia

Verna Trout
B: 1901 west virginia
D: September 1974 PA

Charles Lee Richmond
B: december 30 1947 USA
M:
D:

Melva Marie Smith
B: august 27 1931 virginia
D: december 24 2004 USA

Arby Roy Smith
B: april 6 1906 Virginia
D: april 4 1980 virginia

Mary Olive Phillips
B: 6 Sep 1909 West Virginia
D: 6 Oct 1994 United States

Charity Marie Richmond
B: july 10 1977 Quinwood west virginia
D:

Aldon George
B: 9- 16-1917 Falls, WV
M:
D: 2-16-1982 Quinwood, WV

Walter Greg George
B: 10-8-1894 WV
D: 10-12-1972 Marfrance, WV

Virgie Delta Cales
B: 4-1-1897 Hominey Falls WV
D: 6-25-1942 Ronceverte, WV

Nancy Kay George
B: 12-13-1952 Marfrance, WV
D:

Susie Elizabeth Burdiss
B: 7-3-1923 Van Wood, WV
D: 3-21-1998 Quinwood, WV

Edward Peter Burdiss
B: 5-4-1889 ohio
D: 8-13-1952 west, virginia

Susie Belle Hundley
B: 1892 WV
D: 1972 kansas city kansas

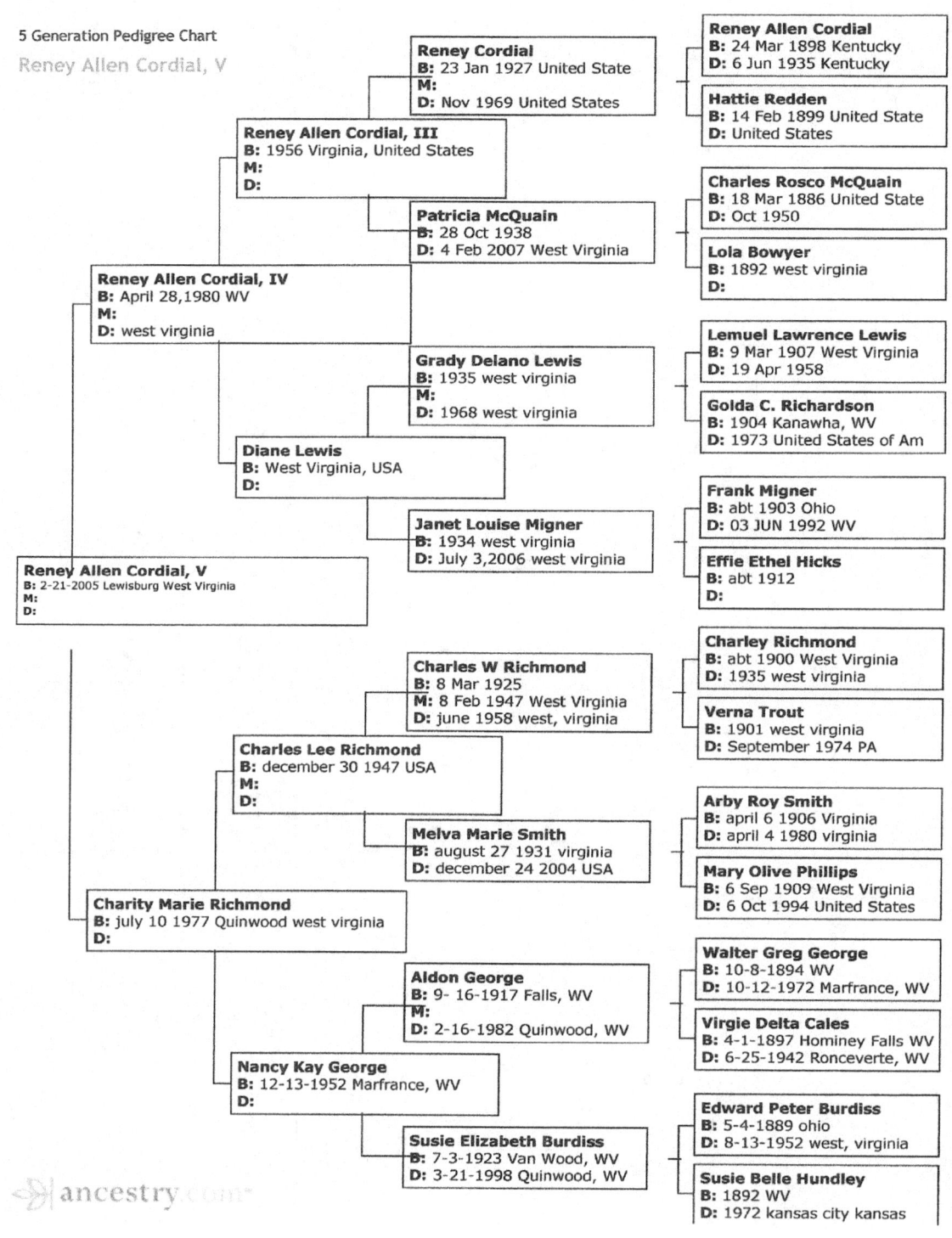

Reney Cordial
B: 23 Jan 1927 United State
M:
D: Nov 1969 United States

Reney Allen Cordial, III
B: 1956 Virginia, United States
M:
D:

Patricia McQuain
B: 28 Oct 1938
D: 4 Feb 2007 West Virginia

Reney Allen Cordial, IV
B: April 28,1980 WV
M:
D: west virginia

Grady Delano Lewis
B: 1935 west virginia
M:
D: 1968 west virginia

Diane Lewis
B: West Virginia, USA
D:

Janet Louise Migner
B: 1934 west virginia
D: July 3,2006 west virginia

Reney Allen Cordial, V
B: 2-21-2005 Lewisburg West Virginia
M:
D:

Reney Allen Cordial
B: 24 Mar 1898 Kentucky
D: 6 Jun 1935 Kentucky

Hattie Redden
B: 14 Feb 1899 United State
D: United States

Charles Rosco McQuain
B: 18 Mar 1886 United State
D: Oct 1950

Lola Bowyer
B: 1892 west virginia
D:

Lemuel Lawrence Lewis
B: 9 Mar 1907 West Virginia
D: 19 Apr 1958

Golda C. Richardson
B: 1904 Kanawha, WV
D: 1973 United States of Am

Frank Migner
B: abt 1903 Ohio
D: 03 JUN 1992 WV

Effie Ethel Hicks
B: abt 1912
D:

Charles W Richmond
B: 8 Mar 1925
M: 8 Feb 1947 West Virginia
D: june 1958 west, virginia

Charles Lee Richmond
B: december 30 1947 USA
M:
D:

Melva Marie Smith
B: august 27 1931 virginia
D: december 24 2004 USA

Charity Marie Richmond
B: july 10 1977 Quinwood west virginia
D:

Aldon George
B: 9- 16-1917 Falls, WV
M:
D: 2-16-1982 Quinwood, WV

Nancy Kay George
B: 12-13-1952 Marfrance, WV
D:

Susie Elizabeth Burdiss
B: 7-3-1923 Van Wood, WV
D: 3-21-1998 Quinwood, WV

Charley Richmond
B: abt 1900 West Virginia
D: 1935 west virginia

Verna Trout
B: 1901 west virginia
D: September 1974 PA

Arby Roy Smith
B: april 6 1906 Virginia
D: april 4 1980 virginia

Mary Olive Phillips
B: 6 Sep 1909 West Virginia
D: 6 Oct 1994 United States

Walter Greg George
B: 10-8-1894 WV
D: 10-12-1972 Marfrance, WV

Virgie Delta Cales
B: 4-1-1897 Hominey Falls WV
D: 6-25-1942 Ronceverte, WV

Edward Peter Burdiss
B: 5-4-1889 ohio
D: 8-13-1952 west, virginia

Susie Belle Hundley
B: 1892 WV
D: 1972 kansas city kansas

66

Hope Marie Boone

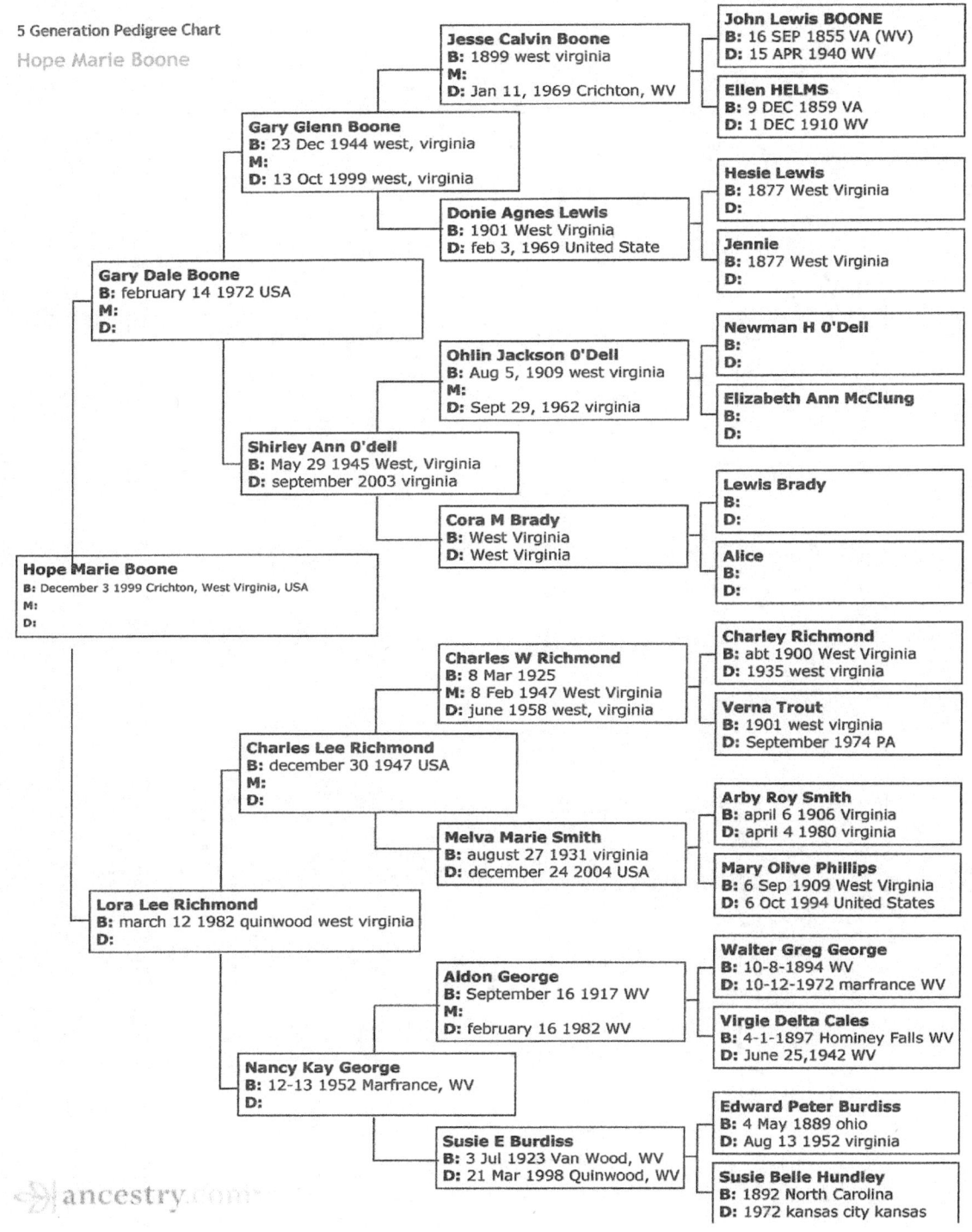

Jesse Calvin Boone
B: 1899 west virginia
M:
D: Jan 11, 1969 Crichton, WV

John Lewis BOONE
B: 16 SEP 1855 VA (WV)
D: 15 APR 1940 WV

Ellen HELMS
B: 9 DEC 1859 VA
D: 1 DEC 1910 WV

Gary Glenn Boone
B: 23 Dec 1944 west, virginia
M:
D: 13 Oct 1999 west, virginia

Donie Agnes Lewis
B: 1901 West Virginia
D: feb 3, 1969 United State

Hesie Lewis
B: 1877 West Virginia
D:

Jennie
B: 1877 West Virginia
D:

Gary Dale Boone
B: february 14 1972 USA
M:
D:

Ohlin Jackson O'Dell
B: Aug 5, 1909 west virginia
M:
D: Sept 29, 1962 virginia

Newman H O'Dell
B:
D:

Elizabeth Ann McClung
B:
D:

Shirley Ann O'dell
B: May 29 1945 West, Virginia
D: september 2003 virginia

Cora M Brady
B: West Virginia
D: West Virginia

Lewis Brady
B:
D:

Alice
B:
D:

Hope Marie Boone
B: December 3 1999 Crichton, West Virginia, USA
M:
D:

Charles W Richmond
B: 8 Mar 1925
M: 8 Feb 1947 West Virginia
D: june 1958 west, virginia

Charley Richmond
B: abt 1900 West Virginia
D: 1935 west virginia

Verna Trout
B: 1901 west virginia
D: September 1974 PA

Charles Lee Richmond
B: december 30 1947 USA
M:
D:

Melva Marie Smith
B: august 27 1931 virginia
D: december 24 2004 USA

Arby Roy Smith
B: april 6 1906 Virginia
D: april 4 1980 virginia

Mary Olive Phillips
B: 6 Sep 1909 West Virginia
D: 6 Oct 1994 United States

Lora Lee Richmond
B: march 12 1982 quinwood west virginia
D:

Aldon George
B: September 16 1917 WV
M:
D: february 16 1982 WV

Walter Greg George
B: 10-8-1894 WV
D: 10-12-1972 marfrance WV

Virgie Delta Cales
B: 4-1-1897 Hominey Falls WV
D: June 25,1942 WV

Nancy Kay George
B: 12-13 1952 Marfrance, WV
D:

Susie E Burdiss
B: 3 Jul 1923 Van Wood, WV
D: 21 Mar 1998 Quinwood, WV

Edward Peter Burdiss
B: 4 May 1889 ohio
D: Aug 13 1952 virginia

Susie Belle Hundley
B: 1892 North Carolina
D: 1972 kansas city kansas

Gary Dale Boone Jr

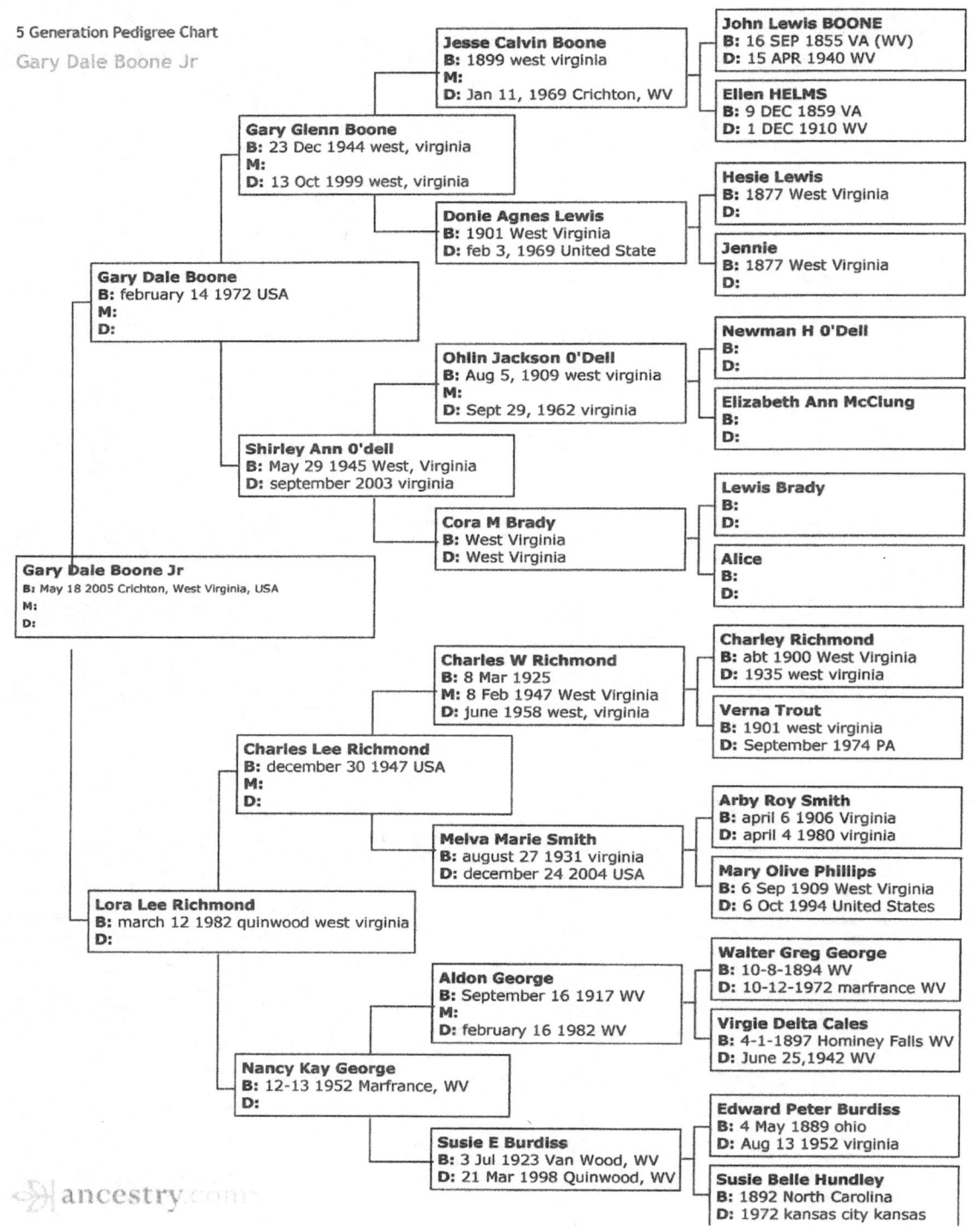

Gary Glenn Boone
B: 23 Dec 1944 west, virginia
M:
D: 13 Oct 1999 west, virginia

Jesse Calvin Boone
B: 1899 west virginia
M:
D: Jan 11, 1969 Crichton, WV

John Lewis BOONE
B: 16 SEP 1855 VA (WV)
D: 15 APR 1940 WV

Ellen HELMS
B: 9 DEC 1859 VA
D: 1 DEC 1910 WV

Donie Agnes Lewis
B: 1901 West Virginia
D: feb 3, 1969 United State

Hesie Lewis
B: 1877 West Virginia
D:

Jennie
B: 1877 West Virginia
D:

Gary Dale Boone
B: february 14 1972 USA
M:
D:

Shirley Ann O'dell
B: May 29 1945 West, Virginia
D: september 2003 virginia

Ohlin Jackson O'Dell
B: Aug 5, 1909 west virginia
M:
D: Sept 29, 1962 virginia

Newman H O'Dell
B:
D:

Elizabeth Ann McClung
B:
D:

Cora M Brady
B: West Virginia
D: West Virginia

Lewis Brady
B:
D:

Alice
B:
D:

Gary Dale Boone Jr
B: May 18 2005 Crichton, West Virginia, USA
M:
D:

Lora Lee Richmond
B: march 12 1982 quinwood west virginia
D:

Charles Lee Richmond
B: december 30 1947 USA
M:
D:

Charles W Richmond
B: 8 Mar 1925
M: 8 Feb 1947 West Virginia
D: june 1958 west, virginia

Charley Richmond
B: abt 1900 West Virginia
D: 1935 west virginia

Verna Trout
B: 1901 west virginia
D: September 1974 PA

Melva Marie Smith
B: august 27 1931 virginia
D: december 24 2004 USA

Arby Roy Smith
B: april 6 1906 Virginia
D: april 4 1980 virginia

Mary Olive Phillips
B: 6 Sep 1909 West Virginia
D: 6 Oct 1994 United States

Nancy Kay George
B: 12-13 1952 Marfrance, WV
D:

Aldon George
B: September 16 1917 WV
M:
D: february 16 1982 WV

Walter Greg George
B: 10-8-1894 WV
D: 10-12-1972 marfrance WV

Virgie Delta Cales
B: 4-1-1897 Hominey Falls WV
D: June 25,1942 WV

Susie E Burdiss
B: 3 Jul 1923 Van Wood, WV
D: 21 Mar 1998 Quinwood, WV

Edward Peter Burdiss
B: 4 May 1889 ohio
D: Aug 13 1952 virginia

Susie Belle Hundley
B: 1892 North Carolina
D: 1972 kansas city kansas

PART FOUR

Generational Charts

Generations from Nancy George (Richmond) to King Charlemagne

Nancy George (Richmond), daughter of
Aldon George, son of
Virgie Delta Cales, daughter of
Amanda Alice McClung, daughter of
Hamilton McClung, son of
James McClung, son of
John McClung, son of
Abigail Dickinson (Dickson), daughter of
Joseph Carpenter, son of
Joseph Carpenter, son of
Tamar Wright Coles, daughter of
Mercy Wright, daughter of
Nicholas Wright, son of
Nicholas Wright, son of
Nicholas Wright, son of
Ann Beaupre, daughter of
Margery Wiseman, daughter of
John Wiseman, son of
Isabel Wyndham, daughter of
John Wyndham, son of
Margaret Seagrave, daughter of
Alice Fitzalan, daughter of
Edmund Fitzalan, son of
Richard Fitzalan, son of
John Fitzalan, son of
John Fitzalan, son of
John Fitzalan, son of
William Fitzalan, son of
Alan Fitzflaald, son of
Fladaldus Senescal, son of
Alan Senescal, son of
Constance, daughter of
King William I (William the Conquerer), son of
Robert I of Normandy, son of
Richard of Normandy, son of
Richard I of Normandy, son of
Sporte DeBretagne, daughter of
Hubert Senlis, son of
Pepin I De Vermandois, son of
King Bernard of Italy, son of
King Pepin of Italy, son of
King Charlemagne (Charles I) Holy Roman Emperor - 39th Great Grandfather of Nancy George (Richmond)

Generations from Nancy George (Richmond) to King Alfred the Great of England

Nancy George (Richmond), daughter of
Aldon George, son of
Virgie Delta Cales, daughter of
Amanda Alice McClung, daughter of
Hamilton McClung, son of
James McClung, son of
John McClung, son of
Abigale Dickinson (Dickson), daughter of
Joseph Carpenter, son of
Joseph Carpenter, son of
Tamar Wright Coles, daughter of
Mercy Wright, daughter of
Nicholas Wright, son of
Nicholas Wright, son of
Nicholas Wright, son of
Ann Beaupre, daughter of
Margery Wiseman, daughter of
John Wiseman, son of
Isabel Wyndham, daughter of
John Wyndham, son of
Margaret Seagrave, daughter of
Alice Fitzalan, daughter of
Edmund Fitzalan, son of
Richard Fitzalan, son of
John Fitzalan, son of
John Fitzalan, son of
John Fitzalan, son of
William Fitzalan, son of
Alan Fitzflaaid, son of
Guenta Verch Griffith, daughter of
Queen Ealdgyth of England, daughter of
Elfgifu, daughter of
King Ethelred of England, son of
King Edgar of England, son of
King Edmund of England, son of
King Edward of England, son of
King Alfred (The Great) of England - 34th Great Grandfather of Nancy George (Richmond)

Generations from Charles Lee Richmond to Henry Adams

Charles Lee Richmond, son of
Melva Marie Smith, daughter of
Mary Olive Phillips, daughter of
Webster Phillips, son of
Edward Phillips, son of
Lewis Anderson Phillips, son of
John George Phillips, son of
John Phillips, son of
Sarah Holland, daughter of
Sarah Streeter, daughter of
Ursula Adams, daughter of
Henry Adams -10th Great Grandfather of Charles Lee Richmond

Generations from Charles Lee Richmond to Sir Thomas Phillips of England

Charles Lee Richmond, son of
Melva Marie Smith, daughter of
Mary Olive Phillips, daughter of
Webster Phillips, son of
Edward Phillips, son of
Lewis Anderson Phillips, son of
John George Phillips, son of
John Phillips, son of
Jonathan Phillips, son of
George Phillips, son of
Christopher Phillips, son of
John Phillips, son of
Simon Phillips, son of
Owen Phillips, son of
Sir Thomas Phillips - 13th Great Grandfather of Charles Lee Richmond

CHAPTER THREE

HISTORICAL DOCUMENTS

*Birth Certificates
*Marriage Certificates
*Death Certificates
*Newspaper Articles
*Passenger Immigration Lists
*US Federal Census Records
*Military Records
*Court Records
*Property Records

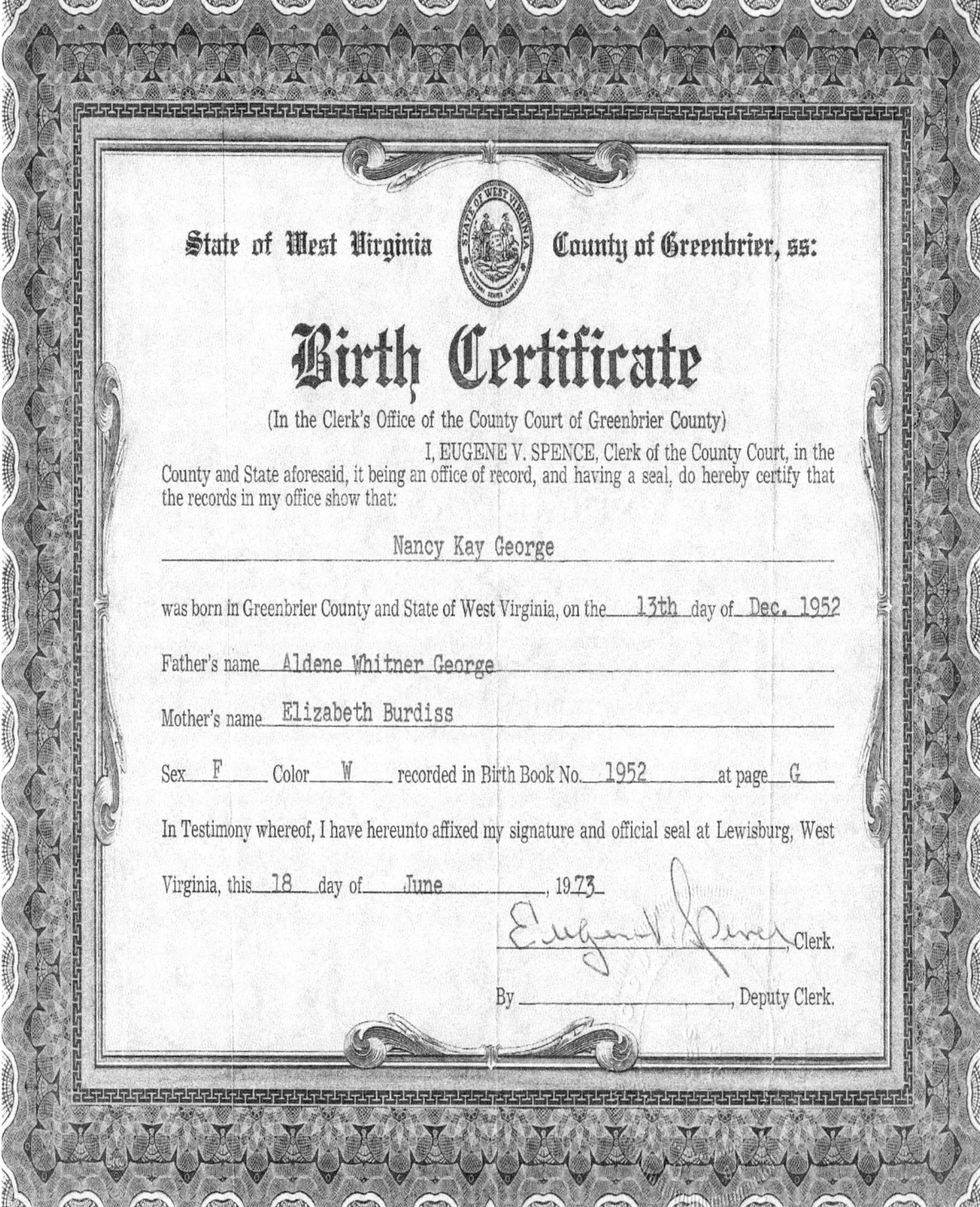

State of West Virginia   County of Greenbrier, ss:

Birth Certificate

(In the Clerk's Office of the County Court of Greenbrier County)

I, EUGENE V. SPENCE, Clerk of the County Court, in the County and State aforesaid, it being an office of record, and having a seal, do hereby certify that the records in my office show that:

Nancy Kay George

was born in Greenbrier County and State of West Virginia, on the ___13th___ day of __Dec. 1952__

Father's name___Aldene Whitner George_____

Mother's name___Elizabeth Burdiss_____

Sex___F___ Color___W___ recorded in Birth Book No.___1952___ at page___G___

In Testimony whereof, I have hereunto affixed my signature and official seal at Lewisburg, West

Virginia, this___18___ day of ___June___, 19_73_

_____, Clerk.

By _____, Deputy Clerk.

State of West Virginia   County of Greenbrier, ss:

Birth Certificate

(In the Clerk's Office of the County Commission of Greenbrier County)

I, R. SANDRA MORGAN, Clerk of the County Commission in the County and State aforesaid, it being an office of record, and having a seal, do hereby certify that the records in my office show that:

Charles Lee Richmond

was born in Greenbrier County and State of West Virginia, on the __30th__ day of __DEC.,1947__

Father's name __Charles Wyatt Richmond__

Mother's name __Melva Marie Smith__

Sex __M__ Color __W__ recorded in Birth Book No. __1947__ at page __"R"__

In Testimony whereof, I have hereunto affixed my signature and official seal at Lewisburg, West

Virginia, this __16th__ day of __JUNE__, __1999__.
Year

This certificate was recorded _R. Sandra Morgan_, Clerk.
in said Clerk's Office
before Jan. 1, 1948.   By _____, Deputy Clerk.

75

United States Marine Corps

Certificate of Acceptance

This is to certify that _____CHARLES LEE RICHMOND_____ has successfully passed the required mental, moral and physical examinations and has been accepted for enlistment in the United States Marine Corps.

The defense of our country and our freedoms is the duty and privilege of every citizen. The Marine Corps has a proud tradition of outstanding service to our country in peace and war. Voluntary enlistment in this elite military organization is a clear demonstration of those American qualities of patriotism and loyalty to God and country.

Presented this ___20th___ day of ___February___ , 19 _65_.

E M Ringley

By the Officer In Charge
Marine Corps Recruiting Station South Charleston, W. Va.
E. M. RINGLEY, Capt USMC

NAVMC 6648 (Rev.)

76

1. LAST NAME - FIRST NAME - MIDDLE NAME RICHMOND, Charles Lee	**2. SERVICE NUMBER** 2139380	**3a. GRADE, RATE OR RANK** Pvt (E-1)	**b. DATE OF RANK** (Day, Month, Year) 17Jun65

PERSONAL DATA

4. DEPARTMENT, COMPONENT AND BRANCH OR CLASS USMC	**5. PLACE OF BIRTH** (City and State or Country) Crichton,Greenbrier, W. Virginia	**6. DATE OF BIRTH** — DAY 30 / MONTH Dec / YEAR 47

7a. RACE	**b. SEX** Male	**c. COLOR HAIR** Brown	**d. COLOR EYES** Blue	**e. HEIGHT** 76"	**f. WEIGHT** 160	**8. U.S. CITIZEN** ☒YES ☐NO	**9. MARITAL STATUS** Single

10a. HIGHEST CIVILIAN EDUCATION LEVEL ATTAINED High School - 4	**b. MAJOR COURSE OR FIELD** Commercial

TRANSFER OR DISCHARGE DATA

11a. TYPE OF TRANSFER OR DISCHARGE Discharge	**b. STATION OR INSTALLATION AT WHICH EFFECTED** Camp Lejeune, North Carolina	
c. REASON AND AUTHORITY 264 - Paragraph 13265.1C Marine Corps Personnel, Manual		**d. EFFECTIVE DATE** — DAY 08 / MONTH Apr / YEAR 66

12. LAST DUTY ASSIGNMENT AND MAJOR COMMAND 2dBn, 6thMar, 2dMarDiv, FMF, CamLej, NC 12171	**13a. CHARACTER OF SERVICE** UNDER HONORABLE CONDITIONS	**b. TYPE OF CERTIFICATE ISSUED** DD-257MC

SELECTIVE SERVICE DATA

14. SELECTIVE SERVICE NUMBER Not Available	**15. SELECTIVE SERVICE LOCAL BOARD NUMBER, CITY, COUNTY AND STATE** Not Available	**16. DATE INDUCTED** Not Applicable

17. DISTRICT OR AREA COMMAND TO WHICH RESERVIST TRANSFERRED N/A

SERVICE DATA

18. TERMINAL DATE OF RESERVE OBLIGATION — DAY / MONTH / YEAR N/A	**19. CURRENT ACTIVE SERVICE OTHER THAN BY INDUCTION** **a. SOURCE OF ENTRY** ☒ ENLISTED (First Enlistment) ☐ ENLISTED (Prior Service) ☐ REENLISTED ☐ OTHER:	**b. TERM OF SERVICE** (Years) Four	**c. DATE OF ENTRY** — DAY 17 / MONTH Jun / YEAR 65

20. PRIOR REGULAR ENLISTMENTS None	**21. GRADE, RATE OR RANK AT TIME OF ENTRY INTO CURRENT ACTIVE SERVICE** Private (E-1)	**22. PLACE OF ENTRY INTO CURRENT ACTIVE SERVICE** (City and State) South Charleston, Kanawha, W. Virginia		

23. HOME OF RECORD AT TIME OF ENTRY INTO ACTIVE SERVICE (Street, RFD, City, County and State) Box 45, Quinwood, Greenbrier, W. Virginia	**24. STATEMENT OF SERVICE**		**YEARS**	**MONTHS**	**DAYS**
	a. CREDITABLE FOR BASIC PAY PURPOSES	(1) NET SERVICE THIS PERIOD	00	06	08
		(2) OTHER SERVICE	00	03	26
		(3) TOTAL (Line (1) + line (2))	00	09	34
25a. SPECIALTY NUMBER AND TITLE BasicPers&Admin Man: 0100	**b.** TOTAL ACTIVE SERVICE		00	06	08
b. RELATED CIVILIAN OCCUPATION AND D.O.T. NUMBER 1-04.01 Clerk, General (Clerical)	**c.** FOREIGN AND/OR SEA SERVICE		00	00	00

26. DECORATIONS, MEDALS, BADGES, COMMENDATIONS, CITATIONS AND CAMPAIGN RIBBONS AWARDED OR AUTHORIZED Rifle M-14 Marksman

27. WOUNDS RECEIVED AS A RESULT OF ACTION WITH ENEMY FORCES (Place and date, if known) N/A

28. SERVICE SCHOOLS OR COLLEGES, COLLEGE TRAINING COURSES AND/OR POST-GRADUATE COURSES SUCCESSFULLY COMPLETED			**29. OTHER SERVICE TRAINING COURSES SUCCESSFULLY COMPLETED**
SCHOOL OR COURSE a	**DATES** (From - To) b	**MAJOR COURSES** c	
N/A	N/A	N/A	N/A

VA DATA

30a. GOVERNMENT LIFE INSURANCE IN FORCE ☐YES ☒NO	**b. AMOUNT OF ALLOTMENT** N/A	**c. MONTH ALLOTMENT DISCONTINUED** N/A

31a. VA BENEFITS PREVIOUSLY APPLIED FOR (Specify type) N/A	**b. VA CLAIM NUMBER** c- N/A

AUTHENTICATION

32. REMARKS Good Conduct Medal Period commenced 17Jun65 Check excess leave for 2 days From 20Nov65 To 21Nov65 No lump sum leave settlement due Social Security No. Applied For

33. PERMANENT ADDRESS FOR MAILING PURPOSES AFTER TRANSFER OR DISCHARGE (Street, RFD, City, County and State) Box 45, Quinwood, Greenbrier, W. Virginia	**34. SIGNATURE OF PERSON BEING TRANSFERRED OR DISCHARGED** *Charles L. Richmond*
35a. TYPED NAME, GRADE AND TITLE OF AUTHORIZING OFFICER R. L. BONIFAY, 2ndLt. BnAdj.	**b. SIGNATURE OF OFFICER AUTHORIZED TO SIGN**

DD FORM 1 NOV 55 **214** — REPLACES EDITION OF 1 JUL 52 WHICH IS OBSOLETE. — **ARMED FORCES OF THE UNITED STATES REPORT OF TRANSFER OR DISCHARGE** — SR/OQR OR HQMC—2

USMC

Certificate of Marriage

STATE OF WEST VIRGINIA,

GREENBRIER COUNTY, TO-WIT:

I, W. J. Livesay, Sr. , Clerk of the County Commission in and for said County and State (the same being a Court of Record), also, the Custodian of the Marriage Records, do hereby certify that the Marriage Record discloses the following facts that Charles Lee Richmond and Nancy Kay George Murray were united in marriage by Rev. Ronald George , on the 24th. day of September , 1977 .

His parents, Father Charles Wyatt Richmond Mother Melva Smith

Her parents, Father Aldon George Mother Susie Burdiss

His age is 29 years. Her age is 24 years.

He was born December 30 , 1947 She was born December 13 , 1952

He was born at Crichton in Greenbrier County, State of WV

She was born at Marfrance in Greenbrier County, State of WV

Given under my hand and official seal this the 30th. day

of October , 2002 .

_____
Clerk County Commission, Greenbrier County, West Virginia

Recorded in Marriage Record No. 34 , Page 369 .

Dayton Legal Blank, Inc.

No. 24-A

Marriage License
Application

WHITE

To the Clerk of the County Court of Greenbrier County, West Virginia:

Pursuant to the provisions of Sec. 6, Article 1, Chapter 48, Official Code of W. Va. as amended by Chapter 124 of the Acts of the Legislature of West Virginia, Regular Session 1937, the undersigned hereby makes application for a marriage license, __ he being one of the parties of the contemplated marriage, and makes the following statements in support thereof:

The Full Names of the Parties to be Married are

Aldon Whitmer George and Susie Elizabeth Burdiss

His parents, Father Walter George   Mother Virgie George

Her parents, Father Edward Burdiss   Mother Bell Burdiss

His age is 26 years. Single XXXXXXX XXXXXX Her age is 21 years. XXXXX XXXXX Divorced.

He was born September 16 1917 She was born July 4, 1922

He was born at Honiny Falls in Nicholas County, State of W. Va.

She was born at Van Wood in Raleigh County, State of W. Va.

His place of residence is Quinwood in Greenbrier County, State of W. Va.

Her place of residence is East Rainelle in Greenbrier County, State of W. Va.

Are contracting parties related? No. If so give degree of relationship

Has either of contracting parties been previously married? Yes, she

Has either party been divorced? Yes When? April 1943 Where? Greenbrier County

Dated this the 1st day of December, 1943.

Aldon Whitmer George

Susie Elizabeth Burdiss
Applicant or Applicants.

STATE OF WEST VIRGINIA,
County of Greenbrier, } To-wit:

Upon being duly sworn, the applicant __ S __, whose name __ XXX are signed to the foregoing application, say __ that the facts as therein contained are true to the best of __ their __ knowledge and belief.

Given under my hand this the 1st day of December 194 43

Paul C. Hogsett
Clerk, Notary Public, Justice of the Peace

My commission expires x

Filed in the Clerk's office December 1, 194 3, at 2:50 o'clock P. M.

Consent For Issuing

His Parents Consent, Father __ , Mother __

Her Parents Consent, Father __ , Mother __

His Guardian Consent, __ Her Guardian Consent __

Issuance of license directed by __ , Judge of Circuit Court,

__ , County, West Virginia, dated __

Order Book No. __ Page __ .

License
West Virginia, County of Greenbrier, to-wit:

To Any Person Licensed to Celebrate Marriages:

You are hereby authorized to join together IN THE HOLY STATE OF MATRIMONY, according to the rites and ceremonies of your church or religious denomination, and the laws of the STATE OF WEST VIRGINIA,

Aldon Whitmer George and Susie Elizabeth Burdiss

GIVEN UNDER MY HAND, as Clerk of the County Court of the County of Greenbrier, this __ day of December, 1943.

By __ Deputy. Paul S Hogsett Clerk County Court, Greenbrier County.

Minister's Return or Endorsement

I, Paul L. Flanagan __ , a Minister of the Gospel,

do certify that on the 6th day of December, 1943, at Rainelle, West Virginia

I united in marriage the above named and described parties under authority of the foregoing license.

A Copy Teste: Paul S Hogsett Clerk   Paul L. Flanagan Minister

79

Certificate of Marriage

STATE OF WEST VIRGINIA,

GREENBRIER COUNTY, TO-WIT:

I, _____Paul C. Hogsett_____, Clerk of the County Court in and for

said County and State (the same being a Court of Record), also, the Custodian of the Marriage

Records, do hereby certify that the Marriage Record discloses the following facts that

Aldon Whitmer George and _Susie Elizabeth Burdiss_

were united in marriage by _Rev. Paul L. Flanagan_, on the _6th_

day of _December_, 19_43_

His parents, Father _Walter George_ Mother _Virgie George_

Her parents, Father _Edward Burdiss_ Mother _Bell Burdiss_

His age is _26_ years. Her age is _21_ years.

He was born _September 16,_ 1_917_ She was born _July 4,_ 1922

He was born at _Hominy Falls_ in _Nicholas_ County, State of _W. Va._

She was born at _Van Wood_ in _Raleigh_ County, State of _W. Va._

Given under my hand and official seal this the _19th_ day

of _October_ 19_65_

Clerk County Court, Greenbrier County, West Virginia

Recorded in Marriage Record No. _19_, Page _54_

80

Marriage License
Application

To the Clerk of the County Court of Greenbrier County, West Virginia:

Pursuant to the provisions of Sec. 6, Article 1, Chapter 48, Official Code of W. Va. as amended by Chapter 124 of the Acts of the Legislature of West Virginia, Regular Session 1937, the undersigned hereby makes application for a marriage license, _____he being one of the parties of the contemplated marriage, and makes the following statements in support thereof:

The Full Names of the Parties to be Married are

Charles Wyatt Richmond _____ and _____ Melba Maria Smith

His parents, Father _____ Charles Richmond (deceased) _____ Mother _____ Verna Richmond

Her parents, Father _____ Arby Smith _____ Mother _____ Mary Smith

His age is _____ 21 _____ years. Single, _____ Her age is _____ 18 _____ years. Single,

He was born _____ March 8 _____ 1925 _____ She was born _____ August 27 _____ 1928

He was born at _____ Carl _____ in _____ Nicholas _____ County, State of _____ W. Va.

She was born at _____ Beards Fork _____ in _____ Fayette _____ County, State of _____ W. Va.

His place of residence is _____ Quinwood _____ in _____ Greenbrier _____ County, State of _____ W. Va.

Her place of residence is _____ Crichton _____ in _____ Greenbrier _____ County, State of _____ W. Va.

Are contracting parties related? _____ No _____ If so give degree of relationship _____

Has either of contracting parties been previously married? _____ No

Has either party been divorced? _____ No _____ When? _____ Where? _____

Dated this the _____ 3rd _____ day of _____ February _____, 194 7.

Charles W. Richmond
_____
Applicant or Applicants.

STATE OF WEST VIRGINIA, }
County of Greenbrier, } To-wit:

Upon being duly sworn, the applicant _____, whose name _____ is _____ signed to the foregoing application, say _____ that the facts as therein contained are true to the best of _____ his _____ knowledge and belief.

Given under my hand this the _____ 3rd _____ day of _____ February _____ 194 7.

Paul C. Hogsett
Clerk,

Filed in the Clerk's office _____ February 3rd _____, 194 7, at _____ 9:50 _____ o'clock _____ A. _____ M.

Consent For Issuing

His Parents Consent, Father _____ , Mother _____

Her Parents Consent, Father _____ Arby Smith _____, Mother _____ Mary Smith

His Guardian Consent, _____ Her Guardian Consent _____

Issuance of license directed by _____, Judge of Circuit Court,

_____, County, West Virginia, dated _____

_____ Order Book No. _____ Page _____

License

West Virginia, County of Greenbrier, to-wit:

To Any Person Licensed to Celebrate Marriages:

You are hereby authorized to join together IN THE HOLY STATE OF MATRIMONY, according to the rites and ceremonies of your church or religious denomination, and the laws of the STATE OF WEST VIRGINIA,

Charles Wyatt Richmond _____ and _____ Melba Maria Smith

GIVEN UNDER MY HAND, as Clerk of the County Court of the County of Greenbrier, this _____ 6th _____ day of February _____, 194 7. _____ Paul C. Hogsett

By _____ C Watts _____ Deputy. _____ Clerk County Court, Greenbrier County.

Minister's Return or Endorsement

I _____ Laurence B Fairfax _____, a Minister of the Gospel, do certify that on the _____ 8th _____ day of _____ Feb _____ 194 7 at _____ Quinwood, West Va. _____ I united in marriage the above named and described parties under authority of the foregoing license.

A Copy Teste _____ Paul C. Hogsett _____ Clerk. _____ Rev. L B Fairfax _____ Minister.

☆   ☆   ☆   YOUNG AMERICAN PATRIOTS

RICHMOND, CHARLES W.

S 1/c, U. S. Navy. Born Mar. 8, 1925. Entered service July 23, 1943, Great Lakes, Ill.; Shoemaker, Calif.; S. Pacific Theatre; Pearl Harbor; Gilberts; Marshalls; Saipan; Guam; Okinawa; Bainbridge, Md. Awarded 3 BS, P. Unit Cit., G. Cond. M., VM, Amer., AP. Attended Crichton schools. Methodist. Son of Mrs. Vernie Richmond, Quinwood, W. Va. Husband of Mrs. Melva Marie Smith Richmond, Crichton, W. Va.

CHARLES W RICHMOND

RANK: SERGEANT FIRST CLASS
BRANCH: UNITED STATES NAVY
BIRTH DATE: 8 MAR 1925
SERVICE DATE: 23 JUL 1943
PARENT I NAME: MRS. VERNIE RICHMOND
SPOUSE NAME: MRS. MELVA MARIE SMITH RICHMOND
STATE: WEST VIRGINIA
COUNTY: GREENBRIER

World War II Young American Patriots, 1941-1945

Name:	**Charles W Richmond**
Rank:	**Sergeant First Class**
Branch:	**United States Navy**
Birth Date:	**8 Mar 1925**
Service Date:	**23 Jul 1943**
Parent 1 Name:	**Mrs. Vernie Richmond**
Spouse Name:	**Mrs. Melva Marie Smith Richmond**
State:	**West Virginia**
County:	**Greenbrier**

Source Information:
Ancestry.com. *World War II Young American Patriots, 1941-1945* [database on-line]. Provo, UT, USA: The Generations Network, Inc., 2007. Original data: *Young American Patriots*. Richmond, VA, USA: National Publishing Co., 1946.

Description:
This database is a collection of books compiled to preserve the lives of the American men and women who served in World War II. These books are arranged by state. Currently this database includes the volumes for 9 states. Information available in a soldier's biography includes: name, branch of military served in, birth date, date and place entered service, and parents' names. Learn more...

Birth Certificate

STATE OF WEST VIRGINIA,

COUNTY OF NICHOLAS, ss:

I, SPURGEON HINKLE, Clerk of the County Court of Nicholas County, and as such, Custodian

of the Records of Births, do certify that the said Records show that _____Aldon George_____

was born at _____Hominy Falls_____ in Nicholas County and State of West Virginia, on

the _____16th_____ day of _____September_____, _____1917_____, and that the parents' names are

as follows:

Father's name _____Walter George_____ Mother's name _____Vergie Cales George_____

Book No. _____2_____, page _____68_____

In Testimony Whereof, I have hereunto affixed my

signature and official Seal at Summersville, West

[SEAL]

Virginia, this _____17th_____ day of _____August_____

19 72.

Spurgeon Hinkle , Clerk.

bfe

84

WEST VIRGINIA STATE DEPARTMENT OF HEALTH -- DIVISION OF VITAL STATISTICS

SUPPORTING AFFIDAVIT FOR DELAYED CERTIFICATE OF BIRTH

THE FOLLOWING INFORMATION RELATES TO THE FACTS OF BIRTH OF THE APPLICANT:

FULL NAME AT BIRTH __Susie Elizabeth Burdiss__

DATE OF BIRTH __7-3-1923__ COLOR OR RACE __W__ SEX __F__

PLACE OF BIRTH: (CITY OR TOWN) __Van Wood__ (COUNTY) __Raleigh__ (STATE) __W. Va.__

FATHER'S FULL NAME __Edward P. Burdiss__ BIRTHPLACE (STATE) __Virginia__

MOTHER'S MAIDEN NAME __Susie Bell Hunley__ BIRTHPLACE (STATE) __Virginia__

PERSON SWEARING TO THE ABOVE FACTS (MUST BE AT LEAST TEN YEARS OLDER THAN THE APPLICANT):

I, __WILLIAM K. GRAVELY__ , being duly sworn, state that my age is __67 YRS.__
     (PRINT OR TYPE NAME)

that I am: (1) related to the applicant as __1ST COUSIN__ , OR,

(2) a friend who has personal knowledge of the facts of birth of the applicant,

and, that the above are the true facts of birth of the applicant.

SIGNATURE: __William K. Gravely__
                  (PERSON MAKING AFFIDAVIT)

__108 Roosevelt St.__
                  (STREET ADDRESS)

__Beckley,__   __W. Va.__
     (CITY)   (STATE)

SUBSCRIBED IN MY PRESENCE AND SWORN TO BEFORE ME THIS __19th__ DAY OF __February__ , 19__76__

NOTARY PUBLIC __Kenneth D. Christian__ MY COMMISSION EXPIRES __11-23-83__

FORM VS 420 (REV. 10/70)

85

Army of the United States

Honorable Discharge

This is to certify that

ALDON GEORGE, 35 425 521, TECHNICIAN FOURTH GRADE,

COMPANY C, 708TH MILITARY POLICE BATTALION,

Army of the United States

is hereby Honorably Discharged from the military service of the United States of America.

This certificate is awarded as a testimonial of Honest and Faithful Service to this country.

Given at   SEPARATION CENTER, FORT GEORGE G. MEADE, MARYLAND.

Date   2 FEBRUARY 1946

Recorded in Discharge Record
BOOK 13 PAGE 289
Greenbrier County, West Va.
This 13th day of Dec 19 51

Paul C. Hoyett
Clerk

Richard C O'Connell
RICHARD C O'CONNELL
LT COL   AGD

86

29

ENLISTED RECORD AND REPORT OF SEPARATION
HONORABLE DISCHARGE

4411-3

1. LAST NAME - FIRST NAME - MIDDLE INITIAL	2. ARMY SERIAL NO.	3. GRADE	4. ARM OR SERVICE	5. COMPONENT
George Aldon	35 425 521	TEC 4	CMP	AUS

6. ORGANIZATION	7. DATE OF SEPARATION	8. PLACE OF SEPARATION
Co C 708th MP Bn	2 Feb 46	Separation Center Fort Geo G Meade Md

9. PERMANENT ADDRESS FOR MAILING PURPOSES	10. DATE OF BIRTH	11. PLACE OF BIRTH
C/O PM East Rainelle Greenbrier Co W Va	16 Sep 17	Homoney Falls W Va

12. ADDRESS FROM WHICH EMPLOYMENT WILL BE SOUGHT	13. COLOR EYES	14. COLOR HAIR	15. HEIGHT	16. WEIGHT	17. NO.DEPEND.
See 9	Blue	Brown	5'10"	160 LBS.	1

18. RACE			19. MARITAL STATUS			20. U.S. CITIZEN		21. CIVILIAN OCCUPATION AND NO.
WHITE	NEGRO	OTHER (specify)	SINGLE	MARRIED	OTHER (specify)	YES	NO	Miner I 5-21.010
X				X		X		

MILITARY HISTORY

22. DATE OF INDUCTION	23. DATE OF ENLISTMENT	24. DATE OF ENTRY INTO ACTIVE SERVICE	25. PLACE OF ENTRY INTO SERVICE
2 Apr 42		2 Apr 42	Ft Thomas Ky

SELECTIVE SERVICE DATA	26. REGISTERED		27. LOCAL S.S. BOARD NO.	28. COUNTY AND STATE	29. HOME ADDRESS AT TIME OF ENTRY INTO SERVICE
	YES	NO	1	Greenbrier Co W Va	Marfrance W Va
	X				

30. MILITARY OCCUPATIONAL SPECIALTY AND NO.	31. MILITARY QUALIFICATION AND DATE (i.e., infantry, aviation and marksmanship badges, etc.)
Cook 060	MKM 30 Cal Rifle SS Carbine

32. BATTLES AND CAMPAIGNS

None

33. DECORATIONS AND CITATIONS

Good Conduct Medal   American Theater Ribbon   European African Middle Eastern Theater Ribbon   World War II Victory Ribbon

34. WOUNDS RECEIVED IN ACTION

None

35. LATEST IMMUNIZATION DATES				36. SERVICE OUTSIDE CONTINENTAL U.S. AND RETURN		
SMALLPOX	TYPHOID	TETANUS	OTHER (specify)	DATE OF DEPARTURE	DESTINATION	DATE OF ARRIVAL
Jul 43	Jul 45	Aug 44	Typhus Jul 43	25 Jun 43	Oran	19 Jul 43
				6 Nov 43	United States	21 Nov 43

37. TOTAL LENGTH OF SERVICE						38. HIGHEST GRADE HELD
CONTINENTAL SERVICE			FOREIGN SERVICE			
YEARS	MONTHS	DAYS	YEARS	MONTHS	DAYS	TEC 4
3	5	4	0	4	27	

39. PRIOR SERVICE

None

40. REASON AND AUTHORITY FOR SEPARATION

AR 615-365 & RR 1-1 & TWX WDGAP dtd 15 Jan 46

41. SERVICE SCHOOLS ATTENDED	42. EDUCATION (Years)		
None	Grammar	High School	College
	4	0	0

PAY DATA

43. LONGEVITY FOR PAY PURPOSES			44. MUSTERING OUT PAY		45. SOLDIER DEPOSITS	46. TRAVEL PAY	47. TOTAL AMOUNT, NAME OF DISBURSING OFFICER
YEARS	MONTHS	DAYS	TOTAL	THIS PAYMENT	None	$ 13.95	$342.27 G M PEERSON
3	10	1	$ 300.00	$ 100.00			CAPTAIN FD

INSURANCE NOTICE

IMPORTANT   IF PREMIUM IS NOT PAID WHEN DUE OR WITHIN THIRTY-ONE DAYS THEREAFTER, INSURANCE WILL LAPSE. MAKE CHECKS OR MONEY ORDERS PAYABLE TO THE TREASURER OF THE U. S. AND FORWARD TO COLLECTIONS SUBDIVISION, VETERANS ADMINISTRATION, WASHINGTON 25, D.C.

48. KIND OF INSURANCE			49. HOW PAID		50. Effective Date of Allotment Discontinuance	51. Date of Next Premium Due (One month after 50)	52. PREMIUM DUE EACH MONTH	53. INTENTION OF VETERAN TO		
Nat. Serv.	U.S. Govt.	None	Allotment	Direct to V. A.	28 Feb 46	31 Mar 46	$ 2.01	Continue	Continue Only	Discontinue
X			X							X

54.	55. REMARKS (This space for completion of above items or entry of other items specified in W. D. Directives)
[RIGHT THUMB PRINT]	Lapel button issued No days lost under AW 107 ASR SCORE 46

BOOK __ PAGE 269

56. SIGNATURE OF PERSON BEING SEPARATED	57. PERSONNEL OFFICER (Type name, grade and organization - signature)
Aldon George	G A EICHENBERGER 2ND LT WAC *G A Eichenberger*

WD AGO FORM 53 - 55
1 November 1944

This form supersedes all previous editions of WD AGO Forms 53 and 55 for enlisted persons entitled to an Honorable Discharge, which will not be used after receipt of this revision.

87

WEST VIRGINIA DEPARTMENT OF HEALTH & HUMAN RESOURCES
DIVISION OF HEALTH - VITAL REGISTRATION OFFICE
PHYSICIAN'S/MEDICAL EXAMINER'S CERTIFICATE OF DEATH
BLDG. 3, RM. 513, CAPITOL COMPLEX, CHARLESTON, WV 25305

STATE FILE NUMBER

TYPE/PRINT IN PERMANENT BLACK INK

DECEDENT

1. DECEDENT'S NAME (First, Middle, Last)	2 SEX	3 DATE OF DEATH (Month, Day, Year)
Susie E George	F	March 21, 1998

4 SOCIAL SECURITY NUMBER	5a. AGE-Last Birthday (Years)	5b. UNDER 1 YEAR Months Days	5c. UNDER 1 DAY Hours Minutes	6 DATE OF BIRTH (Month, Day, Year)	7 BIRTHPLACE (City and State or Foreign Country)
236 38 7124	74			July 3, 1923	Beckley, WV

8 WAS DECEDENT EVER IN US ARMED FORCES? (Yes or no)	9a PLACE OF DEATH (Check only one: see instructions on other side)
No	HOSPITAL: ☒ Inpatient ☐ ER/Outpatient ☐ DOA OTHER: ☐ Nursing Home ☐ Residence ☐ Other (Specify)

9b. FACILITY NAME (If not institution, give street and number)	9c. CITY, TOWN, OR LOCATION OF DEATH	9d COUNTY OF DEATH
Columbia Gbr. Valley Hospital	Fairlea	Greenbrier

10. MARITAL STATUS—Married, Never Married, Widowed, Divorced (Specify)	11 SURVIVING SPOUSE (If wife, give maiden name)	12a DECEDENT'S USUAL OCCUPATION (Give kind of work done during most of working life. Do not use retired.)	12b KIND OF BUSINESS/INDUSTRY
Widowed		Homemaker	Her Home

13a. RESIDENCE—STATE	13b. COUNTY	13c. CITY, TOWN, OR LOCATION	13d STREET AND NUMBER
WV	Greenbrier	Quinwood	Box 93

13e. INSIDE CITY LIMITS? (Yes or no)	13f. ZIP CODE	14 WAS DECEDENT OF HISPANIC ORIGIN? (Specify No or Yes—If yes, specify Cuban, Mexican, Puerto Rican, etc) ☒ No ☐ Yes Specify	15 RACE—American Indian, Black, White, etc (Specify)	16 DECEDENT'S EDUCATION (Specify only highest grade completed) Elementary/Secondary (0-12) 2nd College (1-4 or 5 -)
Yes	25981		White	

PARENTS

17 FATHER'S NAME (First, Middle, Last)	18 MOTHER'S NAME (First, Middle, Maiden Surname)
Edward Burdiss	Susie Belle

INFORMANT

19a. INFORMANT'S NAME (Type/Print)	19b MAILING ADDRESS (Street and Number or Rural Route Number, City or Town, State, Zip Code)
Connie Bennett	Gen Del Rupert, WV 25984

DISPOSITION

20a. METHOD OF DISPOSITION	20b PLACE OF DISPOSITION (Name of cemetery, crematory, or other place)	20c LOCATION—City or Town State
☒ Burial ☐ Cremation ☐ Removal from State ☐ Donation ☐ Other (Specify)	Wallace Memorial Cemetery	Clintonville, WV

21 SIGNATURE OF FUNERAL SERVICE LICENSEE OR PERSON ACTING AS SUCH	22 NAME AND ADDRESS OF FACILITY
▶ William F. Wallace	Wallace & Wallace Inc 213 Main Street, Rainelle, WV

PRONOUNCING PHYSICIAN ONLY

ITEMS 24-26 MUST BE COMPLETED BY PERSON WHO PRONOUNCES DEATH

23a To the best of my knowledge, death occurred at the time, date, and place stated Signature and Title ▶ H. W. Walker	23b DATE SIGNED (Month, Day, Year) 3/21/98

24 TIME OF DEATH 3:32 P M	25 DATE PRONOUNCED DEAD (Month, Day, Year) 3-21-98	26 WAS CASE REFERRED TO MEDICAL EXAMINER/CORONER? (Yes or no) NO

CAUSE OF DEATH

27 PART I. Enter the diseases, injuries, or complications that caused the death. Do not enter the mode of dying, such as cardiac or respiratory arrest, shock, or heart failure. List only one cause on each line.

Approximate Interval Between Onset and Death

IMMEDIATE CAUSE (Final disease or condition resulting in death)
a. Septicemia

DUE TO (OR AS A CONSEQUENCE OF)
b. Perforated hollow abdominal viscus

Sequentially list conditions, if any, leading to immediate cause. Enter UNDERLYING CAUSE (Disease or injury that initiated events resulting in death) LAST

DUE TO (OR AS A CONSEQUENCE OF)
c.

DUE TO (OR AS A CONSEQUENCE OF)
d.

PART II. Other significant conditions contributing to death but not resulting in the underlying cause given in Part I Small Cell Cancer of Lung	28a WAS AN AUTOPSY PERFORMED? (Yes or no) No	28b WERE AUTOPSY FINDINGS AVAILABLE PRIOR TO COMPLETION OF CAUSE OF DEATH? (Yes or no)

29. MANNER OF DEATH	30a. DATE OF INJURY (Month, Day, Year)	30b TIME OF INJURY	30c INJURY AT WORK? (Yes or No) No	30d DESCRIBE HOW INJURY OCCURRED
☒ Natural ☐ Pending Investigation ☐ Accident ☐ Suicide ☐ Could not be Determined ☐ Homicide				
	30e. PLACE OF INJURY — At home, farm, street, factory, office building, etc (Specify)		30f LOCATION (Street and Number or Rural Route Number, City or Town, State)	

CERTIFIER

31a. CERTIFIER (Check only one)
☒ CERTIFYING PHYSICIAN (Physician certifying cause of death when another physician has pronounced death and completed Item 23) To the best of my knowledge, death occurred due to the cause(s) and manner as stated

☐ PRONOUNCING AND CERTIFYING PHYSICIAN (Physician both pronouncing death and certifying to cause of death) To the best of my knowledge, death occurred at the time, date, and place, and due to the cause(s) and manner as stated

☐ MEDICAL EXAMINER/CORONER On the basis of examination and/or investigation, in my opinion, death occurred at the time, date, and place, and due to the cause(s) and manner as stated

31b SIGNATURE AND TITLE OF CERTIFIER ▶ Jay Baker MD	31c DATE SIGNED (Month, Day, Year) 3/25/98

32 NAME AND ADDRESS OF PERSON WHO COMPLETED CAUSE OF DEATH (ITEM 27) (Type/Print)
Dr Jay Baker   Gbr. Valley Medical Center, Ronceverte, WV

33. REGISTRAR'S SIGNATURE ▶ Imogene Garland	34 DATE FILED (Month, Day, Year) 3-31-98

Form VS-002 (Rev. 6/92)

88

RATHA BLACK WWII DRAFT CARD

1447

REGISTRATION CARD—(Men born on or after April 28, 1877 and on or before February 16, 1897)

SERIAL NUMBER	1. NAME (Print)			ORDER NUMBER
U 264	Ratha (First)	Black (Middle)	Trout (Last)	

2. PLACE OF RESIDENCE (Print) Quinwood Gbn Wva.
(Number and street) (Town, township, village, or city) (County) (State)

[THE PLACE OF RESIDENCE GIVEN ON THE LINE ABOVE WILL DETERMINE LOCAL BOARD JURISDICTION; LINE 2 OF REGISTRATION CERTIFICATE WILL BE IDENTICAL]

3. MAILING ADDRESS Same
(Mailing address if other than place indicated on line 2. If same insert word same)

4. TELEPHONE None   5. AGE IN YEARS 62   PLACE OF BIRTH Nicholas

DATE OF BIRTH Dec 17 – 1879   W.Va.
(Mo.) (Day) (Yr.) (State or country)

(Exchange) (Number)

7. NAME AND ADDRESS OF PERSON WHO WILL ALWAYS KNOW YOUR ADDRESS Flossie Trout Quinwood Wva.

8. EMPLOYER'S NAME AND ADDRESS None

9. PLACE OF EMPLOYMENT OR BUSINESS Quinwood Gbn Wva.
(Number and street or R. F. D. number) (Town) (County) (State)

I AFFIRM THAT I HAVE VERIFIED ABOVE ANSWERS AND THAT THEY ARE TRUE.

R. B. Trout.
(Registrant's signature)

D. S. S. Form 1
(Revised 4-1-42)   (over)   16—21630-2

REGISTRAR'S REPORT

DESCRIPTION OF REGISTRANT

HEIGHT (Approx.)	WEIGHT (Approx.)	HAIR	EYES	COMPLEXION	
5'9"	175	Blonde	Blue	Sallow	
		Red	Gray	Light	✓
		Brown	Hazel	Ruddy	
		Black ✓	Brown ✓	Dark	
		Gray	Black	Freckled	
		Bald		Light brown	
				Dark brown	
				Black	

RACE
White ✓
Negro
Oriental
Indian
Filipino

(Other obvious physical characteristics that will aid in identification)

None to my knowledge

I certify that my answers are true; that the person registered has read or has had read to him his own answers; that I have witnessed his signature or mark and that all of his answers of which I have knowledge are true, except as follows:

Hoy Hatter
Registrar for Local Board # Nicholas Wva.
(Number) (City or county)

Date of registration April 27 1942

APR 28 1942
STAMP OF LOCAL BOARD

Local Board No. 11
Nicholas County 667 001

Bank building,
Summersville, W. Va.
(This stamp of the Local Board having jurisdiction of the registrant shall be placed in the above space.)

16—21630-1

WEST VIRGINIA STATE DEPARTMENT OF HEALTH—DIVISION OF VITAL STATISTICS

Dist No. _130_

Serial No. _130_

CERTIFICATE OF DEATH

State File No. **8438**

1. NAME OF DECEASED (Type or Print)	a. (First) **Rathe** b. (Middle) **Black**	c. (Last) **Trout**	2. DATE OF DEATH (Month) (Day) (Year) **6/13/55**

3. PLACE OF DEATH

a. COUNTY **Greenbrier**

b. CITY OR TOWN (If outside corporate limits, write RURAL and give district) **Quinwood**

c. LENGTH OF STAY (in this place)

d. FULL NAME OF HOSPITAL OR INSTITUTION (If not in hospital or institution, give street address or location) **M**

4. USUAL RESIDENCE (Where deceased lived. If institution: residence before admission)

a. STATE **W. Va.**   b. COUNTY **Greenbrier**

c. CITY OR TOWN (If outside corporate limits, write RURAL and give district) **Quinwood**

d. STREET ADDRESS (If rural, give location)

5. SEX **Male**	6. COLOR OR RACE **White**	7. MARRIED, NEVER MARRIED, WIDOWED, DIVORCED (Specify) **Widowed**	8. DATE OF BIRTH **12/17/1878**	9. AGE (In years) **76**	If under 1 year / If under 24 hrs Month Days Hours Min.

10. USUAL OCCUPATION **Methodist Minister** 7	10a. KIND OF BUSINESS OR INDUSTRY	11. BIRTHPLACE (State or foreign country) **West Virginia**	12. CITIZEN OF WHAT COUNTRY?

13. FATHER'S NAME **Jack Trout**	14. MOTHER'S MAIDEN NAME **Lizzie Pitsenbarger**

15. WAS DECEASED EVER IN U.S. ARMED FORCES? (Yes, no, or unknown) **No** / If yes, give war or dates of service	16. SOCIAL SECURITY No.	17. INFORMANT **Mrs. Flota Groves**

MEDICAL CERTIFICATION

18. CAUSE OF DEATH Enter only one cause per line for (a), (b), and (c).		INTERVAL BETWEEN ONSET AND DEATH
I. DISEASE OR CONDITION DIRECTLY LEADING TO DEATH* (a)	_Coronary Thrombosis_	_3 Min._
ANTECEDENT CAUSES *This does not mean the mode of dying, such as heart failure, asthenia, etc. It means the disease, injury, or complication which caused death.	Morbid conditions, if any, giving rise to the above cause (a) stating the underlying cause last. DUE TO (b) _Arterio sclerosis_	?
	DUE TO (c) _Generalized_	
II. OTHER SIGNIFICANT CONDITIONS Conditions contributing to the death but not related to the disease or condition causing death.	_4201_	

19a. DATE OF OPERATION	19b. MAJOR FINDINGS OF OPERATION	20. AUTOPSY? Yes ☐ No ☒

21a. ACCIDENT SUICIDE HOMICIDE	(Specify)	21b. PLACE OF INJURY (e.g., in or about home, farm, factory, street, office bldg., etc.)	21c. (CITY, TOWN OR TOWNSHIP) (COUNTY) (STATE)

21d. TIME OF INJURY (Month) (Day) (Year) (Hour)	21e. INJURY OCCURRED While at Work ☐ Not While at Work ☐	21f. HOW DID INJURY OCCUR?	21g. INQUEST Yes ☐ No ☐

22. I hereby certify that I attended the deceased from _4 July_ 19_5_, to _13 June_, 19_55_, that I last saw the deceased alive on _13 June_, 19_55_, and that death occurred at _4_ m., from the causes and on the date stated above.

23a. SIGNATURE _Lee B. Ford_ M. D. (Degree or title)	23b. ADDRESS _Quinwood W. Va._	23c. DATE SIGNED _20 June 1955_

24a. BURIAL, CREMATION, REMOVAL (Specify) **Burial**	24b. DATE **6/15/55**	24c. NAME OF CEMETERY OR CREMATORY **Carl Cemetery**	24d. EMBALMER'S SIGNATURE _Charles E. Butler_	Lic. No. **1184**

DATE REC'D BY LOCAL REG. **6-7-55**	REGISTRAR'S SIGNATURE _Eva W. Hefner_	25. FUNERAL DIRECTOR'S (Signature) _Charles E. Butler_	Lic. No. **823**

VS-002 (3-31-49)   FEDERAL SECURITY AGENCY PUBLIC HEALTH SERVICE

This becomes a legal record when properly executed and will be placed in permanent file.

Write plainly with permanent ink or typewriter.

Physician last in attendance must state cause of death and sign medical certification. If no physician in attendance, health officer (or coroner, if inquest is held) must complete and sign medical certification. Power of signature cannot be delegated.

Cause of death.

Enter only one cause per line for A.B.C. This does not mean mode of dying such as heart failure, asthenia, etc., it means the disease, injury or complication which causes death.

Funeral director or person disposing of body, must file certificate with local registrar within 72 hours after death and prior to transportation by common carrier or removal from state.

All items are to be complete and accurate.

90

WEST VIRGINIA STATE DEPARTMENT OF HEALTH—DIVISION OF VITAL STATISTICS

CERTIFICATE OF DEATH

Dist No. _130_   Serial No. _46_   State File No. _1414_

1. NAME OF DECEASED (Type or Print)	a. (First) John	b. (Middle) Smith	c. (Last)	2. DATE OF DEATH (Month) (Day) (Year) 1/24/55

3. PLACE OF DEATH a. COUNTY Greenbrier	4. USUAL RESIDENCE a. STATE W. Va. b. COUNTY Greenbrier
b. CITY OR TOWN Crichton	c. LENGTH OF STAY	c. CITY OR TOWN Crichton
d. FULL NAME OF HOSPITAL OR INSTITUTION	d. STREET ADDRESS

5. SEX Male	6. COLOR OR RACE White	7. MARRIED... Married	8. DATE OF BIRTH 3/25/1875	9. AGE 79

10. USUAL OCCUPATION Retired Miner	10a. KIND OF BUSINESS OR INDUSTRY Coal	11. BIRTHPLACE West Virginia	12. CITIZEN OF WHAT COUNTRY?

13. FATHER'S NAME Bill Smith	14. MOTHER'S MAIDEN NAME Jeanette Coleman

15. WAS DECEASED EVER IN U.S. ARMED FORCES? No	16. SOCIAL SECURITY No. 233 07 1801	17. INFORMANT Arby Smith

MEDICAL CERTIFICATION

18. CAUSE OF DEATH

I. DISEASE OR CONDITION DIRECTLY LEADING TO DEATH (a) Uremia — Interval: not known

ANTECEDENT CAUSES DUE TO (b) Cerebral Hemorrhage — 1½ Month

DUE TO (c) Arterio-sclerosis — ?

II. OTHER SIGNIFICANT CONDITIONS 331K

20. AUTOPSY? No

22. I hereby certify that I attended the deceased from 24 Jan 1935 to 24 Jan 1955, that I last saw the deceased alive on 24 Jan 1955, and that death occurred at 3:30 m., from the causes and on the date stated above.

23a. SIGNATURE Lee B. Frel (M.D.)   23b. ADDRESS Rainwood   23c. DATE SIGNED 8 Feb 55

24a. BURIAL, CREMATION Burial	24b. DATE 1/26/55	24c. NAME OF CEMETERY OR CREMATORY Willis Branch	24d. EMBALMER'S SIGNATURE Charles E. Austin Lic. No. 1184

DATE REC'D BY LOCAL REG. 2-10-55   REGISTRAR'S SIGNATURE Eva W. Hefner   25. FUNERAL DIRECTOR'S SIGNATURE Charles E. Austin Jr. Lic. No. 823

VS-002 (3-31-48)   FEDERAL SECURITY AGENCY   PUBLIC HEALTH SERVICE

91

1. PLACE OF DEATH (Dist. No. 3461) Series No. 17 Division of Vital Statistics

County Nicholas

District Summersville

West Virginia State Department of Health

CERTIFICATE OF DEATH

13824

(FOR STATE REG. USE ONLY)

Town or City Summersville, W. Va. No._____ St.,_____ Ward

(IF DEATH OCCURRED IN A HOSPITAL OR INSTITUTION, GIVE ITS NAME INSTEAD OF STREET AND NUMBER)

2. FULL NAME King Harry Richmond,

(a) Residence. No._____ St.,_____ Ward.

(USUAL PLACE OF ABODE)   (IF NON-RESIDENT GIVE CITY OR TOWN AND STATE)

Length of residence in city or town where death occurred yrs. mos. days. How long in U.S.A., if of foreign birth? yrs. mos. days.

PERSONAL AND STATISTICAL PARTICULARS	MEDICAL CERTIFICATE OF DEATH

3. SEX Male 4. COLOR OR RACE White 5. Single, Married, Widowed, or Divorced (write the word) Married

21. DATE OF DEATH (month, day and year) October 16, - - - 1932.

5a. IF MARRIED, WIDOWED, OR DIVORCED Husband of (or) Wife of Sarah Taylor Richmond,

22. I HEREBY CERTIFY, That I attended deceased from Aug 1932 to Oct 1932, I last saw him alive on Oct 1 1932, death is said to have occurred on the date stated above, at 7:30 A. m.

6. DATE OF BIRTH (month, day, and year) 1850

7. AGE 82 Years Months Days IF LESS than 1 day,___hrs. or___min.

The principal cause of death and related causes of importance in order of onset were as follows: Date of onset

Typhoid Fever   Aug 19, 1932

(1)

8. TRADE, PROFESSION, or particular kind of work done, as spinner, sawyer, bookkeeper, etc. Farming

9. INDUSTRY OR BUSINESS, in which work was done, as silk mill, saw mill, bank, etc.

10. DATE DECEASED LAST WORKED at this occupation (month and year)

11. TOTAL TIME (years) spent in this occupation

Contributory causes of importance not related to principal cause:

12. BIRTHPLACE (city or town) (State or Country) Virginia.

Name of operation_____ Date of_____

13. NAME Don't know.

What test confirmed diagnosis?

14. BIRTHPLACE (City or Town) (State or Country) Don't know.

Was there an autopsy?

15. MAIDEN NAME Don't know.

23. If death was due to external causes, fill in also the following:

16. BIRTHPLACE (City or Town) (State or Country) Don't know.

(Check) Accident—Suicide—Homicide? Date of injury_____ 19__

Where did injury occur?

(Specify City or Town, County, and State)

17. INFORMANT John Sears, (Address) Rainelle, W. Va.

Check whether injury occurred in industry____ home____ public place____

Manner of injury

18. BURIAL, CREMATION, OR REMOVAL Place Carl, W. Va. Date Oct. 18, 1932.

Nature of injury

19. UNDERTAKER H. C. White (Address) Summersville, W. Va.

24. Was disease or injury in any way related to occupation of deceased? If so, specify

20. FILED Nov 3, 1932 S. H. Horron Register.

(Signed) F N Brown M.D.

(Address) Summersville, W Va

MARRIAGE RECORD 25

Wm. Lilienthal & Sons, Cambridge, O.—75650   SP–F-1

In the matter of		Probate Court, Shelby County, Ohio.

Marvin J. Murray
Nancy Kay George   and

No. ....

MARRIAGE LICENSE APPLICATION

To the Honorable Judge of the Probate Court of said County:

The undersigned respectfully makes application for a Marriage License for said parties, and upon oath states:

That said........Marvin J. Murray........was 20
years of age, on the......5th......day of......December......19 70,
his residence is........Sidney, Ohio........,
his place of birth is........Clinton, Tennessee........
his occupation is........U. S. Army........
his father's name is........Elvin Murray........,
his mother's maiden name was........Vivian Hammons........,

that he was......never......previously married........
and that he has no wife living.

	State and
Date Divorced............ Case No............	County............

Minor Children ....

Name of former wife............

That said........Nancy Kay George........was 18
years of age, on the......13th......day of......December......19 70,
her residence is......512-1/2 N. Main, Sidney......and Shelby County, Ohio,
her place of birth is......West Virginia........
her occupation is......Unemployed........
her father's name is........Alton George........,
her mother's maiden name was........Susie Burdiss........,
that she was......never......previously married........
and is........................a widow or divorced woman, her married name
being ....
and that she has no husband living.

	State and
Date Divorced............ Case No............	County............

Minor Children ....

Name of former husband............

For record of further divorces, See Page........ Sec........

That neither of said parties is an habitual drunkard, imbecile or insane, and is not under the influence of any intoxicating liquor or narcotic drug. Said parties are not nearer of kin than second cousins, and there is no legal impediment to their marriage.

It is expected that........................is to solemnize the marriage of said parties.

Applicants request that the delay period be waived.

For good cause the delay period is waived.

Sworn to before me and signed in my presence, this......3rd......day of........September......19 71.

Statement of Laboratory and Physician filed......Sept. 3......19 71

Certified Abstract mailed to State Bd. of Health......yes......19......

Lieudell E. Bauer........Probate Judge.

By........................Deputy Clerk.

CONSENT OF PARENTS, GUARDIAN OR COURT

Vivian Murray
Elvin Murray   ....Parents

Witness........

See Marriage Consent   ....Parents

MARRIAGE CERTIFICATE   No. 14528

The State of Ohio, Shelby County, ss:

I Do Hereby Certify, That on the......4th......day of......September......A. D. 19 71 I solemnized the Marriage

of Mr.......Marvin J. Murray........with M iss Nancy Kay George........

Filed and Recorded........September 7......19 71

Lieudell E. Bauer........Probate Judge.

By........................Deputy Clerk.

James H. Bieck........
Sidney Municipal Court Judge........
At........Sidney, Ohio........

U.S. World War II Army Enlistment Records, 1938-1946

Name:	**Aldon George**
Birth Year:	**1917**
Race:	**White, citizen** *(White)*
Nativity State or Country:	**West Virginia**
State of Residence:	**West Virginia**
County or City:	**Greenbrier**
Enlistment Date:	**2 Apr 1942**
Enlistment State:	**Virginia**
Enlistment City:	**Huntington West**
Branch:	**Branch Immaterial - Warrant Officers, USA**
Branch Code:	**Branch Immaterial - Warrant Officers, USA**
Grade Code:	**Private**
Term of Enlistment:	**Enlistment for the duration of the War or other emergency, plus six months, subject to the discretion of the President or otherwise according to law**
Component:	**Selectees (Enlisted Men)**
Education:	**Grammar school**
Civil Occupation:	**Semiskilled miners, and mining-machine operators**
Marital Status:	**Single, without dependents**
Height:	**69**
Weight:	**146**

Source Information:
National Archives and Records Administration. U.S. World War II Army Enlistment Records, 1938-1946 [database on-line]. Provo, UT, USA: The Generations Network, Inc., 2005. Original data: Electronic Army Serial Number Merged File, 1938-1946 [Archival Database]; World War II Army Enlistment Records; Records of the National Archives and Records Administration, Record Group 64; National Archives at College Park, College Park, MD.

Description:
This database contains information on about 8.3 million men and women who enlisted in the U.S. Army during World War II. Information contained in this database usually includes: name of enlistee, army serial number, residence (county and state), place of enlistment, enlistment date, grade, arm or branch, component, term of enlistment, birthplace, year of birth, race and citizenship, height and weight, education, and marital status. Learn more...

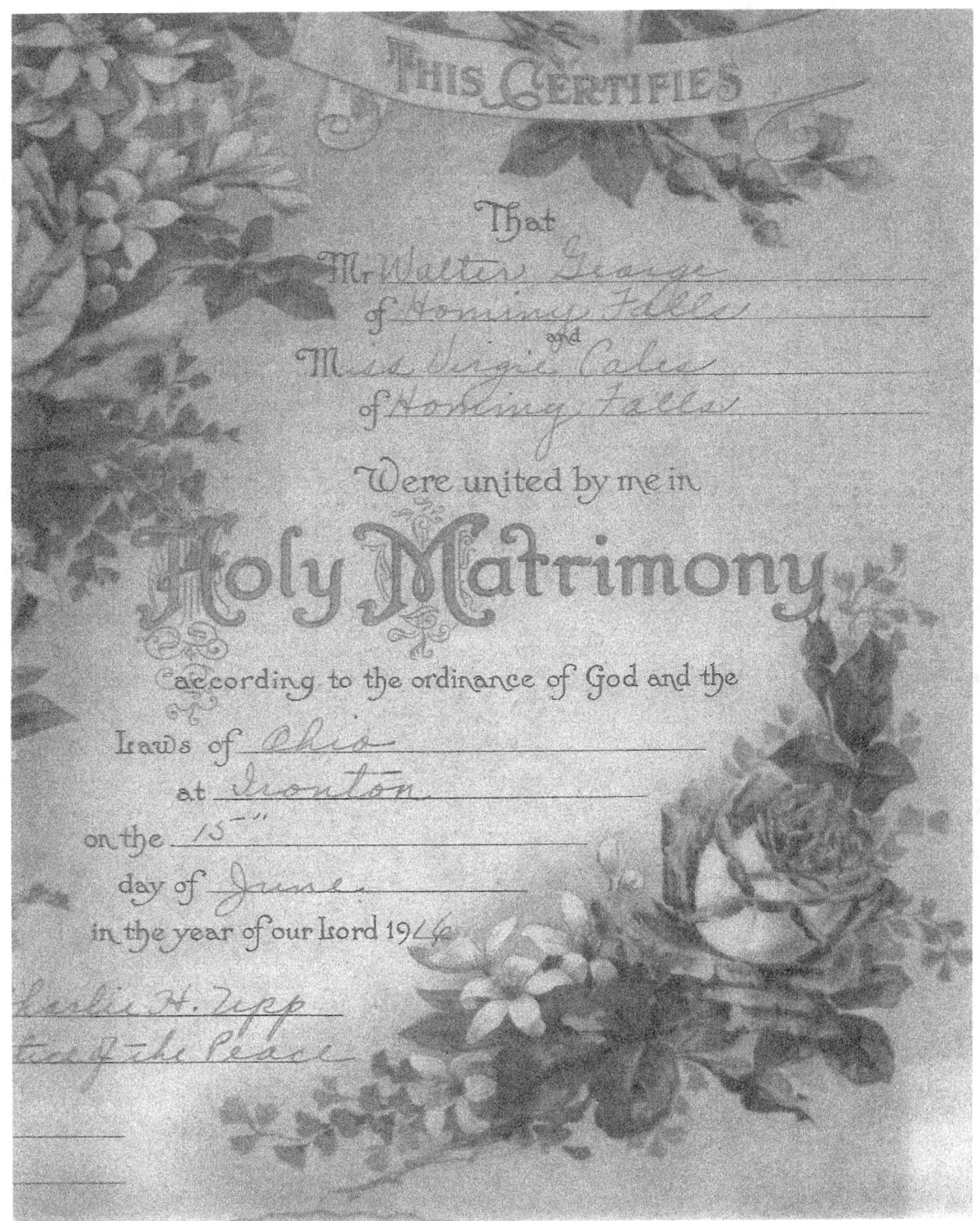

THIS CERTIFIES

That
Mr Walter George
of Hominy Falls
and
Miss Virgie Cales
of Hominy Falls

Were united by me in

Holy Matrimony

according to the ordinance of God and the

Laws of Ohio
at Ironton
on the 15"
day of June
in the year of our Lord 1946

Leslie H. Zipp
tice of the Peace

WALTER George - WWI Draft Card

REGISTRATION CARD—(Men born on or after April 28, 1877 and on or before February 16, 1897)

SERIAL NUMBER | 1 NAME (Print) | ORDER NUMBER

U 1539 | Walter GREY George

2. PLACE OF RESIDENCE (Print) Moyhrave Gbr W.Va

5. AGE IN YEARS 47
DATE OF BIRTH Oct 8 1894
6. PLACE OF BIRTH Red Creek West Virginia

7. NAME AND ADDRESS OF PERSON WHO WILL ALWAYS KNOW YOUR ADDRESS
Vergie George, Marfrance, W.Va.

8. EMPLOYER'S NAME AND ADDRESS
Marquette Coal Corp.

9. PLACE OF EMPLOYMENT OR BUSINESS Marfrance Gbr. W.Va.

Walter George

D. S. S. Form 1 (Revised 4-1-42) (over)

Indexing Search - Indexed Instrument Display   Print Page

Displayed on: Saturday, June 27, 2009 5:01:31 PM

DEEDS Valid From 01/01/1818 Thru 06/25/2009

Index Type: DEEDS	**Date Filed:** 01/01/1924
Book: 74 **Page:** 306	
Kind: DEED	**Scan Pages:**
Description (Not Warranted): [1924] [DEED] 75 3/4A KENTUCKY DIST	

GRANTOR - Record(s) 1

−ALLEN T COLES

GRANTEE - Record(s) 2

GEORGE, VIRGIE
GEORGE, WALTER'

2 Document(s) Selected
Document 1 of 2

First Document | Previous Document | Next Document | Last Document

Search Menu | Advanced Search | Name Directory | Indexed Entries

(George Farm)

98

Nicholas County, West Virginia
Wanda Hendrickson, County Clerk

Index Type: DEEDS	**Date Filed:** 01/01/1936
Book: 89 **Page:** 401	
Kind: DEED	**Scan Pages:** 0
Description (Not Warranted): [1936] [DEED] 52 & MIN KENTUCKY DIST	

GRANTOR - Record(s) 2

```
GEORGE, VIRGIE CALES
GEORGE, WALTER G
```

GRANTEE - Record(s) 1

```
-GAULEY COAL LAND CO
```

2 Document(s) Selected
Document 2 of 2

First Document | Previous Document | Next Document | Last Document

Search Menu | Advanced Search | Name Directory | Indexed Entries

99

State of West Virginia

County of Nicholas, ss:

BIRTH CERTIFICATE

I, Wanda G. Hendrickson, Clerk of the County Commission, of Nicholas County, West Virginia, it

being an office of record, and having a seal, do hereby certify that the records in my office show

that <u>AMANDA MCCLUNG</u> was born at <u>HOMINY CREEK</u>

in Nicholas County and State of West Virginia, on the <u>NO DAY</u> day of <u>JAN, 1855</u>
<u>GIVEN</u>
and the parents names are as follows:

Father <u>HAMILTON MCCLUNG</u> Mother <u>SUSAN (NO LAST NAME GIVEN)</u>

Sex <u>FEMALE</u> as shown by certificate of birth returned by <u>FATHER</u>

and recorded in the Birth Record No. <u>1A</u> at page <u>1855</u> Certificate filed <u>APPROX. TWO MONTHS</u>
<u>AFTER BIRTH</u>

In Testimony whereof, I have hereunto affixed my signature and official Seal at Summersville, West

Virginia, this <u>1ST</u> day of <u>JULY</u> 20 <u>09</u> .

<u>Wanda Hendrickson</u> , Clerk

Casto & Harris, Inc. 2480C-09

CERTIFICATE OF DEATH

Division of Vital Statistics
West Virginia State Department of Health

No. **5601**

D.V.S.—Form 2

1 PLACE OF DEATH (Dist. No. **3467**)   Series No. **1**

County **Nicholas**

District **Kentucky**

or

Town or City **Bamboo**   No.____ St.;

2 FULL NAME **Allen J. Coles**

PERSONAL AND STATISTICAL PARTICULARS

3 SEX **male**

4 COLOR OR RACE **white**

5 SINGLE, MARRIED, WIDOWED, OR DIVORCED, (Write the word) **Married**

6 DATE OF BIRTH **Feb** (Month) **1** (Day) **1848** (Year)

7 AGE **83** yrs. **2** mos. **28** ds. IF LESS than 1 day, ...hrs. or ...min.?

8 OCCUPATION
(a) Trade, profession or particular kind of work **Farmer**
(b) General nature of industry, business, or establishment in which employed (or employer)

9 BIRTHPLACE (State or country) **Summers Co**

PARENTS

10 NAME OF FATHER **Dont Know**

11 BIRTHPLACE OF FATHER (State or country) **Va**

12 MAIDEN NAME OF MOTHER **Dont Know**

13 BIRTHPLACE OF MOTHER (State or country) **Va**

14 THE ABOVE IS TRUE TO THE BEST OF MY KNOWLEDGE
(Informant) **Russell Richmond**
(Address) **Leivacy WVa**

16 Filed **April 30, 81** **G D Odell** REGISTRAR.

MEDICAL CERTIFICATE OF DEATH

16 DATE OF DEATH **April 29 1931** (Month) (Day) (Year)

17 I HEREBY CERTIFY, That I attended deceased from _____, 192___, to _____ 192___
that I last saw h___ alive on _____ 192___
and that death occurred, on the date stated above, at ___ m.

The CAUSE OF DEATH was as follows:
(Primary) **Dropsy**

131 (Duration) ___ yrs. ___ mos. ___ ds.

CONTRIBUTORY (Secondary) _____
(Duration) ___ yrs. ___ mos. ___ ds.

(Signed) _____ M. D.

_____, 192 (Address) _____

NOTE: State the Disease Causing Death. In deaths from Violent Causes, State Means of Injury; and whether Accidental, Suicidal, or Homicidal.

18 LENGTH OF RESIDENCE (FOR HOSPITALS, INSTITUTIONS, TRANSIENTS OR RECENT RESIDENTS)
At place of death ___ yrs. ___ mos. ___ ds. In the State ___ yrs. ___ mos. ___ ds.
Where was disease contracted, if not at place of death? _____
Former or usual residence _____

19 PLACE OF BURIAL OR REMOVAL **Bamboo WVa** DATE OF BURIAL **May 1 1931**

20 UNDERTAKER _____

ADDRESS _____

1850 United States Federal Census

Name:	**James McClung**	
Age:	**52**	
Estimated Birth Year:	**abt 1798**	
Birth Place:	**Virginia**	
Gender:	**Male**	
Home in 1850 (City,County,State):	**District 2 and A Half, Augusta, Virginia**	

Household Members:	Name	Age
	James McClung	52
	Benj H McClung	25
	Andrew I McClung	19
	James McClung	16
	John McClung	14
	David B McClung	13
	Frances W McClung	3
	Elizabeth Tate	46
	Isabella E Tate	11
	William L Tate	9

ISAAC LIPTRAP

1. Isaac Liptrap, founder of the family in America, lived in Middlesex, England, for the first twenty years of his life. He first appears in official records in January, 1772, age 19, while living in the East End of London. (1) He had apparently been orphaned about fourteen years earlier and lived with aunts and uncles until mid-1771. What he did for a living in London is unrecorded, though he had done some farm work as a boy. In 1772, a laborer's wages of 9 to 12 shillings for a 75-hour work week were totally consumed by food, lodging, and clothing needs. London was dirty, overcrowded, using the ditch down the middle of the street as the sewer, very much resembling the worst Charles Dickens could describe 70 years later.

Around the first of May, 1772, Isaac Liptrap stood in the dock at the Old Bailey Justice Hall in London, accused of burglary of the house of one Eliezar Pigot of Endfield, Middlesex. (1) His accomplice, Isaac Francis, testified against him. Three cousins testified to his character, John Liptrap of London, John Allen of Whitechappel, and John Dutton of Ralph's Key. See the transcript of his trial. He was sentenced to death, as was the custom, that sentence commuted to transportation to the colonies.

In July, 1772, Isaac Liptrap, about 20 years of age, boarded the ship *Tayloe* under Captain Dougal McDougal (2) along with 173 other convicts, for the two-month voyage to Virginia. The *Tayloe* sailed for Stewart & Campbell Company, convicts from England to Annapolis Maryland, or to the Rappahannock River ironworks in Virginia, returning iron and/or tobacco to England (3) It is unknown where Isaac Liptrap's indenture was sold, but Captain McDougal was still in Williamsburg in January of 1773. (4) With the outbreak of the American Revolution, the convict trade was lost. The *Tayloe* was anchored in the Thames River in London and became one of the infamous Prison Hulks that held transportable convicts until transportation to Australia was established. (3)

Isaac's indenture was probably sold to a citizen or company in the Rappahannock River area, and nothing is known of him for the next seven years, which would be the typical length of service for an indenture. During those seven years, a considerable portion of American History took place. What part Isaac played in the fight for independence we may never know. He did not serve in any army, at least not under his own name. We have no way of knowing whether he may have been a "substitute" for his master's son, for he would have served under his name instead of his own.

Isaac was married on July 29, 1785, (7) in Augusta County, to Mary Bright, born 1763, died after 1850, daughter of George Adam Bright. (8) The minister officiating was Rev. Archibald Scott (9) of Bethel and Hebron Presbyterian Churches southwest of Staunton, Virginia. (10) Some of Isaac's descendants still attend Bethel Presbyterian Church 200 years later.

Not long after his father-in-law's death, Isaac Liptrap purchased land in the Borden Tract in Augusta County from Robert Wasson on March 10, 1806, (11) paying 200 pounds for 150 acres described as follows:

This land is apparently two miles southeast of the town of Moffatts Creek, Virginia, being along or near Otts Creek about one mile from the Rockbridge County Line. On June 22, 1839, this land was granted to John McNutt; in which deed, (12) seven of the nine heirs to the estate of Isaac Liptrap were named. Isaac died in May or June, 1819, (11) leaving his widow and eight of his nine children. His estate was inventoried and sold in 1820 for $231, less notes and expenses left $9 for this heirs.(13) Mary Liptrap died soon after the Census of 1850. (14)

The Trial of Isaac Liptrap

1. The proceedings on the King's Commission of the Peace, Oyer and Terminer, and the Gaol-Delivery for the County of Middlesex held at Justice-Hall in the Old Bailey between Wednesday, April 29, and Friday, May 8, 1772, before the Right Honourable William Nash, Esquire, Lord Mayor of the City of London, and the Honourable Sir Richard Adams, Knt. one of the Barons of his Majesty's Court of Exchequer. The First Middlesex Jury:

Benjamin Coates	William Dickins	John Elkins	Richard Foster
John Edridge	William Nichol	George Eyres	John Pickering
Thomas Vardy	William King	William Selby	William Lester

ISAAC LIPTRAP was indicted for breaking and entering the dwellinghouse of Eliezar Pigot on the 11th of January, about the hour of one in the night, and stealing two silver tablespoons, value 20s.(1) two silver teaspoons, value 3s. one pair of iron spurs, plated with silver, value 5s. one pair of leather boots, value 10s. one woolen surtout coat, value 7s. one gown, value 10s. two pair of men's leather shoes, value 2s. one pair of men's leather pumps, value 2s. one peruke, value 10s. one pair of silver shoe buckles, value 7s. one silver stock-buckle, value 2s. one hunting whip mounted with silver, value 5s. and a powder-proof piece, value 1s. the property of the said Eliezar Pigott.

Eliezar Pigot: I am a farmer, and live at Endfield; I had been to Edmonton on the 10th of January to pay my rent; I came home about half an hour after eleven o'clock and went to bed; about six o'clock in the morning my maid called me up, and told me my house was broke open; I got up, and found that three panes over the shutter (it was a leaded window) had been taken out, which made room enough for a man to put his arm over the top of the shutter I which was an inside one that took up and down, and fastened only with a button; on the inside of this was the kitchen; and the shutter was buttoned very near the top; the casement was open; my desk, which stood in the kitchen, was broke open, and I lost the powder-proof piece, from the desk; the two teaspoons, the two tablespoons, and a child's pap-spoon, were taken from drawers in the dresser; the spurs, boots, coat, gown, shoes, pumps, peruke, shoe-buckles, stock-buckle, and hunting whip were all taken out of the kitchen; the shoes were, I believe, in the kitchen.

Question: Do you know that they were fast the over night?

Pigot: I saw the window-shutters were put to, but did not observe any thing further; the bureau, I am certain, was locked the over night; I pulled off my boots when I came home, and left them and my spurs and whip in the kitchen; my whip was brought to me when it was advertised, on the 16th of March, by Isaac Francis, who said he had bought it of a neighbour; I took my horse, and went with Mr. Francis to seek for the prisoner, of whom he bought the whip and my spurs; Francis took me to his lodgings; he was not there; we went to a house(2) to drink; while we were there we saw the prisoner go by; Francis went out and brought him into the house, under a pretence to drink; as soon as he came into the house he made a push to get out again; I charged him with having stolen my whip and spurs; he said he bought them of a Jew; Francis told me where he lodged; we searched his lodgings, and there found my powder-proof piece locked up in his box; and there were some other things that belonged to other people; these are my whip and spurs, (producing them) I left the powder-proof piece at Justice Wilmot's, and it is somehow lost; the prisoner denied the fact the first two or three times he was examined; on the 18th of March, after he was fully committed to Newgate, he charged Francis and Walby with being both concerned in breaking into my house, and said he handed the things out at the window to them.

Cross Examination

Question: You said he denied the charge the first or second time he was examined; I suppose the magistrate bid him be upon his guard?

Pigot: The Justice said it would be better for him to impeach(3) at first.

Question: How came he to do it at last?

104

Pigot: I suppose he did not like to be sent to Newgate. (4)

Question: Can you tell what words the magistrate made use of?

Pigot: He told him, if he was fully committed, he could not turn evidence.

Question: Did he make any promises to him of any sort?

Pigot: No.

Elizabeth Pepper: I am servant to Mr. Pigot I went to bed between eleven and twelve o'clock the night the house was broke open; I put the shutters up at the usual time, and they were safe when I went to bed; I buttoned the shutters, and an sure the casement was hasped when I put the shutters up.

Question: Do you know what was in the kitchen?

Pepper: All the things my master has mentioned. I went to bed between eleven and twelve o'clock; when I got up, a little after six in the morning, I found my master's desk broke open, and the shutters took down; I believe the casement was shut.

Question: Did you open it?

Pepper: I don't know that I did; the glass was broke, and the things mentioned in the indictment were gone.

Isaac Francis: I live at Mile-End; the prisoner lodged at one Price's, a brewer's clerk, just by me; he had lodged about the neighborhood five or six months, I bought this whip and spurs of him; I believe it was the 16th of March that Mr. Pigot had them of me, and I had then had them about a month; the prisoner came by me smacking the whip as I stood at my door; he came another day, and said he had a mind to sell it; as I kept a horse, I purchas'd it of him; I bought the spurs some time afterwards.

Question: Is there a name on the whip?

Francis: Yes; I did not take notice of the name then; he said a gentleman had died at Edmonton, and had left his whip, boots, spurs, and a great coat, to his servant, of whom he had them; I went out with two friends to Little Heath, on one side of Wormly, two of us in a chaise, and one on horseback; we stopped to dine there; from thence we went to Edmonton; I lay at a publick-house there; a man at the publick-house examined the whip, and then asked me how I came by it; I told him; he said it belonged to one of his neighbours, and that it was stolen out of Mr. Pigot's house; I told him I had bought a pair of spurs of the same man; my friends and I, and this person, went to the prosecutor's house on the Monday Morning, and shewed Mr. Pigot the whip, which he owned.

Cross Examination

Question: Where did he sell you the whip?

Francis: I was at my door; we went down to Mr. Horsenail's, and I agreed with him and paid him there.

Question: It was not done in any private way, was it?

Francis: None in the least, it was open to all the people that were in company. He was fully committed on Thursday, and on Saturday Mr. Wilmot sent for me; I went to Mr. Wilmot, who informed me that the prisoner had sworn against me, and that he must commit me. I sent for my father and several of my friends, and Mr. Wilmot indulged me with going to a sponging-house instead of a goal; we were fully committed a second time, I and one Walby, who is a man of character and property; we were re-examined on Wednesday before six justices, and, when the justices had heard the whole of the case related, we were honourably acquitted; we were committed to the bailiff's house from Saturday till Wednesday.

William Piner: I am servant to Mr. Pigot; my master came to the stable to me, and told me the window was broke open; I went to the house, and there were three panes taken out of the window.

--- Flanagan: The prosecutor gave me the spurs and whip to bring to Hick's hall.

Question: Did the justice deliver the powder-proof piece to you?

Flanagan: No; he said it did not signify, for Mr. Pigot could not swear to it.

Pigot: I did swear it was my property before Justice Wilmot.

Court: So he said he would not deliver it, because it was not sworn to?

Flanagan: He said he could not just immediately find it, and there were things enough already.

I leave it to my council; I know nothing at all about it.

For the Prisoner

John Liptrap: I was with the prisoner before Justice Wilmot; the first time he was questioned was about the boots and spurs, and he said he bought them of a Jew; the Justice told me afterwards, if he would impeach any confederates, he would admit him an evidence; and I told him that.

John Allen: I am a butcher at Red-lion-street, White-chappel, and have known the prisoner 14 years; he lived four or five years with my uncle as a carter and plowman, and bears the best of characters.

Francis Lee: I live at Ponder's end; the prisoner lived at a publick-house just by me, and I never heard any impeachment of his character before this.

--- Ballard: I live at Marybone, and have known the prisoner about two years and a half, I made him two suits of cloaths, and he paid me very honestly; he always behaved well.

John Dutton: I am a wharfinger, and live at Ralph's key; I knew the prisoner about twelve years ago, when he lived with my father; he bore a good character then, but I have known nothing of him since.

Verdict: GUILTY

Sentence: DEATH (5)

Isaac Liptrap was reprieved in July, 1772; and his sentence was commuted to transportation to America (considered by many to be a worse fate than hanging) in July of 1772. He was ordered transported for 14 years, twice the usual term. Duncan Campbell, of the company Stewart & Campbell, contracted (8) for the transportation of Isaac and 41 other Middlesex convicts on 22 July 1772, and Captain Dougal McDougal certified that they were shipped aboard the ship *Tayloe* 23 July 1772.(6,8) According to English Law and custom, Stewart & Campbell, was paid £5 for transporting each prisoner, who was then sold privately for as much as £10 in Virginia. A total of 174 prisoners were consigned to Campbell and McDougal between 22-25 July for the trip on the *Tayloe*, for which Campbell was paid £870.(8) On this voyage, the *Tayloe* stopped at the ironworks on the Rappahannock River in Virginia, and in Annapolis, Maryland.(9) To whom Isaac Liptrap's indenture was sold is unknown, but Captain McDougal apparently sold him for the more usual seven years, as "Isack Cliptrap" appears on the tax rolls of Rockbridge County, Virginia, in September of 1780.(7)

(1) In 1772, a laborer's wages were 9 to 12 shillings for a 75-hour work week.
(2) a public-house, or inn
(3) to name his accomplices
(4) The main gaol (jail) in London had no water, no sanitation, no separation of 1700 prisoners, no beds, no bail or bond, prisoners required to pay their guards upon entering and leaving, and an inconceivable stench.

WORLD WAR I DRAFT REGISTRATION CARDS, 1917-1918

GEORGE WASHINGTON GEORGE

COUNTY: GREENBRIER
STATE: WEST VIRGINIA
BIRTH DATE: 2 MAY 1873
RACE: WHITE
ROLL: 1992481
DRAFTBOARD: 0

WORLD WAR I DRAFT REGISTRATION CARDS, 1917-1918

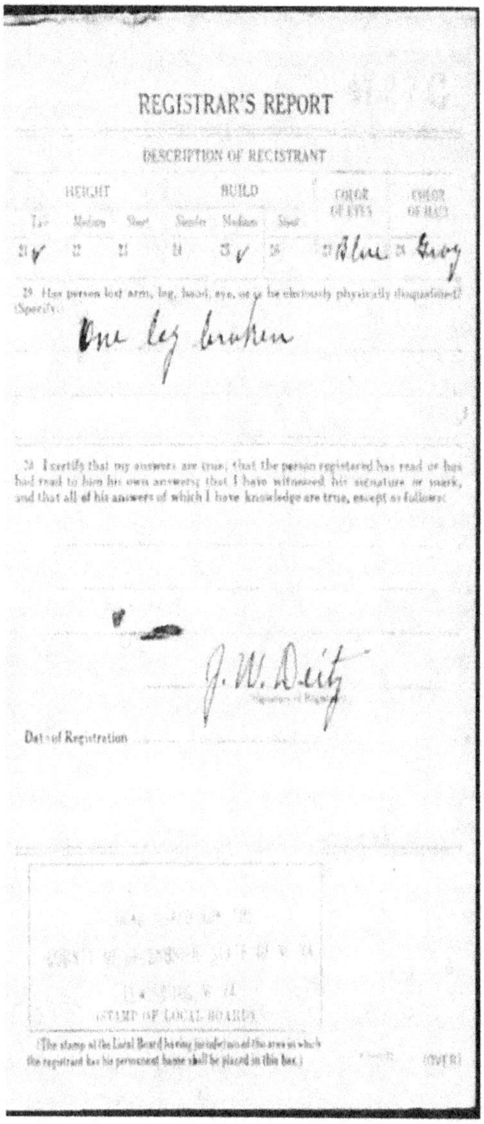

REGISTRAR'S REPORT

DESCRIPTION OF REGISTRANT

HEIGHT			BUILD			COLOR OF EYES	COLOR OF HAIR
Tall	Medium	Short	Slender	Medium	Stout		
21 ✓	22	23	24	25 ✓	26	27 Blue	28 Gray

29 Has person lost arm, leg, hand, eye, or is he obviously physically disqualified? (Specify.)

One leg broken

30 I certify that my answers are true; that the person registered has read or has had read to him his own answers; that I have witnessed his signature or mark, and that all of his answers of which I have knowledge are true, except as follows:

J. W. Deitz
(Signature of Registrar)

Date of Registration

(STAMP OF LOCAL BOARD)

(The stamp of the Local Board having jurisdiction of the area in which the registrant has his permanent home shall be placed in this box.)

(OVER)

GEORGE WASHINGTON GEORGE

COUNTY: GREENBRIER
STATE: WEST VIRGINIA
BIRTH DATE: 2 MAY 1873
RACE: WHITE
ROLL: 1992481
DRAFTBOARD: 0

SOURCE INFORMATION: WWW.ANCESTRY.COM **DATABASE:** WORLD WAR I DRAFT REGISTRATION CARDS, 1917-1918 **DETAIL: REGISTRATION LOCATION:** GREENBRIER COUNTY, WEST VIRGINIA; **ROLL:** 1992481; **DRAFT BOARD:** 0.

Children (1)
George Washington George   B. 1872

William Jasper George

B:1840 in Ohio
D:1880 in west virginia

Phoebe E Vanmeter B: 7-15-1840 in Virginia

U.S. Civil War Soldier Records and Profiles

Name:	**William J George**
Age at Enlistment:	**25**
Enlistment Date:	**4 Oct 1863**
Rank at enlistment:	**Private**
State Served:	**Ohio**
Survived the War?:	**Yes**
Service Record:	**Enlisted in** Company K, Ohio 36th Infantry Regiment **on 10 Apr 1863.** **Mustered out on 27 Jul 1865 at Wheeling, WV.**
Birth Date:	**abt 1838**
Sources:	**Official Roster of the Soldiers of the State of Ohio**

Edward Peter Burdiss

County: Raleigh
State: West Virginia
Birthplace: Ohio United States of America
Birth Date: 4 May 1889
Race: Caucasian (White)
Roll: 1992959
DraftBoard: 0

WORLD WAR I DRAFT REGISTRATION CARDS, 1917-1918

EDWARD PETER BURDISS

COUNTY: RALEIGH
STATE: WEST VIRGINIA
BIRTHPLACE: OHIO, UNITED STATES
OF AMERICA
BIRTH DATE: 4 MAY 1889
RACE: CAUCASIAN (WHITE)
ROLL: 1992959
DRAFTBOARD: 0

Edward Burdiss WWII DRAFT CARD

1337

REGISTRATION CARD—(Men born on or after April 28, 1877 and on or before February 16, 1897)   ORDER NUMBER

SERIAL NUMBER | 1. NAME (Print)
U 314 | Edward *(First)* *(Middle)* Peter Burdiss *(Last)*

2. PLACE OF RESIDENCE (Print) (Snake Island) East Rainelle Gbr. W. Va.
(Number and street) *(Town, township, village, or city)* *(County)* *(State)*
[THE PLACE OF RESIDENCE GIVEN ON THE LINE ABOVE WILL DETERMINE LOCAL BOARD
JURISDICTION; LINE 2 OF REGISTRATION CERTIFICATE WILL BE IDENTICAL]

3. MAILING ADDRESS Same
(Mailing address if other than place indicated on line 2. If same insert word same)

4. TELEPHONE None | 5. AGE IN YEARS 53 | 6. PLACE OF BIRTH Jacksonville *(Town or county)*
DATE OF BIRTH May 2 1888 | Ohio *(State or country)*
(Exchange) *(Number)* | *(Mo.)* *(Day)* *(Yr.)*

7. NAME AND ADDRESS OF PERSON WHO WILL ALWAYS KNOW YOUR ADDRESS
Lacey Cole, East Rainelle, W. Va.

8. EMPLOYER'S NAME AND ADDRESS Low Ash Smokeless Fuel Co, East Rainelle W. Va.

9. PLACE OF EMPLOYMENT OR BUSINESS Snake Island East Rainelle Gbr. W. Va.
(Number and street or R.F.D. number) *(Town)* *(County)* *(State)*

I AFFIRM THAT I HAVE VERIFIED ABOVE ANSWERS AND THAT THEY ARE TRUE.

E P Burdiss
(Registrant's signature)

D. S. S. Form 1
(Revised 4-1-42)   (over)   16—21530-2

REGISTRAR'S REPORT

DESCRIPTION OF REGISTRANT

RACE		HEIGHT (Appx.) 5-8	WEIGHT (Appx.) 137	COMPLEXION	
White	X	EYES		Sallow	
Negro		Blue	X	Light	X
Oriental		Gray		Ruddy	
Indian		Hazel		Dark	
Filipino		Brown		Freckled	
		Black		Light brown	
		HAIR		Dark brown	X
		Blonde		Black	
		Red			
		Brown	X		
		Black			
		Gray			
		Bald			

Other obvious physical characteristics that will aid in identification

I certify that my answers are true; that the person registered has read or has had read to him his own answers; that I have witnessed his signature or mark, and that all of his answers of which I have knowledge are true, except as follows:

 Auh Irwin
(Signature of registrar)
Registrar for Local Board 2 Harrison WVa
(City or county)

4/27/42
Date of registration

LOCAL BOARD # 2. SELECTIVE SERVICE
447 W. PIKE STREET
CLARKSBURG (HARRISON CO.), W. VA
(STAMP OF LOCAL BOARD)

(The stamp of the Local Board hereby jurisdiction of the registrant shall be placed in the above space.)
16—21530-2

112

MARRIAGE  LICENSE.

West Virginia, County of Raleigh, to-wit:

TO ANY PERSON LICENSED TO CELEBRATE MARRIAGES.

You are hereby authorized to join together in the Holy State of Matrimony, according to the rites and ceremonies of your Church or religious denomination, and the laws of the STATE OF WEST VIRGINIA, *Edward P. Burdiss* and *Belle Hunley,*

GIVEN under my hand, as Clerk of the County Court of the County of Raleigh, this *4.* day of *March,* 1910

M. J. Meadow
Clerk County Court of Raleigh County.

CLERK'S CERTIFICATE.

Preliminary inquiries and answers thereto, made and ascertained by *M. J. Meadow* Clerk of the County Court of RALEIGH COUNTY, STATE OF WEST VIRGINIA, relative to Mr. *Edward P. Burdiss* of *Raleigh* County and State of *West Virginia* and Miss *Belle Hunley* of *Raleigh* County and State of *West Virginia* to whom the accompanying Marriage License is issued.

The full names of the parties are as follows:

His full name is *Edward P. Burdiss,*
Her full name is *Belle Hunley,*
His age is *20 Years* Her age is *17 Years,*
He was born in *Ohio* County and State of *Ohio*
She was born in County and State of *N. C.,*
His place of residence is *Raleigh County West Virginia*
Her place of residence is " " "
The name of the party giving the foregoing information is *Edward Burdiss,* of *Raleigh* County and State of *West Virginia*

GIVEN under my hand, this *4.* day of *Mch.* 1910,

M. J. Meadow
Clerk County Court.

MINISTER'S RETURN OR INDORSEMENT.

I, *H. A. Spadling* a *Minister of the Seymill Baptist Church* do certify that, on the *1st* day of *March* 1910 at *Beckley, W. Va.* I united in marriage the above named and described parties, under authority of the foregoing License.

H. A. Spadling

KANSAS STATE DEPARTMENT OF HEALTH
Division of Vital Statistics
CERTIFICATE OF DEATH

NOV. - 1, 1972

72 016816

DECEASED — NAME	FIRST	MIDDLE	LAST	SEX	DATE OF DEATH (MONTH, DAY, YEAR)	
1.	Susie	Belle	Burdiss	2. Female	3. October 25, 1972	

RACE WHITE, NEGRO, AMERICAN INDIAN, ETC. (SPECIFY)	AGE — LAST BIRTHDAY (YEARS)	UNDER 1 YEAR MOS. DAYS	UNDER 1 DAY HOURS MIN.	DATE OF BIRTH (MONTH, DAY, YEAR)	COUNTY OF DEATH
4. White	5a. 87	5b.	5c.	5d. June 25, 1885	6. Johnson

CITY, TOWN, OR LOCATION OF DEATH	INSIDE CITY LIMITS (SPECIFY YES OR NO)	HOSPITAL OR OTHER INSTITUTION — NAME (IF NOT IN EITHER, GIVE STREET AND NUMBER)
7a. DeSoto	7b. Yes	7c. DeSoto Nursing Home

STATE OF BIRTH (IF NOT IN U.S.A., NAME COUNTRY)	CITIZEN OF WHAT COUNTRY	MARRIED, NEVER MARRIED, WIDOWED, DIVORCED (SPECIFY)	SURVIVING SPOUSE (IF WIFE, GIVE MAIDEN NAME)
8. W. Virginia	9. U.S.A.	10. Widowed	11. None

SOCIAL SECURITY NUMBER	USUAL OCCUPATION (GIVE KIND OF WORK DONE DURING MOST OF WORKING LIFE, EVEN IF RETIRED)	KIND OF BUSINESS OR INDUSTRY
12. None	13a. Housewife	13b. Home

RESIDENCE — STATE	COUNTY	CITY, TOWN, OR LOCATION	INSIDE CITY LIMITS (SPECIFY YES OR NO)	STREET AND NUMBER
14a. Kansas	14b. Wyandotte	14c. Kansas City	14d. No	14e. 7015 Berry Rd.

FATHER — NAME	FIRST	MIDDLE	LAST	MOTHER — MAIDEN NAME	FIRST	MIDDLE	LAST
15.	John	Hunley		16.	Susie Belle		No Data

INFORMANT — NAME	MAILING ADDRESS (STREET OR R.F.D. NO., CITY OR TOWN, STATE, ZIP)
17c. Mr. Tom P. Burdiss	17h. 7015 Berry Rd. Kansas City, Kansas 66106

PART I.	DEATH WAS CAUSED BY:	(ENTER ONLY ONE CAUSE PER LINE FOR (a), (b), AND (c))	APPROXIMATE INTERVAL BETWEEN ONSET AND DEATH
18. 4270	IMMEDIATE CAUSE (a)	Cerebral anoxia	minutes
CONDITIONS, IF ANY, WHICH GAVE RISE TO IMMEDIATE CAUSE (a), STATING THE UNDERLYING CAUSE LAST	DUE TO, OR AS A CONSEQUENCE OF: (b)	Pulmonary Edema	hours
	DUE TO, OR AS A CONSEQUENCE OF: (c)	Congestive heart failure	weeks

PART II.	OTHER SIGNIFICANT CONDITIONS: CONDITIONS CONTRIBUTING TO DEATH BUT NOT RELATED TO CAUSE GIVEN IN PART I (a)	AUTOPSY (YES OR NO)	IF YES WERE FINDINGS CONSIDERED IN DETERMINING CAUSE OF DEATH
	Arteriosclerosis	19a. NO	19b.

ACCIDENT, SUICIDE, HOMICIDE, OR UNDETERMINED (SPECIFY)	DATE OF INJURY (MONTH, DAY, YEAR)	HOUR	HOW INJURY OCCURRED (ENTER NATURE OF INJURY IN PART I OR PART II, ITEM 18)
20a.	20b.	20c. M. 20d.	

INJURY AT WORK (SPECIFY YES OR NO)	PLACE OF INJURY AT HOME, FARM, STREET, FACTORY, OFFICE BLDG., ETC. (SPECIFY)	LOCATION (STREET OR R.F.D. NO., CITY OR TOWN, STATE)
20e.	20f.	20g.

CERTIFICATION — PHYSICIAN: I ATTENDED THE DECEASED FROM	MONTH DAY YEAR	TO	MONTH DAY YEAR	AND LAST SAW HIM/HER ALIVE ON MONTH DAY YEAR	I DID/DID NOT VIEW THE BODY AFTER DEATH.	DEATH OCCURRED AT THE PLACE, ON THE DATE, AND, TO THE BEST OF MY KNOWLEDGE, DUE TO THE CAUSE(S) STATED. HOUR
21a.	2 28 72	21b.	10 25 72	21c. 10-20 72	21d. Did Not	21e. 4 05 P M.

CERTIFICATION — MEDICAL EXAMINER OR CORONER: ON THE BASIS OF THE EXAMINATION OF THE BODY AND/OR THE INVESTIGATION, IN MY OPINION, DEATH OCCURRED ON THE DATE AND DUE TO THE CAUSE(S) STATED.	HOUR OF DEATH	THE DECEDENT WAS PRONOUNCED DEAD MONTH DAY YEAR HOUR
22a.	M. 22b.	22c.

CERTIFIER — NAME (TYPE OR PRINT)	SIGNATURE	DEGREE OR TITLE	DATE SIGNED (MONTH, DAY, YEAR)
23a. Robert C. LaHue DO	23b. Robert C. LaHue	23c.	23d. 10-26-72

MAILING ADDRESS — CERTIFIER	STREET OR R.F.D. NO.	CITY OR TOWN	STATE	ZIP
24.	5811 Truman Road	Kansas City, Missouri		

BURIAL, CREMATION, REMOVAL (SPECIFY)	CEMETERY OR CREMATORY — NAME	LOCATION	CITY OR TOWN	STATE
24a. Burial	24b. Maple Hill Cemetery	24c. Kansas City, Kansas		

DATE (MONTH, DAY, YEAR)	FUNERAL HOME — NAME AND ADDRESS (STREET OR R.F.D. NO., CITY OR TOWN, STATE, ZIP)	
24e. Oct. 28, 1972	25a. Simmons Funeral Home 1404 S. 37th Kansas City, Kansas	66106

FUNERAL DIRECTOR — SIGNATURE	REGISTRAR — SIGNATURE	DATE RECEIVED BY LOCAL REGISTRAR
25b. Donald L. Simmons	Harold H. Bair	26b. October 30, 1972

114

Mrs. Susie Belle Burdiss

Services for Mrs. Susie Belle Burdiss, 7015 Berry Rd., will be at 11 a.m. Saturday at the Simmons Funeral Home.

Burial will be in the Maple Hill Cemetery. Friends may call after 4 p.m. today at tha funeral home.

Mrs. Burdiss, died Wednesday at a nursing home in De Soto in Johnson County. Born in Beckley, W. Va., she lived in Wyandotte County 14 years.

Surviving are four sons, Robert C. Burdiss, Kansas City, Mo.; Basil W. Burdiss, Sidney, Ohio, Tom P. Burdiss, of the home, and Cecil K. Burdiss, Denver; three daughters, Mrs. Margaret Mary Coy, Denver; Mrs. Margaret Richmond, De Soto, and Mrs. Susan George, Marfrance, W. Va.; a sister, Mrs. Elizabeth Gravely, Beckley; 30 grandchildren and 10 great-grandchildren.

nsas City Since 1905

115

Dist. No. 180
Serial No. 196

WEST VIRGINIA STATE DEPARTMENT OF HEALTH—DIVISION OF VITAL STATISTICS
CERTIFICATE OF DEATH

10062

State File No.

1. NAME OF DECEASED (Type or Print)	a. (First) Edward	b. (Middle) P.	c. (Last) Burdiss	2. DATE OF DEATH (Month) Aug. (Day) 13 (Year) 1952

3. PLACE OF DEATH
a. COUNTY Greenbier
b. CITY OR TOWN Charmco
c. LENGTH OF STAY (in this place)
d. FULL NAME OF HOSPITAL OR INSTITUTION

4. USUAL RESIDENCE
a. STATE W. Va. b. COUNTY Greenbier
c. CITY OR TOWN Charmco
d. STREET ADDRESS

5. SEX Male	6. COLOR OR RACE white	7. MARRIED, NEVER MARRIED, WIDOWED, DIVORCED (Specify) married	8. DATE OF BIRTH May 4, 1888	9. AGE (In years) 61

10. USUAL OCCUPATION Coal miner 2
10a. KIND OF BUSINESS OR INDUSTRY
11. BIRTHPLACE (State or foreign country) Ohio
12. CITIZEN OF WHAT COUNTRY? U.S.A.

13. FATHER'S NAME James Burdiss
14. MOTHER'S MAIDEN NAME Martha

15. WAS DECEASED EVER IN U.S. ARMED FORCES? no
16. SOCIAL SECURITY No.
17. INFORMANT Bernard Burdiss

18. CAUSE OF DEATH
Enter only one cause per line for (a), (b), and (c)

MEDICAL CERTIFICATION

I. DISEASE OR CONDITION DIRECTLY LEADING TO DEATH (a) Cornary Thrombosis

ANTECEDENT CAUSES
Morbid conditions, if any, giving rise to the above cause (a) stating the underlying cause last.
DUE TO (b) 4.201
DUE TO (c)

INTERVAL BETWEEN ONSET AND DEATH few minute

II. OTHER SIGNIFICANT CONDITIONS
Conditions contributing to the death but not related to the disease or condition causing death.

19a. DATE OF OPERATION
19b. MAJOR FINDINGS OF OPERATION

20. AUTOPSY? Yes ☐ No ☒

21a. ACCIDENT SUICIDE HOMICIDE (Specify)
21b. PLACE OF INJURY (e.g., in or about home, farm, factory, street, office bldg., etc.)
21c. (CITY, TOWN OR TOWNSHIP) (COUNTY) (STATE)

21d. TIME OF INJURY (Month) (Day) (Year) (Hour)
21e. INJURY OCCURRED While at Work ☐ Not While at Work ☐
21f. HOW DID INJURY OCCUR?
21g. INQUEST Yes ☐ No ☐

22. I hereby certify that I attended the deceased from 13th Aug 1952 and that death occurred at 6 am from the causes and on the date stated above.

23a. SIGNATURE Mellen R. Huntley MD
23b. ADDRESS (Degree or title) Rupert W. Va.
23c. DATE SIGNED 9-15-52

24a. BURIAL, CREMATION, REMOVAL (Specify) burial
24b. DATE Aug. 15, 52
24c. NAME OF CEMETERY OR CREMATORY Wildwood Cemetery
24d. EMBALMER'S SIGNATURE Charles E. Buster
Lic. No.

DATE REC'D BY LOCAL REG. Aug 22-52
REGISTRAR'S SIGNATURE Eva W. Hefner
25. FUNERAL DIRECTOR'S (Signature) Charles E. Buster Jr.
Lic. No. 1823

Edward P. Burdiss Dies Unexpectedly

CHARMCO, Aug. 13 — Edward P. Burdiss, 64, of Charmco, died unexpectedly today of a heart ailment.

Employed at the Betty-Page Coal Co., in Rupert, he became ill while working in the mine and died while enroute to the office of a physician.

He was born on May 4, 1888 in Ohio and was a former resident of Raleigh County.

Surviving are his wife, Mrs. Belle Hundley Burdiss, Charmco; three daughters, Mrs. Aldon George, Marfrance; Mrs. Tom Coy and Miss Margaret Burdiss, Charmco; six sons, Basil, East Rainelle; George, McAlpin, Robert, Bernard, Lloyd and Cecil, Charmco; one sister, Mrs. Brydia Spencer, Columbus, Ohio, and one brother, George Burdiss, Coal City.

The body is at the Wallace and Wallace Funeral Home pending completion of funeral arrangements.

Children (1)
Edward Peter Burdiss   B: 1889

James Burdiss

B:1848 in England
D:West Virginia

Martha Madge Bennett B:1859 in Kentucky

New York Passenger Lists, 1820-1957

Name:	**James Burdess**
Arrival Date:	**2 Sep 1850**
Estimated Birth Year:	**abt 1848**
Age:	**2**
Gender:	**Male**
Port of Departure:	**Liverpool, England**
Ship Name:	**West Point**
Search Ship Database:	Search the West Point in the 'Passenger Ships and Images' database
Port of Arrival:	**New York, New York**
Line:	**17**
Microfilm Serial:	**M237**
Microfilm Roll:	**M237_92**
List Number:	**1005**

Source Citation: Year: 1850; Microfilm serial: M237; Microfilm roll: M237_92; Line: 17; List number: 1005.

Source Information:
Ancestry.com. New York Passenger Lists, 1820-1957 [database on-line]. Provo, UT, USA: The Generations Network, Inc., 2006. Original data:

Passenger Lists of Vessels Arriving at New York, New York, 1820-1897; (National Archives Microfilm Publication M237, 675 rolls); Records of the U.S. Customs Service, Record Group 36; National Archives, Washington, D.C.

Passenger and Crew Lists of Vessels Arriving at New York, New York, 1897-1957 (National Archives Microfilm Publication T715, 8892 rolls); Records of the Immigration and Naturalization Service; National Archives, Washington, D.C.

Description:
This database is an index to the passenger lists of ships arriving from foreign ports at the port of New York from 1820-1957. In addition, the names found in the index are linked to actual images of the passenger lists. Information contained in the index includes given name, surname, age, gender, arrival date, port of arrival, port of departure and ship name. Learn more...

NAMES.	AGE.		SEX.	OCCUPATION.	The country to which they severally belong.	The country in which they intend to become inhabitants	Died on the voyage.
	Years.	Months.					
Robert MacSweeney	19	"	"	Clerk	Ireland	United States	
Pat. d°	20	"	"	d°			"
Joseph Green	20	"	"	Baker	England		"
James Colan	15	"	"	Labourer	Ireland		"
Bridget Brady	30	"	Female	Servant	"		"
Mary d°	16	"	"	d°	"		"
Bridget Spencer	15	"	"	d°	"		"
Bridget Smith	20	"	"	d°	"		"
Thomas Beaven	30	"	Male	Wool Comber	"		"
Nane George	16	"	Female	Married	"		"
James McGuire	15	"	Male	Sailor	England		"
George Bingham	48	"	"	Farmer	Scotland		"
Mrs d°	39	"	Female	Married	"		"
Mary d°	13	"	"		"		"
George d°	5	"	Male		"		"
Alexander d°	3	"	"		"		"
James d°	2	"			"		"
John Tudor	63	"	"	Retired from business	England		"
Mrs d°	61	"	"	Married	"		"
Miss d°	25	"	"		"		"
Maria d°	18	"	"		"		"
Eliza Peel	36	"	d°	Married	"		"
Thomas d°	Infant		Male	Infant	"		"
Margaret Hudson	35	"	Female	Widow	England		"
S.W. Samuel	39	"	Male	Glazier	"		"
John d°	20	"	"	"	"		"
Charles d°	16	"	"	"	"		"
F. d°	4	"	"	"	"		"
Riley d°	50	"	Female		"		"
Sarah d°	46	"	"		"		"
Ann d°	22	"	"		"		"
John Lord	22	"	Male	Grocer			"
Charles Crocker	30	"	"	Brick maker			"
Richard Creighton	17	"	"	Labourer	Ireland		"
James Sage	17	"	"	Cordwainer	England		"
Martha d°	37	"	Female	Married			"
Harriett d°	12	"	"				"
Mary Johnson	28	"	"	Married			"
George d°	12	"	Male				"
W. d°	8	"	"		"		"
Charles d°	6	"	"	" "			"
Alfred d°	4	"	"				"
John Middleton	24	"	"	Joiner			"
Fanny d°	24	"	Female	"			"
William d°	Infant		Male	"			"

119

Children (1)				Parents
James Burdiss		B: 1848		UNKNOWN

George Burdiss

Ba800 in scotland

D:united states

UNKNOWN

Unknown Mother B:

New York Passenger Lists, 1820-1957

Name:	**George Burdess**
Arrival Date:	**2 Sep 1850**
Estimated Birth Year:	**abt 1802**
Age:	**48**
Gender:	**Male**
Port of Departure:	**Liverpool, England**
Ship Name:	**West Point**
Search Ship Database:	Search the West Point in the 'Passenger Ships and Images' database
Port of Arrival:	**New York, New York**
Line:	**12**
Microfilm Serial:	**M237**
Microfilm Roll:	**M237_92**
List Number:	**1005**

Source Citation: Year: 1850; Microfilm serial: M237; Micro-film roll: M237_92; Line: 12; List number: 1005.

Source Information:
Ancestry.com. *New York Passenger Lists, 1820-1957* [database on-line]. Provo, UT, USA: The Generations Network, Inc., 2006. Original data:

Passenger Lists of Vessels Arriving at New York, New York, 1820-1897. (National Archives Microfilm Publication M237, 675 rolls); Records of the U.S. Customs Service, Record Group 36; National Archives, Washington, D.C.

Passenger and Crew Lists of Vessels Arriving at New York, New York, 1897-1957. (National Archives Microfilm Publication T715, 8892 rolls); Records of the Immigration and Naturalization Service; National Archives, Washington, D.C.

Description
This database is an index to the passenger lists of ships arriving from foreign ports at the port of New York from 1820-1957. In addition to the names listed in the index are those file actual images of the passenger lists. Information contained in the index includes given name, surname, age, gender, arrival date, port of arrival, port of departure and ship name. Learn more...

CHAPTER FOUR

PHOTOGRAPHS

Five Generations of Nancy George (Richmond) family
Five Generations of Charles Lee Richmond family

Edward P Burdiss (and son Lloyd) -grandfather of Nancy George Richmond

Susie B Hundley Burdiss - grandmother of Nancy George Richmond

Walter Greg George (seated with child on his lap)
and
Virgie Cales George (standing behind Walter)

Grandparents of Nancy George Richmond

Arby Roy Smith and Mary Olive Phillips Smith

Grandparents of Charles Lee Richmond

Charlie Richmond and Vernie Trout Richmond and son Charles Wyatt

Grandparents of Charles Lee Richmond

Aldon George and Susie Burdiss George

Parents of Nancy George Richmond

Charles Wyatt Richmond and Melva Smith Richmond and sons Charles and Curtis

Parents of Charles Lee Richmond

Nancy George Richmond and Charles Lee Richmond

Tammy Murray Workman and Ronnie Joseph Workman

Daughter and Son-In-Law of Nancy George Richmond

Misty Murray Walkup, James Roy Walkup Jr. and children
James Roy Walkup 3rd, Tia Dawn Walkup and Jesse James Walkup

Daughter, Son-In-Law and grandchildren of Nancy George Richmond

Charity Richmond and Fiancé Reney Cordial 4th
With
Victoria Francis and Reney Allen Cordial 5th

Daughter and grandchildren of Charles Lee Richmond and Nancy George Richmond

Bethany Ellard-Richmond and Thor Richmond

Daughter-In-Law and Son of Charles Lee Richmond and Nancy George Richmond

**Gary Dale Boone and Lora Richmond Boone and children
Hope Marie Boone and Gary Dale Boone Jr.**

Son-In-Law, Daughter and grandchildren of Charles Lee and Nancy George Richmond

ABOUT THE AUTHOR

Nancy Richmond has been writing for over thirty years, first as a newspaper and magazine columnist, and later as the author of several books. She lives in Lewisburg, WV with her husband Charles, who is also an author.

ABOUT THE COVER

The cover photograph features Aachen Cathedral in Germany. It was built by the Holy Roman Emperor Charlemagne, and is his final resting place. Charlemagne is the author's 39th great grandfather.

www.ingramcontent.com/pod-product-compliance
Lightning Source LLC
Chambersburg PA
CBHW081353280526
45788CB00009B/2861